Prestwick House
AP* Language and
Composition

BY DOUGLAS GRUDZINA

Prestwick House

Writer
Douglas Grudzina

Senior Editor
Paul Moliken

Cover and Text Design
Larry Knox

Production
Jeremy Clark

Prestwick House

© 2010 Copyrighted by Prestwick House, Inc.

All rights reserved. No portion may be reproduced
without permission in writing from the publisher. Printed
in the United States of America. Revised, 2012.

ISBN: 978-1-935466-68-0

Prestwick House
AP* Language and Composition

BY DOUGLAS GRUDZINA

Prestwick House

Prestwick House AP Language and Composition

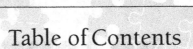

Table of Contents

Prestwick House AP Language and Composition

Acknowledgments

Anthony, Susan B. "On Woman's Right to the Suffrage." Speech delivered in 1873.

Catton, Bruce. "Grant and Lee: A Study in Contrasts." *The American Story*. Ed. Earl Schenck Miers.
  • Reprinted by permission of the U.S. Capitol Historical Society.

Churchill, Winston. "We Shall Fight…." Address to the House of Commons, 4 June 1940
  • Reproduced with permission of Curtis Brown Ltd, London on behalf of The Estate of Winston Churchill
       Copyright © Winston S. Churchill

Churchill, Winston. "Blood, Sweat and Tears." Address to the House of Commons, 13 May 1940
  • Reproduced with permission of Curtis Brown Ltd, London on behalf of The Estate of Winston Churchill
       Copyright © Winston S. Churchill

Darwin, Charles. from *Narrative of the Surveying Voyages of His Majesty's Ships Adventure and Beagle*.

Eagleton, Terry. "Introduction: What is Literature?" from *Literary Theory: An Introduction* by Terry Eagleton. University of Minnesota Press, 1983.
  • All rights reserved. No part of this publication may be reproduced, stored in a retrieval system, or transmitted, in any form or by any means, electronic, mechanical, photocopying, recording, or otherwise, without the prior written permission of the publisher.

Epstein, Joseph. "Obama's Good Students: A dissent on the 'valedictocracy.'"
- This article is reprinted with permission of *The Weekly Standard*, where it first appeared on 8 Dec. 2008. For more information visit www. weeklystandard.com.

Epstein, Joseph. "A Genius of Temperament: Joseph Epstein remembers Irving Kristol"
- This article is reprinted with permission of *The Weekly Standard*, where it first appeared on 5 Oct. 2009. For more information visit www.weeklystandard.com.

Goldman, Emma. *The Tragedy of Woman's Emancipation.* New York: Mother Earth Publishing Association, 1906.

James, Henry. *Portraits of Places, second edition.* Boston: J.R. Osgood, 1885.

Jones, Absalom. "A Thanksgiving Sermon." Delivered in St. Thomas's Church, Philadelphia, 1 Jan. 1808.

Kennedy, John Fitzgerald. *Inaugural Address.* Delivered 20 Jan. 1961.

King, Martin Luther, Jr. "Letter from Birmingham Jail."
- Reprinted by arrangement with The Heirs to the Estate of Martin Luther King, Jr., c/o Writers House as agent for the proprietor New York, NY.

   Copyright 1963 Dr. Martin Luther King, Jr.; copyright renewed 1991 Coretta Scott King

"A Call for Unity: Statement by Alabama Clergymen"
- Reprinted by arrangement with The Heirs to the Estate of Martin Luther King, Jr., c/o Writers House as agent for the proprietor New York, NY.

   Copyright 1963 Dr. Martin Luther King, Jr.; copyright renewed 1991 Coretta Scott King

Laga, Barry. "What is Literature? A paraphrase, summary, and adaptation of the opening chapter of Terry Eagleton's *Introduction to Literary Theory.*"
- © 1998 by Dr. Barry Laga. Reprinted by permission of the author.

Lincoln, Abraham. *Second Inaugural Address.* Delivered 4 Mar. 1865.

Marquis, Don. "The Almost Perfect State."

Paine, Thomas. *The Crisis,* Number I.

Smith, Margaret Chase. "Declaration of Conscience."
Statement on the Floor of the U.S. Senate, 1 June 1950.
Special thanks to the Margaret Chase Smith Library.

Stevenson, Adlai E. Veto Statement to "An Act to Provide Protection to
Insectivorous Birds by Restraining Cats" ("Cat Bill Veto") 23 April 1949. *Veto
Messages of Adlai E. Stevenson, Governor of Illinois, on Senate and House Bills Passed
by the 66th General Assembly of Illinois.* Springfield:
State of Illinois, 1949.

Truth, Sojourner. "Ain't I a Woman?" Three versions of a speech delivered at the
Women's Convention in Akron, Ohio. 29 May 1851.

Wells, H.G. "The World in Space," from *A Short History of the World.*

Wiesel, Elie. Nobel Lecture: Hope, Despair and Memory. 10 Dec. 1986.
  • Mr. Wiesel is the sole author of the text.

    © The Nobel Foundation 1986.

Wiesel, Elie. The Nobel Peace Prize Lecture. 11 Dec. 1986.
  • Mr. Wiesel is the sole author of the text.

    © The Nobel Foundation 1986.

Wirt, William. *Sketches of the Life and Character of Patrick Henry.*
Philadelphia: 1836.

The sample essays for Joseph Epstein's "A Genius of Temperament: Joseph
Epstein remembers Irving Kristol" and "Obama's Good Students: A dissent on
the 'valedictocracy,'" Adlai Stevenson's "Cat Bill Veto," Winston Churchill's *Blood,
Sweat and Tears* speech, and the Alabama clergymen's "Call for Unity" were
written by Derek Spencer and are the property of Prestwick House, Inc.

Prestwick House AP Language and Composition

Introduction: *How to Use this Book*

To the Student

Prestwick House AP Language and Composition was written with you in mind. The AP Language and Composition exam is a demanding exercise that requires both a deep knowledge of the writer's craft and the application of strong analytical skills. Each chapter in this book focuses on a specific element of that craft: purpose, adherence to conventions of language, use of literary and rhetorical devices, and so on.

After some instructional material—definitions, explanations, and the like—we provide you with a nonfiction passage, the type of passage that is likely to appear on an AP English Language exam. In some cases, the passage has appeared on the exam. Many of the passages are listed as suggested reading by the Common Core State Standards initiative, so they are well-recommended and worth your attention.

The first passage in each chapter is annotated to reflect the kind of thinking a top-notch AP student would do while reading. The passage is then followed by five multiple-choice questions with the answers revealed. These are not to "test" your understanding of the passage but to show you the often fine distinctions between the "best" answer and some of the other choices that might seem "right" as well. Following the questions are explanations of each choice—why it is wrong, why it is right but not the best. Again, all of this is to model for you the type of thinking you'll want to have mastered before you take the exam.

Finally, we present you with an AP-style essay question for that same passage— followed by a model student essay.

Look over the passage and model test items as often as you need until you feel confident that you understand the chapter's focus. When you're ready to try it on your own, we provide you another high-quality nonfiction passage, multiple-choice questions, and writing prompt. Use the exercise as a practice test—and you can check your answers in the answer key at the end of the book.

Prestwick House AP Language and Composition follows the same format chapter after chapter, including the section on the Synthesis Essay. Here, too, we provide two models of quality student work for you to examine before you work on your own synthesis problems.

Whether you've bought this book for your own use at home or are using it as a text book in your AP class, we are confident you'll benefit from the models and exercises and will approach your AP English Language exam with confidence.

One important note: All of the passages and excerpts that are attributed to actual persons are accurately and authentically replicated with the appropriate permissions.

Some of the sources and data presented in this book, however,—especially in Synthesis Exercise Two—have been created solely for the purpose of the exercise. You are, therefore, urged to exercise caution and to verify all information before citing any of the sources in this book for your own research project. (You should be doing your own research anyway, right?)

To the Teacher

Prestwick House AP Language and Composition was written with you in mind. We know as well as you do that the AP Language and Composition exam is a demanding exercise that requires both a deep knowledge of the writer's craft and the application of strong analytical skills. We also know as well as you do that, in the wealth of AP test-prep materials on the market, there is precious little that is truly useable as a core text for your class. We know that your task is not only to prepare your students for the exam but to prepare them to meet your district and state's graduation requirements.

Toward that end, we've made every effort to fill this book with important nonfiction titles—the types of works that are likely to appear on the AP exam as well as those suggested by groups like the Common Core State Standards initiative. Thus, this book is useable as a core text for nonfiction even for classes that do not have an Advanced Placement emphasis.

For AP classes, however, you'll find the added benefit of the popular and effective teach-model-and-practice approach in every chapter. Each chapter focuses on a specific element of the craft: purpose, adherence to conventions of language, use of literary and rhetorical devices, and so on and could be a self-contained, weeklong unit.

It is your choice the extent to which you use this as a "homework text" or an "in-class text": use the annotated passages to foster class discussion; examine with the students the often fine distinctions between the "best" answer and some of the other choices that might also seem "right"; discuss the exercise passages in class or assign them as out-of-class reading; have the students do the exercise multiple-choice questions as a classroom activity or homework assignment; or have your students write the exercise essays for a grade or for pure practice.

Students can check their own understanding with the answer keys at the end of the book, or you can use the explanatory keys to help your students develop the analytical skills they will need to demonstrate on the exam.

Prestwick House AP Language and Composition is flexible and adaptable. It allows you to be as involved or as removed as you want and your students need.

One important note: All of the passages and excerpts that are attributed to actual persons are accurately and authentically replicated with the appropriate permissions.

Some of the sources and data presented in this book, however,—especially in Synthesis Exercise Two—have been created solely for the purpose of the exercise. Students are, therefore, urged to exercise caution and to verify all information before citing any of the sources in this book for their own research projects. (They should be doing their own research anyway, right?)

CHAPTER 1

A S A WRITER, you've probably already been taught to think always about your "audience and purpose." Audience and purpose may actually be specified in your writing assignments or the prompts on some of the writing tests you have taken. As a writer, you've probably also been taught that your awareness of purpose governs many of the decisions you will make in terms of organizational pattern, amount of information from outside, cited sources (and how you present it), tone, word choice, sentence structure, and so on.

The writers whose works you read have also been taught to be aware of audience and purpose, and awareness of purpose has the same implications for how they write as it does for you. It follows, then, that a *reader's* awareness of the author's purpose will help him or her understand, analyze, and evaluate the piece.

The three most common purposes for writing are to inform, to persuade, and to entertain. Certainly, these purposes are not mutually exclusive; most professional, published writers hope to entertain as well as inform and/or persuade. It is, therefore, helpful for readers to know why the piece they are reading was written and avoid being misinformed or misled.

 To inform

It almost goes without saying that to inform others is probably the most common purpose for writing. Even bloggers, tweeters, and people writing on social networks, for the most part, write to inform. Textbooks are written primarily to inform, as are newspapers and magazines (including electronic publications), and nonfiction books.

The person who is writing to inform is not pressing an agenda or arguing a point—at least not openly. Informative writing exists primarily for the information it conveys and should be evaluated in terms of the quality of that information and the effectiveness with which the writer communicates it.

Consider the following passage, an excerpt from Charles Darwin's account of his famous voyage to the Galapagos Islands. It has been annotated to point out to you the types of issues—word choice, sentence structure, use of figurative devices—that a careful reader would need to examine in a close reading, an analysis, or an evaluation of Darwin's account.

After you examine the passage and the accompanying notes, look at how a student taking the AP Language exam might respond to multiple-choice questions and a free-response item dealing with how Darwin communicates the information at the heart of his narrative.

from:

Narrative of the Surveying Voyages of His Majesty's Ships Adventure and Beagle (1839)

CHARLES DARWIN (1809-1882)

1 SEPTEMBER 15th.—This archipelago[1] consists of ten principal islands, of which five exceed the others in size. They are situated under the Equator, and between five and six hundred miles westward of the coast of America. They are all formed of volcanic rocks;[2] a few fragments of granite curiously glazed and altered by the heat, can hardly be considered as an exception. Some of the craters, surmounting the larger islands, are of immense size, and they rise to a height of between three and four thousand feet. Their flanks are studded by innumerable smaller orifices.[3] I scarcely hesitate to affirm, that there must be in the whole archipelago at least two thousand craters. These consist either of lava or scoriae, or of finely-stratified, sandstone-like tuff. Most of the latter are beautifully symmetrical; they owe their origin to eruptions of volcanic mud without any lava: it is a remarkable circumstance that every one of the twenty-eight tuff-craters which were examined, had their southern sides either much lower than the other sides, or quite broken down and removed.[4] As all these craters apparently have been formed when standing in the sea, and as the waves from the trade wind and the swell from the open Pacific here unite their forces on the southern coasts of all the islands, this singular uniformity in the broken state of the craters, composed of the soft and yielding tuff, is easily explained.[5]

Sample Student Commentary

[1] The antecedent to the demonstrative pronoun, this, is understood to be the Galapagos Archipelago, which is the title of this chapter.

[2] Note the use of the semicolon. Darwin is not simply combining two main clauses; they are closely connected by subject matter—the geologic makeup of the islands.

[3] Because this in an informative essay, Darwin is not overly concerned with narrative style or voice. Note the long string of basic, subject-verb sentences.

[4] Even the few instances of narrative intrusion—"can hardly be considered," "I scarcely hesitate to affirm," "it is a remarkable circumstance"—do little to alter the reader's understanding of, or reaction to, the essential facts of the description.

[5] The explanation, while logical and carefully laid out for the reader, is actually speculation. Darwin admits this when he says the craters were "apparently" formed.

2   Considering that these islands are placed directly under the equator, the climate is far from being excessively hot; this seems chiefly caused by[6] the singularly low temperature of the surrounding water, brought here by the great southern Polar current. Excepting during one short season, very little rain falls, and even then it is irregular; but the clouds generally hang low. Hence,[7] whilst the lower parts of the islands are very sterile, the upper parts, at a height of a thousand feet and upwards, possess a damp climate and a tolerably luxuriant vegetation. This is especially the case on the windward sides of the islands, which first receive and condense the moisture from the atmosphere.[8]

3   In the morning (17th) we landed on Chatham Island, which, like the others,[9] rises with a tame and rounded outline, broken here and there by scattered hillocks, the remains of former craters. Nothing could be less inviting [10] than the first appearance. A broken field of black basaltic lava, thrown into the most rugged waves, and crossed by great fissures, is everywhere covered by stunted, sun-burnt brushwood, which shows little signs of life. The dry and parched surface, being heated by the noon-day sun, gave to the air a close and sultry feeling, like that from a stove:[11] we fancied even that the bushes smelt unpleasantly. Although I diligently tried to collect as many plants as possible, I succeeded in getting very few; and such wretched-looking little weeds would have better become an arctic than an equatorial Flora. The brushwood appears, from a short distance, as leafless as our trees during winter; and it was some time before I discovered that not only almost every plant was now in full leaf, but that the greater number were in flower. The commonest bush is one of the *Euphorbiaceae*: an acacia and a great odd-looking cactus are the only trees which afford any shade. After the season of heavy rains, the islands are said to appear for a short time partially green. The volcanic island of Fernando Noronha, placed in many respects under nearly similar conditions, is the only other country where I have seen a vegetation at all like this of the Galapagos Islands.

4   The Beagle sailed round Chatham Island, and anchored in several bays. One night I slept on shore on a part of the island, where black truncated cones were extraordinarily numerous: from one small eminence I counted sixty of them, all surmounted by craters more or less perfect. The greater number consisted merely of a ring of red scoriae or slags, cemented together: and their height above the plain of lava was not more than from fifty to a hundred feet; none had been very lately active. The entire surface of this part of the island seems to have been permeated, like a sieve,[12] by the subterranean vapours: here and there the lava, whilst soft, has been blown into great bubbles; and in other

---

Sample Student Commentary

[6] Again, Darwin presents us with an unproven conclusion, though it is, again, based on an observation, and he does share with the reader the basis of the conclusion.

[7] The "hence" suggests that Darwin is certain of this cause-and-effect relationship. He is not hypothesizing the reason for the high-altitude vegetation.

[8] Notice how every observation is followed by a detailed explanation.

[9] This is a literal prepositional phrase, not a SIMILE.

[10] This is a nice example of LITOTES, one of the rare rhetorical devices in this essay.

[11] This is indeed a SIMILE but, like the earlier narrative intrusions, does not really alter the meaning or impact of the passage.

[12] Here is another SIMILE. Again, it is almost a literal comparison and does nothing to create tone, mood, or voice.

parts, the tops of caverns similarly formed have fallen in, leaving circular pits with steep sides. From the regular form of the many craters, they gave to the country an artificial appearance, which vividly reminded me of those parts of Staffordshire, where the great iron-foundries are most numerous. The day was glowing hot, and the scrambling over the rough surface and through the intricate thickets, was very fatiguing; but I was well repaid by the strange Cyclopean[†] scene. As I was walking along I met two large tortoises, each of which must have weighed at least two hundred pounds: one was eating a piece of cactus, and as I approached, it stared at me and slowly walked away; the other gave a deep hiss, and drew in its head. These huge reptiles, surrounded by the black lava, the leafless shrubs, and large cacti, seemed to my fancy like some antediluvian animals.[13] The few dull-coloured birds cared no more for me than they did for the great tortoises. 🍎

[†]Rather than alluding to the mythological Cyclops, Darwin is probably referring here to Cyclopean masonry, an ancient building technique in which stones are stacked with minimal gaps and no mortar between them.

Sample Student Commentary

[13]This SIMILE and the earlier LITOTES are the only two figurative or rhetorical uses in this essay. Darwin's intent has been to share information, not persuade, entertain, or express his personal opinion or feelings.

Sample multiple-choice questions:

1. In the line "Most of the latter are beautifully symmetrical," (paragraph 1) "latter" refers to
   A. "their southern sides."
   B. "innumerable smaller orifices."
   C. "lava and scoriae."
   D. "sandstone-like tuff."
   E. "eruptions of volcanic mud."

2. Darwin's reference to "[t]he volcanic island of Fernando Noronha" (paragraph 3) serves primarily to
   A. illustrate the extent of his travels.
   B. compare the Galapagos with a more familiar island.
   C. intensify the hostility of the island geography.
   D. orient the reader to the *Beagle's* location.
   E. allude to an earlier portion of Darwin's book.

3. The primary focus of the author's observation in the sentence beginning "I scarcely hesitate to affirm..." (paragraph 1) is the
   A. number of craters.
   B. ubiquity of the craters.
   C. origin of the craters.
   D. size of the craters.
   E. substance of the craters.

4. Which of the following organizational plans does Darwin employ most frequently in this essay?

    A. sequential order

    B. order of magnitude

    C. chronological order

    D. cause and effect

    E. *comparison and contrast*

5. The strongest personal evaluation in the essay emphasizes the

    A. ruggedness of the landscape.

    B. disinterest of the wildlife.

    C. incongruity of the climate.

    D. *inhospitable nature of the islands.*

    E. remoteness of the archipelago.

Answers and Explanations:

1. "Latter" must refer to the second of two items mentioned previously. Therefore, (A) and (E) are immediately excluded since they occur later in the passage. (B) occurs too much earlier to be the referent for "the latter," nor is it the second of two items. Only (C) and (D) remain, and (D) is the second in the pairing. **Thus (D) is the correct answer. It is the tuff-craters that are "beautifully symmetrical."**

2. As the overall purpose of this passage is clearly to provide a clear and factual description of the flora, fauna, and geology of the Galapagos, (A) is unlikely. (C) is true but relies on the reader's knowing something about Fernando Noronha; otherwise it is a pointless reference. Likewise (D) is impossible if the reader has no prior knowledge of Fernando Noronha. (E) is possible, as an earlier chapter may be where the reader learned of Fernando Noronha, but there is nothing in *this* passage to suggest that. **Therefore, (B) is the best answer. The comparison to Fernando Noronha is meaningful to the reader only if the reader has some prior familiarity with this island.**

3. The affirmation that Darwin makes without hesitation is that there were "at least two thousand craters." **Thus (A) is the correct answer**. That the craters are found everywhere in the archipelago (B), how they formed (C), their size (D), and makeup (E) are all mentioned, but only in the aftermath of Darwin's amazed affirmation of how many craters there were.

4. Throughout the passage, Darwin uses comparisons with places and objects the reader should know: the air was hot "like that from a stove," the islands had apparently been permeated by volcanic gas "like a sieve." The plant life is compared to the island of Fernando Noronha, and even the description of the archipelago itself contrasts the

humid upper altitudes with the arid lower altitudes and the smooth uniformity of the southern sides of the craters. Both Darwin's description of the plant life and the climate contrast the equator with the poles. **Thus, (E) is the correct answer.** (C) and (D) may be tempting since the chapter itself seems to be organized by date, almost like a journal or diary, and Darwin does hypothesize about the causes and origins of the phenomena he observes, but the preponderance of details strongly support (E). There is nothing in the passage to suggest (A) or (B).

5. Because it is an informative passage of an essentially scientific nature, there is relatively little authorial intrusion and little attention to style and effect. The two similes are almost literal explanations. The most notable rhetorical devices for effect or emphasis are the litotes in paragraph 3 and the final simile. This simile, comparing the Galapagos tortoises to antediluvian creatures, while descriptive, is not evaluative. The litotes, however, "Nothing could be less inviting," *is* an evaluation, and nearly every detail in the passage illustrates and emphasizes, not just the oddity of the islands, but their harshness and ugliness (A), (B), and (C). (E) is suggested in the first paragraph, but as a manner of fact, not evaluation. **Thus, (D) is the best answer**.

Sample free-response item:

Carefully read the excerpt from Charles Darwin's 1839 study, *Narrative of the Surveying Voyages of His Majesty's Ships* Adventure *and* Beagle. In the chapter from which this passage was excerpted, Darwin provides a physical description of the Galapagos archipelago's plant and animal life and geological features. After reading the passage, write an essay in which you analyze Darwin's organizational pattern, especially how he uses transitional elements to add cohesion to his description.

Sample Student Essay

Charles Darwin's famous *Narrative of the Surveying Voyages of His Majesty's Ships* Adventure and Beagle is essentially a scientific report. As such, it must be clear and factual, untainted by opinion or bias. One of the primary issues the writer of such a piece faces is how to organize the data when there is no obvious or necessary organizational pattern. Given the details Darwin is going to relate in the four paragraphs of this passage, he selects an order of size or magnitude, from largest or most general, to smallest and most specific. He is also extremely careful to link the details in each paragraph to at least imply a relationship between them and contribute a sense of cohesion to the passage.

The four categories of detail that Darwin explores are geology, climate, plant life, and animal life. He deals with them in an order of decreasing magnitude, from that which could be observed of all the islands immediately upon their approach, to that which Darwin found on only one island during a relatively intimate examination.

The essay begins with Darwin's referencing "this archipelago." The paragraph that follows is an overall description of the islands, details that could be observed without too close a study of any particular island—the location, geologic features, mineral makeup, and so on. The overall view opens the passage, begins to give the reader an impression of the odd and exotic place, but serves almost as a backdrop to the more detailed descriptions that follow.

Second in magnitude, what would be next noticeable without too intimate a knowledge of any particular island is the climate. Darwin's description of the low-hanging clouds and the difference between the humid upper elevations and the arid lower ground does require a closer examination than does his observation of the craters, but it is still not the intimate view that will come with the descriptions of the plant and animal life in the final paragraphs.

Darwin's description of the archipelago's plant life begins with the expedition's landing on a specific island: Chatham Island. The description of the flora, however, stays relatively general, mentioning "wretched-looking little weeds" and "brushwood." Even when Darwin mentions specific plant species, he does not talk about any specific plant.

Finally, however, Darwin provides an intimate look at the island, beginning with his revealing that he actually spent a night on the island, rather than on the ship. It is the morning after this night that Darwin encounters the two tortoises, both of whom indicate an awareness of him as well. Clearly, then, from the first paragraph's overall account of the islands' geophysical situation to an intimate encounter with two of the islands' exotic inhabitants, Darwin has increasingly narrowed his focus and led his reader to a close-up view of this unearthly archipelago.

As an aid in achieving this narrower focus, Darwin is careful to provide his reader with topical transitions both within and between his paragraphs. While establishing the location of the Galapagos, he writes that the islands "are situated under the Equator." This is a description of physical location, yet Darwin uses the same phraseology when beginning his discussion of the islands' climate in the next paragraph: "Considering that these islands are placed directly under the equator..." Thus, he achieves both a link to and a transition from the information in the first paragraph. Similarly, in the middle of Darwin's climate paragraph, when he is contrasting the humid mountains above one thousand feet to the arid lower elevations, he introduces the topic of vegetation, which becomes the primary topic of the third paragraph. The final paragraph would seem to return to the earlier, broader view, except for the fact that this paragraph begins with Darwin's actually spending a night on the island: the detailed description of this island's geology, this island's climate, and finally this island's vegetation feeding this island's animal life, specifically two tortoises encountered by the author.

Thus, from an introduction of "ten principal islands" to a face-to-face encounter with two reptiles, one of whom hisses at him, Charles Darwin leads his reader through a process of narrowing focus, more or less an order of decreasing magnitude, in order to provide his reader with an accurate and understandable description of the unprecedented phenomena of the exotic archipelago. ❧

Exercise One:

Questions 1-5. Read the following passage carefully before you choose your answers.

This passage is the first essay of Thomas Paine's The Crisis. The Crisis *is a collection of articles written by Thomas Paine during the American Revolutionary War between December 1776 and April 1783. They reported Paine's continued support for the cause of American independence and provided inspiration to the struggling Americans throughout the war. General Washington found this first essay, dated 23 December 1776 so inspiring that he ordered it to be read to his troops at Valley Forge.*

1 THESE ARE THE TIMES THAT TRY MEN'S SOULS. The summer soldier and the sunshine patriot will, in this crisis, shrink from the service of their country; but he that stands by it now deserves the love and thanks of man and woman. Tyranny, like hell, is not easily conquered; yet we have this consolation with us, that the harder the conflict, the more glorious the triumph. What we obtain too cheap, we esteem too lightly: it is dearness only that gives every thing its value. Heaven knows how to put a proper price upon its goods; and it would be strange indeed if so celestial an article as FREEDOM should not be highly rated. Britain, with an army to enforce her tyranny, has declared that she has a right (not only to TAX) but "to BIND us in ALL CASES WHATSOEVER," and if being bound in that manner, is not slavery, then is there not such a thing as slavery upon earth. Even the expression is impious; for so unlimited a power can belong only to God.

[handwritten margin notes: to engage / hook / emotion / passion / "poetry" / fervent]

2 Whether the independence of the continent was declared too soon, or delayed too long, I will not now enter into as an argument; my own simple opinion is, that had it been eight months earlier, it would have been much better. We did not make a proper use of last winter, neither could we, while we were in a dependent state. However, the fault, if it were one, was all our own; we have none to blame but ourselves. But no great deal is lost yet. All that Howe has been doing for this month past, is rather a ravage than a conquest, which the spirit of the Jerseys, a year ago, would have quickly repulsed, and which time and a little resolution will soon recover.

[handwritten margin notes: TS / calmer / still intense / inspire / encourage / firm / earnest]

3 I have as little superstition in me as any man living, but my secret opinion has ever been, and still is, that God Almighty will not give up a people to military destruction, or leave them unsupportedly to perish, who have so earnestly and so repeatedly sought to avoid the calamities of war, by every decent method which wisdom could invent. Neither have I so much of the infidel in me, as to suppose that He has relinquished the government of the world, and given us up to the care of devils; and as I do not, I cannot see on what grounds the king of Britain can look up to heaven for help against us: a common murderer, a highwayman, or a house-breaker, has as good a pretence as he.

4 'Tis surprising to see how rapidly a panic will sometimes run through a country. All nations and ages have been subject to them. Britain has trembled like an ague at the report of a French fleet of flat-bottomed boats; and in the fourteenth [fifteenth] century the whole English army, after ravaging the kingdom of France, was driven back like men petrified with fear; and this brave exploit was performed by a few broken forces collected and headed by a woman, Joan of Arc. Would that heaven might inspire some

Jersey maid to spirit up her countrymen, and save her fair fellow sufferers from ravage and ravishment! Yet panics, in some cases, have their uses; they produce as much good as hurt. Their duration is always short; the mind soon grows through them, and acquires a firmer habit than before. But their peculiar advantage is, that they are the touchstones of sincerity and hypocrisy, and bring things and men to light, which might otherwise have lain forever undiscovered. In fact, they have the same effect on secret traitors, which an imaginary apparition would have upon a private murderer. They sift out the hidden thoughts of man, and hold them up in public to the world. Many a disguised Tory has lately shown his head, that shall penitentially solemnize with curses the day on which Howe arrived upon the Delaware.

5 As I was with the troops at Fort Lee, and marched with them to the edge of Pennsylvania, I am well acquainted with many circumstances, which those who live at a distance know but little or nothing of. Our situation there was exceedingly cramped, the place being a narrow neck of land between the North River and the Hackensack. Our force was inconsiderable, being not one-fourth so great as Howe could bring against us. We had no army at hand to have relieved the garrison, had we shut ourselves up and stood on our defense. Our ammunition, light artillery, and the best part of our stores, had been removed, on the apprehension that Howe would endeavor to penetrate the Jerseys, in which case Fort Lee could be of no use to us; for it must occur to every thinking man, whether in the army or not, that these kind of field forts are only for temporary purposes, and last in use no longer than the enemy directs his force against the particular object which such forts are raised to defend. Such was our situation and condition at Fort Lee on the morning of the 20th of November, when an officer arrived with information that the enemy with 200 boats had landed about seven miles above; Major General [Nathaniel] Green, who commanded the garrison, immediately ordered them under arms, and sent express to General Washington at the town of Hackensack, distant by the way of the ferry —six miles. Our first object was to secure the bridge over the Hackensack, which laid up the river between the enemy and us, about six miles from us, and three from them. General Washington arrived in about three-quarters of an hour, and marched at the head of the troops towards the bridge, which place I expected we should have a brush for; however, they did not choose to dispute it with us, and the greatest part of our troops went over the bridge, the rest over the ferry, except some which passed at a mill on a small creek, between the bridge and the ferry, and made their way through some marshy grounds up to the town of Hackensack, and there passed the river. We brought off as much baggage as the wagons could contain, the rest was lost. The simple object was to bring off the garrison, and march them on till they could be strengthened by the Jersey or Pennsylvania militia, so as to be enabled to make a stand. We staid four days at Newark, collected our out-posts with some of the Jersey militia, and marched out twice to meet the enemy, on being informed that they were advancing, though our numbers were greatly inferior to theirs. Howe, in my little opinion, committed a great error in generalship in not throwing a body of forces off from Staten Island through Amboy, by which means he might have seized all our stores at Brunswick, and intercepted our march into Pennsylvania; but if we believe the power of hell to be limited, we must likewise believe that their agents are under some providential control.

6   I shall not now attempt to give all the particulars of our retreat to the Delaware; suffice it for the present to say, that both officers and men, though greatly harassed and fatigued, frequently without rest, covering, or provision, the inevitable consequences of a long retreat, bore it with a manly and martial spirit. All their wishes centered in one, which was, that the country would turn out and help them to drive the enemy back. Voltaire has remarked that King William never appeared to full advantage but in difficulties and in action; the same remark may be made on General Washington, for the character fits him. There is a natural firmness in some minds which cannot be unlocked by trifles, but which, when unlocked, discovers a cabinet of fortitude; and I reckon it among those kind of public blessings, which we do not immediately see, that God hath blessed him with uninterrupted health, and given him a mind that can even flourish upon care.

7   I shall conclude this paper with some miscellaneous remarks on the state of our affairs; and shall begin with asking the following question, Why is it that the enemy have left the New England provinces, and made these middle ones the seat of war? The answer is easy: New England is not infested with Tories, and we are. I have been tender in raising the cry against these men, and used numberless arguments to show them their danger, but it will not do to sacrifice a world either to their folly or their baseness. The period is now arrived, in which either they or we must change our sentiments, or one or both must fall. And what is a Tory? Good God! What is he? I should not be afraid to go with a hundred Whigs against a thousand Tories, were they to attempt to get into arms. Every Tory is a coward; for servile, slavish, self-interested fear is the foundation of Toryism; and a man under such influence, though he may be cruel, never can be brave.

8   But, before the line of irrecoverable separation be drawn between us, let us reason the matter together: Your conduct is an invitation to the enemy, yet not one in a thousand of you has heart enough to join him. Howe is as much deceived by you as the American cause is injured by you. He expects you will all take up arms, and flock to his standard, with muskets on your shoulders. Your opinions are of no use to him, unless you support him personally, for 'tis soldiers, and not Tories, that he wants.

9   I once felt all that kind of anger, which a man ought to feel, against the mean principles that are held by the Tories: a noted one, who kept a tavern at Amboy, was standing at his door, with as pretty a child in his hand, about eight or nine years old, as I ever saw, and after speaking his mind as freely as he thought was prudent, finished with this unfatherly expression, "Well! give me peace in my day." Not a man lives on the continent but fully believes that a separation must some time or other finally take place, and a generous parent should have said, "If there must be trouble, let it be in my day, that my child may have peace;" and this single reflection, well applied, is sufficient to awaken every man to duty. Not a place upon earth might be so happy as America. Her situation is remote from all the wrangling world, and she has nothing to do but to trade with them. A man can distinguish himself between temper and principle, and I am as confident, as I am that God governs the world, that America will never be happy till she gets clear of foreign dominion. Wars, without ceasing, will break out till that period arrives, and the continent must in the end be conqueror; for though the flame of liberty may sometimes cease to shine, the coal can never expire.

10   America did not, nor does not want force; but she wanted a proper application of

that force. Wisdom is not the purchase of a day, and it is no wonder that we should err at the first setting off. From an excess of tenderness, we were unwilling to raise an army, and trusted our cause to the temporary defense of a well-meaning militia. A summer's experience has now taught us better; yet with those troops, while they were collected, we were able to set bounds to the progress of the enemy, and, thank God! they are again assembling. I always considered militia as the best troops in the world for a sudden exertion, but they will not do for a long campaign. Howe, it is probable, will make an attempt on this city [Philadelphia]; should he fail on this side the Delaware, he is ruined. If he succeeds, our cause is not ruined. He stakes all on his side against a part on ours; admitting he succeeds, the consequence will be, that armies from both ends of the continent will march to assist their suffering friends in the middle states; for he cannot go everywhere, it is impossible. I consider Howe as the greatest enemy the Tories have; he is bringing a war into their country, which, had it not been for him and partly for themselves, they had been clear of. Should he now be expelled, I wish with all the devotion of a Christian, that the names of Whig and Tory may never more be mentioned; but should the Tories give him encouragement to come, or assistance if he come, I as sincerely wish that our next year's arms may expel them from the continent, and the Congress appropriate their possessions to the relief of those who have suffered in well-doing. A single successful battle next year will settle the whole. America could carry on a two years' war by the confiscation of the property of disaffected persons, and be made happy by their expulsion. Say not that this is revenge, call it rather the soft resentment of a suffering people, who, having no object in view but the good of all, have staked their own all upon a seemingly doubtful event. Yet it is folly to argue against determined hardness; eloquence may strike the ear, and the language of sorrow draw forth the tear of compassion, but nothing can reach the heart that is steeled with prejudice.

Quitting this class of men, I turn with the warm ardor of a friend to those who have nobly stood, and are yet determined to stand the matter out: I call not upon a few, but upon all: not on this state or that state, but on every state: up and help us; lay your shoulders to the wheel; better have too much force than too little, when so great an object is at stake. Let it be told to the future world, that in the depth of winter, when nothing but hope and virtue could survive, that the city and the country, alarmed at one common danger, came forth to meet and to repulse it. Say not that thousands are gone, turn out your tens of thousands; throw not the burden of the day upon Providence, but "show your faith by your works," that God may bless you. It matters not where you live, or what rank of life you hold, the evil or the blessing will reach you all. The far and the near, the home counties and the back, the rich and the poor, will suffer or rejoice alike. The heart that feels not now is dead; the blood of his children will curse his cowardice, who shrinks back at a time when a little might have saved the whole, and made them happy. I love the man that can smile in trouble, that can gather strength from distress, and grow brave by reflection. 'Tis the business of little minds to shrink; but he whose heart is firm, and whose conscience approves his conduct, will pursue his principles unto death. My own line of reasoning is to myself as straight and clear as a ray of light. Not all the treasures of the world, so far as I believe, could have induced me to support an offensive war, for I think it murder; but if a thief breaks into my house, burns and destroys my property,

25

and kills or threatens to kill me, or those that are in it, and to "bind me in all cases whatsoever" to his absolute will, am I to suffer it? What signifies it to me, whether he who does it is a king or a common man; my countryman or not my countryman; whether it be done by an individual villain, or an army of them? If we reason to the root of things we shall find no difference; neither can any just cause be assigned why we should punish in the one case and pardon in the other. Let them call me rebel and welcome, I feel no concern from it; but I should suffer the misery of devils, were I to make a whore of my soul by swearing allegiance to one whose character is that of a sottish, stupid, stubborn, worthless, brutish man. I conceive likewise a horrid idea in receiving mercy from a being, who at the last day shall be shrieking to the rocks and mountains to cover him, and fleeing with terror from the orphan, the widow, and the slain of America.

TS **12**   There are cases which cannot be overdone by language, and this is one. There are persons, too, who see not the full extent of the evil which threatens them; they solace themselves with hopes that the enemy, if he succeed, will be merciful. It is the madness of folly, to expect mercy from those who have refused to do justice; and even mercy, where conquest is the object, is only a trick of war; the cunning of the fox is as murderous as the violence of the wolf, and we ought to guard equally against both. Howe's first object is, partly by threats and partly by promises, to terrify or seduce the people to deliver up their arms and receive mercy. The ministry recommended the same plan to Gage, and this is what the Tories call making their peace, "a peace which passeth all understanding" indeed! A peace which would be the immediate forerunner of a worse ruin than any we have yet thought of. Ye men of Pennsylvania, do reason upon these things! Were the back counties to give up their arms, they would fall an easy prey to the Indians, who are all armed: this perhaps is what some Tories would not be sorry for. Were the home counties to deliver up their arms, they would be exposed to the resentment of the back counties who would then have it in their power to chastise their defection at pleasure. And were any one state to give up its arms, that state must be garrisoned by all Howe's army of Britons and Hessians to preserve it from the anger of the rest. Mutual fear is the principal link in the chain of mutual love, and woe be to that state that breaks the compact. Howe is mercifully inviting you to barbarous destruction, and men must be either rogues or fools that will not see it. I dwell not upon the vapors of imagination; I bring reason to your ears, and, in language as plain as A, B, C, hold up truth to your eyes.

TS **13**   I thank God, that I fear not. I see no real cause for fear. I know our situation well, and can see the way out of it. While our army was collected, Howe dared not risk a battle; and it is no credit to him that he decamped from the White Plains, and waited a mean opportunity to ravage the defenseless Jerseys; but it is great credit to us, that, with a handful of men, we sustained an orderly retreat for near an hundred miles, brought off our ammunition, all our field pieces, the greatest part of our stores, and had four rivers to pass. None can say that our retreat was precipitate, for we were near three weeks in performing it, that the country might have time to come in. Twice we marched back to meet the enemy, and remained out till dark. The sign of fear was not seen in our camp, and had not some of the cowardly and disaffected inhabitants spread false alarms through the country, the Jerseys had never been ravaged. Once more we are again collected and collecting; our new army at both ends of the continent is recruiting fast, and we shall be able to open the next campaign with sixty thousand men, well armed and clothed. This is our situation, and who will may know it. By perseverance and fortitude we have the prospect of a glorious issue; by cowardice and submission, the sad choice of a variety of evils—a ravaged country—a depopulated city—habitations without safety, and slavery without hope—our homes turned into barracks and bawdy-houses for Hessians, and a future race to provide for, whose fathers we shall doubt of. Look on this picture and weep over it! and if there yet remains one thoughtless wretch who believes it not, let him suffer it unlamented. ❦

December 23, 1776

Multiple-choice questions:

1. The opening paragraph of this essay employs all of the following rhetorical devices EXCEPT

    A. sententia.

    B. simile.

    C. metaphor.

    D. exemplum.

    E. antithesis.

2. Paine claims not to be superstitious (paragraph 3) in order to

    A. emphasize his comparison of the king to a murderer.

    B. contrast his lack of belief with his political infidelity.

    C. remind his reader that the colonies tried to avoid war.

    D. invoke Divine Wrath on the king of Britain.

    E. validate his claim that God supports the American cause.

3. The antecedent of the pronoun *they*, as it is used in the line "they are the touchstones of sincerity and hypocrisy" (paragraph 4) is

    A. nations.

    B. countrymen.

    C. panics.

    D. traitors.

    E. curses.

4. The fifth paragraph begins a temporary shift in tone and purpose from___to___

    A. expressive to informative.

    B. informative to inspirational.

    C. persuasive to informative.

    D. inspirational to academic.

    E. academic to persuasive.

5. The tone of the eleventh paragraph, which begins, "Quitting this class of men, I turn with the warm ardor of a friend," can best be described as

A. ardent.

B. fervent.

C. torpid.

D. vitriolic.

E. hostile.

Free Response Item:

Carefully read the 23 December 1776 essay from Thomas Paine's *The Crisis*. Then, write an essay in which you analyze the various tones Paine adopts and the apparent purpose of each. Do not merely summarize Paine's argument or the information he provides.

To persuade

A good deal of nonfiction is written, not only to inform, but to persuade the reader or hearer to agree with the author or speaker, possibly even to take some action that is encouraged in the piece. The vast majority of political writing and speaking, especially campaign messages, is persuasive in nature. Television commercials, many (but not all) editorials, and letters to the editor are persuasive.

Remember that the goal of a truly persuasive piece is not merely to express an opinion or to disseminate information. The writer who is writing to persuade is pressing an agenda; he or she is arguing a point. A persuasive piece, then, should be evaluated in terms of its overall effect on the reader or hearer. Has the writer communicated a clear thesis; has he or she demonstrated the validity of that thesis; are you, the reader, at all tempted to reevaluate the position you currently hold and at least consider (if not completely embrace) the position espoused in the passage?

Consider the following passage, Senator Margaret Chase Smith's famous 1950 "Declaration of Conscience." Smith was a Republican Senator from Maine, the first woman from Maine to have held that office. In the face of what she considered abuses of senatorial authority and a lack of leadership from the executive branch, she drafted this declaration, which she presented on the floor of the Senate. The passage has been annotated to point out to you the types of issues—statement of thesis, presentation of clear and specific evidence, use of rhetorical devices, lapses into potential propaganda, and so on—that a careful reader would need to examine in a close reading, an analysis, or an evaluation of a passage written with "an agenda," one written to persuade its audience to assume a certain view or take a particular action.

After you examine the passage and the accompanying notes, look at how a student taking the AP Language exam might respond to the multiple-choice questions and a free-response item dealing with how Margaret Chase Smith states, develops, and supports her argument.

Declaration of Conscience

1 *My creed is that public service must be more than doing a job efficiently and honestly. It must be a complete dedication to the people and to the nation with full recognition that every human being is entitled to courtesy and consideration, that constructive criticism is not only to be expected but sought, that smears are not only to be expected but fought, that honor is to be earned but not bought.*

—Senator Margaret Chase Smith
For Release Upon Delivery

Statement of Senator Margaret Chase Smith
June 1, 1950

Mr. President:

2 I would like to speak briefly and simply about a serious national condition. It is a national feeling of fear and frustration that could result in national suicide and the end of everything that we Americans hold dear. It is a condition that comes from the lack of effective leadership in either the Legislative Branch or the Executive Branch of our Government.[1]

3 That leadership is so lacking that serious and responsible proposals[2] are being made that national advisory commissions be appointed to provide such critically needed leadership.

4 I speak as briefly as possible because too much harm has already been done with irresponsible words of bitterness and selfish political opportunism. I speak as simply as possible because the issue is too great to be obscured by eloquence. I speak simply and briefly in the hope that my words will be taken to heart.

Sample Student Commentary

[1] Senator Smith has clearly identified her thesis: a national condition exists that could threaten the very existence of the United States. Further, the condition reflects a lack of leadership from both the President and the Congress.

[2] Note Senator Smith's subtle, yet effective, use of adjectives. The "proposals" to which she alludes are "serious and responsible." The reader is almost lulled into accepting the Senator's assertion as verified fact.

5   I speak as a Republican, I speak as a woman. I speak as a United States Senator. I speak as an American.[3]

6   The United States Senate has long enjoyed worldwide respect as the greatest deliberative body in the world.[4] But recently that deliberative character has too often been debased to the level of a forum of hate and character assassination sheltered by the shield of congressional immunity.[5]

7   It is ironical that we Senators can in debate in the Senate directly or indirectly, by any form of words impute to any American, who is not a Senator, any conduct or motive unworthy or unbecoming an American—and without that non-Senator American having any legal redress against us—yet if we say the same thing in the Senate about our colleagues we can be stopped on the grounds of being out of order.[6]

8   It is strange that we can verbally attack anyone else without restraint and with full protection and yet we hold ourselves above the same type of criticism here on the Senate Floor.[7] Surely the United States Senate is big enough to take self-criticism and self-appraisal. Surely we should be able to take the same kind of character attacks that we dish out to outsiders.

9   I think that it is high time for the United States Senate and its members to do some soul searching—for us to weigh our consciences—on the manner in which we are performing our duty to the people of America—on the manner in which we are using or abusing our individual powers and privileges.

10   I think that it is high time that we remembered that we have sworn to uphold and defend the Constitution. I think that it is high time that we remembered; that the Constitution, as amended, speaks not only of the freedom of speech but also of trial by jury instead of trial by accusation.[8]

11   Whether it be a criminal prosecution in court or a character prosecution in the Senate, there is little practical distinction when the life of a person has been ruined.[9]

12   Those of us who shout the loudest about Americanism in making character assassinations are all too frequently those who, by our own words and acts, ignore some of the basic principles of Americanism—[10]

The right to criticize;

Sample Student Commentary

[3] With her repetition of the clause "I speak," Senator Smith is also effectively applying the rhetorical device anaphora.

[4] A careful reader needs to discern how much of this statement is fact and how much is hyperbole.

[5] This statement is also an assessment, a statement of opinion. Careful readers will withhold agreement or disagreement until they see what facts and examples the Senator offers as support.

[6] This is a long and complicated sentence. The main idea of the sentence is that Senators can impugn defenseless citizens with no fear of legal retribution, but cannot hold colleagues in the Senate accountable without being reprimanded themselves.

[7] This much simpler sentence reiterates the same idea.

[8] The Senator's references to the Constitution are all verifiable, thus giving the reader a sound basis for agreeing or disagreeing with her conclusions.

[9] "Whether it be…" is a subjunctive construction, establishing this statement as hypothetical.

[10] Notice the Senator's use of first person. She is, at least rhetorically, including herself in her criticism.

The right to hold unpopular beliefs;

The right to protest;

The right of independent thought.[11]

13 The exercise of these rights should not cost one single American citizen his reputation or his right to a livelihood nor should he be in danger of losing his reputation or livelihood merely because he happens to know someone who holds unpopular beliefs. Who of us doesn't?[12] Otherwise none of us could call our souls our own. Otherwise thought control would have set in.

14 The American people are sick and tired of being afraid to speak their minds lest they be politically smeared as "Communists" or "Fascists" by their opponents. Freedom of speech is not what it used to be in America. It has been so abused by some that it is not exercised by others. The American people are sick and tired of seeing innocent people smeared and guilty people whitewashed. But there have been enough proved cases to cause nationwide distrust and strong suspicion that there may be something to the unproved, sensational accusations.

15 As a Republican, I say to my colleagues on this side of the aisle that the Republican Party faces a challenge today that is not unlike the challenge that it faced back in Lincoln's day. The Republican Party so successfully met that challenge that it emerged from the Civil War as the champion of a united nation—in addition to being a Party that unrelentingly fought loose spending and loose programs.[13]

16 Today our country is being psychologically divided by the confusion and the suspicions that are bred in the United States Senate to spread like cancerous tentacles of "know nothing, suspect everything" attitudes.[14] Today we have a Democratic Administration that has developed a mania for loose spending and loose programs.[15] History is repeating itself—and the Republican Party again has the opportunity to emerge as the champion of unity and prudence.

17 The record of the present Democratic Administration[16] has provided us with sufficient campaign issues without the necessity of resorting to political smears. America is rapidly losing its position as leader of the world simply because the Democratic Administration has pitifully failed to provide effective leadership.[17]

18 The Democratic Administration has completely confused the American people by its daily contradictory grave warnings and optimistic assurances—that show the people that

---

Sample Student Commentary

[11] These are clearly not verbatim from the Bill of Rights, but they are fairly close paraphrases, verifiable by consulting the actual amendments.

[12] Here, the Senator's rhetorical use of the first person draws the reader—even the reader who is inclined to disagree with the thesis—into complicity.

[13] The Senator's reference to the Civil War is verifiable as fact. The reader must determine the point and effectiveness of her reference to "loose spending and loose programs."

[14] This is a return to Margaret Chase Smith's original thesis.

[15] Again, however, the reader must question the relevance of references to spending and programs.

[16] Senator Smith is referring to the administration of President Harry S. Truman.

[17] This reiterates what the Senator said at the beginning of her Declaration. There is, however, no further development or elaboration.

our Democratic Administration has no idea of where it is going.[18]

19   The Democratic Administration has greatly lost the confidence of the American people by its complacency to the threat of communism here at home and the leak of vital secrets to Russia through key officials of the Democratic Administration. There are enough proved cases to make this point without diluting our criticism with unproved charges.

20   Surely these are sufficient reasons to make it clear to the American people that it is time for a change and that a Republican victory is necessary to the security of this country.[19] Surely it is clear that this nation will continue to suffer as long as it is governed by the present ineffective Democratic Administration.

21   Yet to displace it with a Republican regime[20] embracing a philosophy that lacks political integrity or intellectual honesty would prove equally disastrous to this nation. The nation sorely needs a Republican victory. But I don't want to see the Republican Party ride to political victory on the Four Horsemen of Calumny—Fear, Ignorance, Bigotry and Smear.[21]

22   I doubt if the Republican Party could—simply because I don't believe the American people will uphold any political party that puts political exploitation above national interest. Surely we Republicans aren't that desperate for victory.

23   I don't want to see the Republican Party win that way. While it might be a fleeting victory for the Republican Party, it would be a more lasting defeat for the American people.[22] Surely it would ultimately be suicide for the Republican Party and the two-party system that has protected our American liberties from the dictatorship of a one party system.

24   As members of the Minority Party, we do not have the primary authority to formulate the policy of our Government. But we do have the responsibility of rendering constructive criticism, of clarifying issues, of allaying fears by acting as responsible citizens.

25   As a woman, I wonder how the mothers, wives, sisters and daughters feel about the way in which members of their families have been politically mangled in Senate debate— and I use the word 'debate' advisedly.[23]

26   As a United States Senator, I am not proud of the way in which the Senate has been made a publicity platform for irresponsible sensationalism. I am not proud of the reckless abandon in which unproved charges have been hurled from this side of the aisle.[24] I am

---

Sample Student Commentary

[18] The reader must determine whether these assertions can be supported with specific examples.

[19] An examination of the preceding five paragraphs shows Smith's subtle shift in focus from her original thesis to an apparent campaign address.

[20] Note the very careful word choice. In the United States, the conventional term is "administration." "Regime" connotes an entirely different type of government.

[21] Smith makes an allusion to the Four Horsemen of the Apocalypse, associated with devastation.

[22] "Fleeting victory" contrasted with "lasting defeat" and "Republican Party" contrasted with "American people" provide two strong examples of antithesis.

[23] The reader must determine the extent to which the Senator's gender is relevant and whether her allusion to "mothers, wives, sisters, and daughters" is a valid argument or propaganda.

[24] In earlier paragraphs, Senator Smith was critical of the "Democratic Administration." Now, however, she includes the Republican minority in her criticism.

not proud of the obviously staged, undignified countercharges that have been attempted in retaliation from the other side of the aisle.

27   I don't like the way the Senate has been made a rendezvous for vilification, for selfish political gain at the sacrifice of individual reputations and national unity. I am not proud of the way we smear outsiders from the Floor of the Senate and hide behind the cloak of congressional immunity and still place ourselves beyond criticism on the Floor of the Senate.[25]

28   As an American, I am shocked at the way Republicans and Democrats alike are playing directly into the Communist design of "confuse, divide and conquer." As an American, I don't want a Democratic Administration "white wash" or "cover up" any more than I want a Republican smear or witch hunt.[26]

29   As an American, I condemn a Republican "Fascist" just as much as I condemn a Democrat "Communist." I condemn a Democrat "fascist" just as much as I condemn a Republican "Communist."[27] They are equally dangerous to you and me and to our country. As an American,[28] I want to see our nation recapture the strength and unity it once had when we fought the enemy instead of ourselves.[29]

30   It is with these thoughts I have drafted what I call a "Declaration of Conscience." I am gratified that Senator Tobey, Senator Aiken, Senator Morse, Senator Ives, Senator Thye and Senator Hendrickson have concurred in that declaration and have authorized me to announce their concurrence.[30]

"Declaration of Conscience," copyright ©1999 Margaret Chase Smith Library. 56 Norridgewock Avenue; Skowhegan, Maine 04976. All rights reserved. 🐦

Sample Student Commentary

[25] The reader must determine the extent to which the fact that Smith does not offer specific examples undermines her thesis.

[26] Senator Smith does strive for balance, expressing disapproval of both sides of the question.

[27] In terms of advancing her argument, what does Smith accomplish by transposing direct object in these two consecutive sentences?

[28] Note again the use of anaphora in the repetition of "As an American." Some may also criticize the use as approaching propaganda, possibly virtue words or flag waving.

[29] Contrasting enemy with ourselves is a concise summary of Smith's thesis and an excellent use of the rhetorical device of antithesis.

[30] The reader must ultimately assess how effective the Senator's inclusion of the names of those who agree with her is. Critics might say she was employing the propaganda technique bandwagon.

Sample multiple-choice questions:

1. Through the course of her argument, Margaret Chase Smith identifies herself by all of the following EXCEPT her
   A. gender.
   B. vocation.
   C. cultural role.
   D. nationality.
   E. social class.

2. Senator Smith's reference to the four "basic principles of Americanism" (paragraph 12) can best be characterized as
   A. interpretation.
   B. summary.
   C. paraphrase.
   D. opinion.
   E. thesis.

3. The shift in focus that begins in the sixteenth paragraph can best be described as from _____ to _____.
   A. legal to political.
   B. political to moral.
   C. ethical to political.
   D. political to cultural.
   E. patriotic to political.

4. For the most part, Smith's use of first person plural refers to herself and the
   A. women of America.
   B. Republican party.
   C. Legislative branch.
   D. United States Senate.
   E. Democratic administration.

5. All of the following words and phrases help Senator Smith maintain balance in her argument EXCEPT
   A. "the present Democratic administration." (paragraph 17)
   B. "Republican regime." (paragraph 21)
   C. "champion of a united nation." (paragraph 15)
   D. "Fascist," (paragraph 29)
   E. "Communist." (paragraph 29)

Answers and Explanations:

1. Smith refers to her gender (A) at least twice, once in paragraph 5 ("I speak as a woman") and again in paragraph 25 ("As a woman…"). She mentions her vocation (B) at least twice as well, in paragraph 5 ("I speak as a United States Senator") and again in paragraph 26 ("As a United States Senator…"). (C) is excluded by paragraph 25 in which she admits that "as a woman," she wonders "how the mothers, wives, sisters and daughters feel…"). (D) is excluded by her many references to herself "as an American." Only (E) is not a point of reference. She never alludes to the class into which she was born, in which she was raised, or which she has attained as a United States Senator. **Thus, (E) is the correct answer**.

2. (B) and (C) might both be initially tempting, but the first two principles "the right to criticize," and the "right to hold unpopular beliefs," as well as the last one, "right of independent thought," are too broad to be drawn directly from the Bill of Rights as would be necessary in a summary or paraphrase. (D) and (E), however, are excluded by the fact that the statements are more closely linked to the amendments than a mere assertion. **(A) is the best choice because, while the wording of three of the four principles is not identical to the wording of the actual rights, the principles do reflect an understanding of the denotations and connotations of the words used in the amendments**.

3. (A) might be tempting, but, while Smith does question the behavior of the Senate, she does not reference whether or not the Senate is acting legally, except for a mention of the Constitution and the Amendments in paragraph 10. (B) and (D) can be eliminated by the fact that the beginning of the address is not political. In fact, the Senator clearly criticizes the Legislative and Executive branches without referencing any particular political parties or ideologies. (E) might be tempting, and the shift *is* to a political focus, but "patriotic" is a broad term and not the best available to describe the first part of the declaration. (C) indicates that the Senator's concern at the beginning is clearly with the *rightness* of the *ethical nature* of the government's behavior more than the *legality* of the situation. The focus then shifts to a political discussion of the Republican minority versus the Democratic majority and administration. **Thus, (C) is the best answer**.

4. (A) might tempt a few students, but the Senator really makes only one claim as a woman, in paragraph 25. (B) is an even more tempting choice, but a close examination of the text reveals that this use occurs only once—in paragraph 23: "As members of the Minority Party, we…"). (C) is too vague to really tempt, as Margaret Chase Smith references the Legislative branch only once, with the rest of the declaration criticizing the Senate specifically. (E), also, should not be tempting, as Smith clearly indicates that she is a Republican, and no use of either singular or plural first person would include the Democratic administration. Clearly, however, the vast majority of the times Senator Smith uses first person plural, she is referring to "we Senators": "without that non-Senator

American having any legal redress against us"; "we hold ourselves above the same type of criticism here on the Senate Floor"; "time for the United States Senate and its members to do some soul searching—for us to weigh our consciences"; "we have sworn to uphold and defend the Constitution"; "I am not proud of the way we smear outsiders from the Floor of the Senate…" and so on. **Thus, (D) is clearly the best answer**.

5. In order to answer this question satisfactorily, the student must consider the context of the entire passage. (A) is clearly a partisan criticism, but it is balanced by (C), in which the Senator is clearly criticizing the actions of her own party. Likewise, (D) and (E) achieve balance as the Senator asserts that she opposes abuses and extremism in *both* parties. **Only (C) is not balanced by a positive about the other party. Thus, (C) is the correct answer**.

Sample free-response item:

Carefully read Senator Margaret Chase Smith's 1950 "Declaration of Conscience." Smith (1897-1995) was a Senator from Maine, the first woman to be elected to both the U.S. House of Representatives and the Senate. She was the first woman from Maine to serve in either house, and a liberal Republican; she issued the following declaration as an indictment of Senator Joseph McCarthy's (R. Wisconsin) campaign against suspected Communists in the government and entertainment industry. After reading the passage, write an essay in which you analyze her argument and the techniques she uses to advance that argument.

Sample Student Essay

In her famous 1950 "Declaration of Conscience" the Honorable Margaret Chase Smith, first female Senator from Maine, strongly criticizes the United States Senate, then-President Harry S. Truman, and her own Republican Party for a lack of effective leadership and an abuse of authority. Senator Smith never specifies the exact cause of her anger, but it is clear from the date of her address that she is concerned about the actions in the United States Senate and the resulting atmosphere in the nation that are commonly referred to as "McCarthyism."

While the illegality and unethical nature of Senator McCarthy's "witch hunts" are generally accepted, and the courage it must have taken Smith to draft and present her declaration is unquestionable, the Senator's argument is, unfortunately, weakened by an overall lack of evidence and examples and a partial loss of focus in the middle of the address. The argument is passionate, to be sure, and rhetorically effective, but the rhetoric occasionally drifts dangerously close to propaganda. Overall, those who already agree with the Senator will still agree, while those who don't…won't.

Senator Smith's thesis is clear enough: There is a "serious national condition," a "national feeling of fear and frustration that could result in national suicide"; this condition is the result of "the lack of effective leadership" in both the executive and legislative branches of the federal government. The language with which she identifies and clarifies the condition and her position is powerful, indeed. Anaphora and use of first person create an intimacy between Smith and her reader or hearer. Four times toward the close of her declaration, the Senator asserts that she is speaking "as an American," transcending party and embracing the whole of the people. Earlier, she appeals to her listeners by repeating the phrase, "I speak," each time adopting a different class or group with which she identifies and for whom she speaks. She continues her strong identification with her audience, even enticing her audience into identification with her, by using the first person plural: "Who of us doesn't? [know someone who holds unpopular beliefs]. Otherwise none of us could call our souls our own." This strong identification with her audience, however, approaches propaganda—bandwagon, transfer, and appeal to the common people: "As a woman, I wonder how the mothers, wives, sisters and daughters feel." There is more to this argument than reason and evidence.

These same techniques are apparent in the Senator's appeal "as an American." Her frequent suggestions that the American way of life is threatened—first by the behavior of the government and then by "the present Democratic Administration"— can be interpreted as approaching an appeal to fear.

The impact of Smith's argument, however, is generally strengthened by her effective use of rhetorical devices. Her two biblical and historical allusions, likening the current situation to the apocalypse and the antics of the administration and Congress as the "Four Horsemen of Calumny—Fear, Ignorance, Bigotry and Smear"—as well as invoking the memory of Republican Abraham Lincoln practically sanctify her stance in the eyes of her audience.

Despite the strength of Senator Smith's language, however, the argument itself is not nearly as persuasive as it might be. In her thesis, the Senator never specifies more clearly what exactly the condition is that she is addressing. She does refer to "irresponsible words of bitterness" and "selfish political opportunism." She calls the United States Senate a "forum of hate and character assassination sheltered by the shield of congressional immunity." She describes a circumstance in which Senators can attack private citizens, destroying their lives with accusations of treason and "un-American" activities with no fear of reprisal. When one Senator attempts to hold a colleague accountable, however, she or he is called "out of line" and faced with censure.

The description clearly fits what was occurring in the Senate and the nation in general at the beginning of Joseph McCarthy's Communist scare. Later mentions of the Constitution's protecting "not only of the freedom of speech, but also of trial by jury instead of trial by accusation"; equations between "criminal prosecution in court or a character prosecution in the Senate"; and the "smearing" of innocent people and the "whitewashing" of the guilty further suggest that McCarthyism is the "condition" Smith is decrying. The June 1, 1950, date of the address supports this interpretation, but the argument is weakened in the long term by her failure to specify that this is the issue.

Similarly, Senator Smith asserts that there are "proved cases to cause nationwide distrust and strong suspicion" that render it unnecessary to create false ones. She offers no examples, however. She likewise offers no examples of the "sufficient campaign issues" provided by the majority party's administration that further render "political smears" unnecessary. The Senator provides no specifics when she alludes to Truman's "daily contradictory grave warnings and optimistic assurances" that, she argues, have "completely confused" the American people. These generalities may indeed have ample specifics to support them, but Smith's thesis is weakened by her reliance on others' already knowing them and her failing to provide a single specific.

Lack of specific, factual support, however, is not the only flaw that weakens the Senator's thesis. Approximately two-thirds of the way through the declaration, a piece that started out denouncing a "serious national condition" caused by a "lack of effective leadership in either the Legislative Branch or the Executive Branch of our Government" devolves into something resembling a campaign address criticizing the then-majority political party and the practices of the current administration. What has been an issue involving an abuse of congressional protections, a denial of Constitutional rights to innocent citizens, and an unraveling of the very liberties that define the United States, is suddenly clouded with criticisms of "loose spending and loose programs." While Senator Smith uses this phrase twice in two consecutive paragraphs, she offers no more specific examples than she does the instances of abuse she talks about earlier in her declaration.

Five consecutive paragraphs are devoted to criticisms of "the present Democratic Administration." These unillustrated and unsubstantiated criticisms include a "mania for loose spending and loose programs," a "complacency to the threat of communism," the administration's "completely confus[ing] the American people," and the administration's having "no idea of where it is going." This section of a "declaration of conscience" about the abuses of power and a breakdown in the very fiber of American democracy ends with Smith's proclaiming that a "Republican victory is necessary to the security of this country." In the next paragraph, she reiterates, "The nation sorely needs a Republican victory."

In the final paragraphs, the Senator does return to her balanced criticism of the conduct of the Senate and the threat McCarthyism poses to the United States, but the mid-declaration tangent into partisan politics has done its damage, and it is hard to accept the Senator's concerns as the genuinely broad one her opening paragraphs suggest.

Senator Margaret Chase Smith's famous "Declaration of Conscience," then, is an important document in United States history. It is an undeniably bold and courageous statement in the face of real danger to American liberty. It is rhetorically a very strong and impassioned plea, but it is, ultimately, flawed by Smith's tendency to rely too heavily on rhetoric—sometimes bordering on propaganda—a lack of specific examples and support, and an unnecessary shift in focus. ❧

Exercise Two:

Questions 6-10. Read the following passage carefully before you choose your answers.

This passage is the text of a speech delivered by British Prime Minister Winston Churchill before Parliament on 4 June 1940, relatively early in World War II. Many historians consider it to be the most influential and inspirational speech of the 20th Century.

1   FROM THE MOMENT THAT THE FRENCH defenses at Sedan and on the Meuse were broken at the end of the second week of May, only a rapid retreat to Amiens and the south could have saved the British and French Armies who had entered Belgium at the appeal of the Belgian King; but this strategic fact was not immediately realized. The French High Command hoped they would be able to close the gap, and the Armies of the north were under their orders. Moreover, a retirement of this kind would have involved almost certainly the destruction of the fine Belgian Army of over 20 divisions and the abandonment of the whole of Belgium. Therefore, when the force and scope of the German penetration were realized and when a new French Generalissimo, General Weygand, assumed command in place of General Gamelin, an effort was made by the French and British Armies in Belgium to keep on holding the right hand of the Belgians and to give their own right hand to a newly created French Army which was to have advanced across the Somme in great strength to grasp it.

2   However, the German eruption swept like a sharp scythe around the right and rear of the Armies of the north. Eight or nine armored divisions, each of about four hundred armored vehicles of different kinds, but carefully assorted to be complementary and divisible into small self-contained units, cut off all communications between us and the main French Armies. It severed our own for food and ammunition, which ran first to Amiens and afterwards through Abbeville, and it shore its way up the coast to Boulogne and Calais, and almost to Dunkirk. Behind this armored and mechanized onslaught came a number of German divisions in lorries, and behind them again there plodded comparatively slowly the dull brute mass of the ordinary German Army and German people, always so ready to be led to the trampling down in other lands of liberties and comforts which they have never known in their own.

3   I have said this armored scythe-stroke almost reached Dunkirk—almost but not quite. Boulogne and Calais were the scenes of desperate fighting. The Guards defended Boulogne for a while and were then withdrawn by orders from this country. The Rifle Brigade, the 60th Rifles, and the Queen Victoria's Rifles, with a battalion of British tanks and 1,000 Frenchmen, in all about four thousand strong, defended Calais to the last. The British Brigadier was given an hour to surrender. He spurned the offer, and four days of intense street fighting passed before silence reigned over Calais, which marked the end of a memorable resistance. Only 30 unwounded survivors were brought off by the Navy, and we do not know the fate of their comrades. Their sacrifice, however, was not in vain. At least two armored divisions, which otherwise would have been turned against the British Expeditionary Force, had to be sent to overcome them. They have added another page to the glories of the light divisions, and the time gained enabled the Graveline water

39

lines to be flooded and to be held by the French troops.

4   Thus it was that the port of Dunkirk was kept open. When it was found impossible for the Armies of the north to reopen their communications to Amiens with the main French Armies, only one choice remained. It seemed, indeed, forlorn. The Belgian, British and French Armies were almost surrounded. Their sole line of retreat was to a single port and to its neighboring beaches. They were pressed on every side by heavy attacks and far outnumbered in the air.

5   When, a week ago today, I asked the House to fix this afternoon as the occasion for a statement, I feared it would be my hard lot to announce the greatest military disaster in our long history. I thought—and some good judges agreed with me—that perhaps 20,000 or 30,000 men might be re-embarked. But it certainly seemed that the whole of the French First Army and the whole of the British Expeditionary Force north of the Amiens-Abbeville gap would be broken up in the open field or else would have to capitulate for lack of food and ammunition. These were the hard and heavy tidings for which I called upon the House and the nation to prepare themselves a week ago. The whole root and core and brain of the British Army, on which and around which we were to build, and are to build, the great British Armies in the later years of the war, seemed about to perish upon the field or to be led into an ignominious and starving captivity.

6   That was the prospect a week ago. But another blow which might well have proved final was yet to fall upon us. The King of the Belgians had called upon us to come to his aid. Had not this Ruler and his Government severed themselves from the Allies, who rescued their country from extinction in the late war, and had they not sought refuge in what was proved to be a fatal neutrality, the French and British Armies might well at the outset have saved not only Belgium but perhaps even Poland. Yet at the last moment, when Belgium was already invaded, King Leopold called upon us to come to his aid, and even at the last moment we came. He and his brave, efficient Army, nearly half a million strong, guarded our left flank and thus kept open our only line of retreat to the sea. Suddenly, without prior consultation, with the least possible notice, without the advice of his Ministers and upon his own personal act, he sent a plenipotentiary to the German Command, surrendered his Army, and exposed our whole flank and means of retreat.

7   I asked the House a week ago to suspend its judgment because the facts were not clear, but I do not feel that any reason now exists why we should not form our own opinions upon this pitiful episode. The surrender of the Belgian Army compelled the British at the shortest notice to cover a flank to the sea more than 30 miles in length. Otherwise all would have been cut off, and all would have shared the fate to which King Leopold had condemned the finest Army his country had ever formed. So in doing this and in exposing this flank, as anyone who followed the operations on the map will see, contact was lost between the British and two out of the three corps forming the First French Army, who were still farther from the coast than we were, and it seemed impossible that any large number of Allied troops could reach the coast.

8   The enemy attacked on all sides with great strength and fierceness, and their main power, the power of their far more numerous Air Force, was thrown into the battle or else concentrated upon Dunkirk and the beaches. Pressing in upon the narrow exit, both from the east and from the west, the enemy began to fire with cannon upon the beaches

by which alone the shipping could approach or depart. They sowed magnetic mines in the channels and seas; they sent repeated waves of hostile aircraft, sometimes more than a hundred strong in one formation, to cast their bombs upon the single pier that remained, and upon the sand dunes upon which the troops had their eyes for shelter. Their U-boats, one of which was sunk, and their motor launches took their toll of the vast traffic which now began. For four or five days an intense struggle reigned. All their armored divisions-or what Was left of them-together with great masses of infantry and artillery, hurled themselves in vain upon the ever-narrowing, ever-contracting appendix within which the British and French Armies fought.

9   Meanwhile, the Royal Navy, with the willing help of countless merchant seamen, strained every nerve to embark the British and Allied troops; 220 light warships and 650 other vessels were engaged. They had to operate upon the difficult coast, often in adverse weather, under an almost ceaseless hail of bombs and an increasing concentration of artillery fire. Nor were the seas, as I have said, themselves free from mines and torpedoes. It was in conditions such as these that our men carried on, with little or no rest, for days and nights on end, making trip after trip across the dangerous waters, bringing with them always men whom they had rescued. The numbers they have brought back are the measure of their devotion and their courage. The hospital ships, which brought off many thousands of British and French wounded, being so plainly marked were a special target for Nazi bombs; but the men and women on board them never faltered in their duty.

10   Meanwhile, the Royal Air Force, which had already been intervening in the battle, so far as its range would allow, from home bases, now used part of its main metropolitan fighter strength, and struck at the German bombers and at the fighters which in large numbers protected them. This struggle was protracted and fierce. Suddenly the scene has cleared, the crash and thunder has for the moment—but only for the moment—died away. A miracle of deliverance, achieved by valor, by perseverance, by perfect discipline, by faultless service, by resource, by skill, by unconquerable fidelity, is manifest to us all. The enemy was hurled back by the retreating British and French troops. He was so roughly handled that he did not hurry their departure seriously. The Royal Air Force engaged the main strength of the German Air Force, and inflicted upon them losses of at least four to one; and the Navy, using nearly 1,000 ships of all kinds, carried over 335,000 men, French and British, out of the jaws of death and shame, to their native land and to the tasks which lie immediately ahead. We must be very careful not to assign to this deliverance the attributes of a victory. Wars are not won by evacuations. But there was a victory inside this deliverance, which should be noted. It was gained by the Air Force. Many of our soldiers coming back have not seen the Air Force at work; they saw only the bombers which escaped its protective attack. They underrate its achievements. I have heard much talk of this; that is why I go out of my way to say this. I will tell you about it.

11   This was a great trial of strength between the British and German Air Forces. Can you conceive a greater objective for the Germans in the air than to make evacuation from these beaches impossible, and to sink all these ships which were displayed, almost to the extent of thousands? Could there have been an objective of greater military importance and significance for the whole purpose of the war than this? They tried hard, and they were beaten back; they were frustrated in their task. We got the Army away; and they have paid fourfold for any losses which they have inflicted. Very large formations of German aeroplanes—and we know that they are a very brave race—have turned on several occasions from the attack of one-quarter of their number of the Royal Air Force, and have dispersed in different directions. Twelve aeroplanes have been hunted by two. One aeroplane was driven into the water and cast away by the mere charge of a British aeroplane, which had no more ammunition. All of our types—the Hurricane, the Spitfire and the new Defiant—and all our pilots have been vindicated as superior to what they have at present to face.

12   When we consider how much greater would be our advantage in defending the air above this Island against an overseas attack, I must say that I find in these facts a sure basis upon which practical and reassuring thoughts may rest. I will pay my tribute to these young airmen. The great French Army was very largely, for the time being, cast back and disturbed by the onrush of a few thousands of armored vehicles. May it not also be that the cause of civilization itself will be defended by the skill and devotion of a few thousand airmen? There never has been, I suppose, in all the world, in all the history of war, such an opportunity for youth. The Knights of the Round Table, the Crusaders, all fall back into the past-not only distant but prosaic; these young men, going forth every morn to guard their native land and all that we stand for, holding in their hands these instruments of colossal and shattering power, of whom it may be said that

13   Every morn brought forth a noble chance And every chance brought forth a noble knight, deserve our gratitude, as do all the brave men who, in so many ways and on so many occasions, are ready, and continue ready to give life and all for their native land.

14   I return to the Army. In the long series of very fierce battles, now on this front, now on that, fighting on three fronts at once, battles fought by two or three divisions against an equal or somewhat larger number of the enemy, and fought fiercely on some of the old grounds that so many of us knew so well—in these battles our losses in men have exceeded 30,000 killed, wounded and missing. I take occasion to express the sympathy of the House to all who have suffered bereavement or who are still anxious. The President of the Board of Trade [Sir Andrew Duncan] is not here today. His son has been killed, and many in the House have felt the pangs of affliction in the sharpest form. But I will say this about the missing: We have had a large number of wounded come home safely to this country, but I would say about the missing that there may be very many reported missing who will come back home, some day, in one way or another. In the confusion of this fight it is inevitable that many have been left in positions where honor required no further resistance from them.

15   Against this loss of over 30,000 men, we can set a far heavier loss certainly inflicted upon the enemy. But our losses in material are enormous. We have perhaps lost one-third of the men we lost in the opening days of the battle of 21st March, 1918, but we have lost nearly as many guns—nearly one thousand-and all our transport, all the armored vehicles that were with the Army in the north. This loss will impose a further delay on the expansion of our military strength. That expansion had not been proceeding as far as we had hoped. The best of all we had to give had gone to the British Expeditionary Force, and although they had not the numbers of tanks and some articles of equipment which

were desirable, they were a very well and finely equipped Army. They had the first-fruits of all that our industry had to give, and that is gone. And now here is this further delay. How long it will be, how long it will last, depends upon the exertions which we make in this Island. An effort the like of which has never been seen in our records is now being made. Work is proceeding everywhere, night and day, Sundays and week days. Capital and Labor have cast aside their interests, rights, and customs and put them into the common stock. Already the flow of munitions has leaped forward. There is no reason why we should not in a few months overtake the sudden and serious loss that has come upon us, without retarding the development of our general program.

16   Nevertheless, our thankfulness at the escape of our Army and so many men, whose loved ones have passed through an agonizing week, must not blind us to the fact that what has happened in France and Belgium is a colossal military disaster. The French Army has been weakened, the Belgian Army has been lost, a large part of those fortified lines upon which so much faith had been reposed is gone, many valuable mining districts and factories have passed into the enemy's possession, the whole of the Channel ports are in his hands, with all the tragic consequences that follow from that, and we must expect another blow to be struck almost immediately at us or at France. We are told that Herr Hitler has a plan for invading the British Isles. This has often been thought of before. When Napoleon lay at Boulogne for a year with his flat-bottomed boats and his Grand Army, he was told by someone. "There are bitter weeds in England." There are certainly a great many more of them since the British Expeditionary Force returned.

17   The whole question of home defense against invasion is, of course, powerfully affected by the fact that we have for the time being in this Island incomparably more powerful military forces than we have ever had at any moment in this war or the last. But this will not continue. We shall not be content with a defensive war. We have our duty to our Ally. We have to reconstitute and build up the British Expeditionary Force once again, under its gallant Commander-in-Chief, Lord Gort. All this is in train; but in the interval we must put our defenses in this Island into such a high state of organization that the fewest possible numbers will be required to give effective security and that the largest possible potential of offensive effort may be realized. On this we are now engaged. It will be very convenient, if it be the desire of the House, to enter upon this subject in a secret Session. Not that the government would necessarily be able to reveal in very great detail military secrets, but we like to have our discussions free, without the restraint imposed by the fact that they will be read the next day by the enemy; and the Government would benefit by views freely expressed in all parts of the House by Members with their knowledge of so many different parts of the country. I understand that some request is to be made upon this subject, which will be readily acceded to by His Majesty's Government.

18   We have found it necessary to take measures of increasing stringency, not only against enemy aliens and suspicious characters of other nationalities, but also against British subjects who may become a danger or a nuisance should the war be transported to the United Kingdom. I know there are a great many people affected by the orders which we have made who are the passionate enemies of Nazi Germany. I am very sorry for them, but we cannot, at the present time and under the present stress, draw all the distinctions which we should like to do. If parachute landings were attempted and fierce fighting attendant upon them followed, these unfortunate people would be far better out of the way, for their own sakes as well as for ours. There is, however, another class, for which I feel not the slightest sympathy. Parliament has given us the powers to put down Fifth Column activities with a strong hand, and we shall use those powers subject to the supervision and correction of the House, without the slightest hesitation until we are satisfied, and more than satisfied, that this malignancy in our midst has been effectively stamped out.

19   Turning once again, and this time more generally, to the question of invasion, I would observe that there has never been a period in all these long centuries of which we boast when an absolute guarantee against invasion, still less against serious raids, could have been given to our people. In the days of Napoleon the same wind which would have carried his transports across the Channel might have driven away the blockading fleet. There was always the chance, and it is that chance which has excited and befooled the imaginations of many Continental tyrants. Many are the tales that are told. We are assured that novel methods will be adopted, and when we see the originality of malice, the ingenuity of aggression, which our enemy displays, we may certainly prepare ourselves for every kind of novel stratagem and every kind of brutal and treacherous maneuver. I think that no idea is so outlandish that it should not be considered and viewed with a searching, but at the same time, I hope, with a steady eye. We must never forget the solid assurances of sea power and those which belong to air power if it can be locally exercised.

20   I have, myself, full confidence that if all do their duty, if nothing is neglected, and if the best arrangements are made, as they are being made, we shall prove ourselves once again able to defend our Island home, to ride out the storm of war, and to outlive the menace of tyranny, if necessary for years, if necessary alone. At any rate, that is what we are going to try to do. That is the resolve of His Majesty's Government—every man of them. That is the will of Parliament and the nation. The British Empire and the French Republic, linked together in their cause and in their need, will defend to the death their native soil, aiding each other like good comrades to the utmost of their strength. Even though large tracts of Europe and many old and famous States have fallen or may fall into the grip of the Gestapo and all the odious apparatus of Nazi rule, we shall not flag or fail. We shall go on to the end, we shall fight in France, we shall fight on the seas and oceans, we shall fight with growing confidence and growing strength in the air, we shall defend our Island, whatever the cost may be, we shall fight on the beaches, we shall fight on the landing grounds, we shall fight in the fields and in the streets, we shall fight in the hills; we shall never surrender, and even if, which I do not for a moment believe, this Island or a large part of it were subjugated and starving, then our Empire beyond the seas, armed and guarded by the British Fleet, would carry on the struggle, until, in God's good time, the New World, with all its power and might, steps forth to the rescue and the liberation of the old. ❧

Multiple-choice questions:

6. In this speech, Winston Churchill uses all of the following rhetorical devices EXCEPT

 A. anaphora.

 B. amplification

 C. apostrophe

 D. metaphor.

 E. simile.

7. In the sentence, "It severed our own [communications] for food and ammunition" (paragraph 2), the word *communications* most nearly means

 A. transport routes.

 B. radio transmissions.

 C. messenger networks.

 D. mass media.

 E. international conversation.

8. Churchill primarily supports the main thesis of this address by

 A. appealing to his audience's emotions.

 B. drawing analogies to Britain's history.

 C. forecasting imminent defeat.

 D. recounting recent victories.

 E. citing specific facts and figures.

9. The shift in tone that begins in the twelfth paragraph is essentially from _____ to _____ .

 A. didactic to conciliatory.

 B. informative to inspirational.

 C. reflective to hopeful.

 D. pessimistic to resigned.

 E. mournful to celebratory.

10. The final sentence of this address is a plea for

 A. continued bravery on the part of British subjects.

 B. additional resources from Parliament.

 C. divine or Providential assistance.

 D. military support from the United States.

 E. permission to suspend civil liberties.

Free Response Item:

Carefully read Sir Winston Churchill's address. Then, write an essay in which you analyze Churchill's argument and the techniques he uses to persuade both Parliament and the British people not to consider surrender to Germany as a viable option.

🧩 To entertain

Even nonfiction that is intended primarily to inform or persuade should be a pleasure to read. Few readers will force themselves to continue when faced with dry facts or innumerable examples if the piece does not, on some level, entertain. Other pieces, feature articles, reviews, memoirs, and so forth, are written and read purely for their entertainment value.

What makes a nonfiction piece "entertaining" is even harder to articulate than what makes an article persuasive or informative. There are, however, some common elements that journalists, columnists, and others who write to entertain use in order to appeal to their readership.

Humor, including sarcasm and a lighthearted tone, is common in entertaining nonfiction. Writers will often appeal directly to their readers with first-person narration or direct address. The writer will also, of course, include only those facts, details, and examples that will be most attractive and relevant to their readers.

Consider the following passage, the first chapter of H. G. Wells's multi-volume work *A Short History of the World*. Wells was a turn-of-the-century author, most famous for his science-fiction novels, *The Time Machine* and *The War of the Worlds*. The passage has been annotated to point out those elements that contribute an entertaining value to an essentially informative article.

After you examine the passage and the accompanying notes, look at how a student taking the AP Language exam might respond to multiple-choice questions and a free-response item dealing with how H. G. Wells takes a fairly dull topic and at least attempts to infuse it with humor and a human element.

from:
A Short History of the World
The World in Space

H. G. WELLS

1 	THE STORY OF OUR WORLD is a story that is still very imperfectly known. A couple of hundred years ago men possessed the history of little more than the last three thousand years.[1] What happened before that time was a matter of legend and speculation. Over a large part of the civilized world it was believed and taught that the world had been created suddenly in 4004 B.C., though authorities differed as to whether this had occurred in the spring or autumn of that year.[2] This fantastically precise misconception[3] was based upon a too literal interpretation of the Hebrew Bible, and upon rather arbitrary theological assumptions connected therewith. Such ideas have long since been abandoned by religious teachers, and it is universally recognized that the universe in which we live has to all appearances existed for an enormous period of time and possibly for endless time. Of course there may be deception in these appearances, as a room may be made to seem endless by putting mirrors facing each other at either end. But that the universe in which we live has existed only for six or seven thousand years may be regarded as an altogether exploded idea.[4]

2 	The earth, as everybody knows nowadays,[5] is a spheroid, a sphere slightly compressed, orange fashion,[6] with a diameter of nearly 8,000 miles. Its spherical shape has been known at least to a limited number of intelligent people[7] for nearly 2,500 years, but before that time it was supposed to be flat, and various ideas which now seem fantastic were entertained about its relations to the sky and the stars and planets. We know now that it rotates upon its axis (which is about 24 miles shorter than its equatorial diameter) every twenty-four hours, and that this is the cause of the alternations of day and night, that it circles about the sun in a slightly distorted and slowly variable oval path in a year. Its distance from the sun varies between ninety-one and a half millions at its nearest and ninety-four and a half million miles.[8]

3 	About the earth circles a smaller sphere, the moon, at an average distance of 239,000 miles. Earth and moon are not the only bodies to travel round the sun. There are also the

---

Sample Student Commentary

[1] Is this a sincere statement, or might there be some humor intended in exaggeration?

[2] These are clearly tongue-in-cheek statements, the arbitrarily specific date of 4004 B.C., and the further "attempt" at specifying the actual season of creation.

[3] By acknowledging the previous claims as a "fantastically precise misconception," Wells repudiates the assumption that he was being humorous, but his tone is still clearly sarcastic.

[4] Repetition and adverb-adjective phrases like "universally recognized that the universe"; "altogether exploded" help Wells to maintain his sarcastic tone.

[5] Note the informal use of "nowadays" and the casual "as everybody knows" contributes to the mildly humorous, sarcastic tone.

[6] Merely an image? Or a humorous, sarcastic expression?

[7] Continued sarcasm.

[8] Notice that the single, long sentence that begins "We know now..." expresses a number of facts but in a casual, almost dismissive manner. Apparently none of the ideas warrants its own, independent sentence.

planets, Mercury and Venus, at distances of thirty-six and sixty-seven millions of miles; and beyond the circle of the earth and disregarding a belt of numerous smaller bodies, the planetoids, there are Mars, Jupiter, Saturn, Uranus and Neptune[9] at mean distances of 141, 483, 886, 1,782, and 1,793 millions of miles respectively. These figures in millions of miles are very difficult for the mind to grasp. It may help the reader's imagination if we reduce the sun and planets to a smaller, more conceivable scale.[10]

4   If, then, we represent our earth as a little ball of one inch diameter, the sun would be a big globe nine feet across and 323 yards away, that is about a fifth of a mile, four or five minutes' walking. The moon would be a small pea two feet and a half from the world.[11] Between earth and sun there would be the two inner planets, Mercury and Venus, at distances of one hundred and twenty-five and two hundred and fifty yards from the sun. All round and about these bodies there would be emptiness until you came to Mars, a hundred and seventy-five feet beyond the earth; Jupiter nearly a mile away, a foot in diameter; Saturn, a little smaller, two miles off; Uranus four miles off and Neptune six miles off. Then nothingness and nothingness except for small particles and drifting scraps of attenuated vapour for thousands of miles. The nearest star to earth on this scale would be 40,000 miles away.

5   These figures will serve perhaps to give one some conception of the immense emptiness of space in which the drama of life goes on.

6   For in all this enormous vacancy of space we know certainly of life only upon the surface of our earth. It does not penetrate much more than three miles down into the 4,000 miles that separate us from the centre of our globe, and it does not reach more than five miles above its surface. Apparently all the limitlessness of space is otherwise empty and dead.

7   The deepest ocean dredgings go down to five miles. The highest recorded flight of an aeroplane is little more than four miles. Men have reached to seven miles up in balloons, but at a cost of great suffering. No bird can fly so high as five miles, and small birds and insects which have been carried up by aeroplanes drop off insensible far below that level.[12] ❦

Sample Student Commentary

[9] The discovery of the ninth planet, Pluto, was not confirmed until 1930. *A Short History of the World* was written in 1922. Pluto was demoted to the status of "dwarf planet" in 2006.

[10] Introduction of this "more conceivable scale" will, hopefully, elevate the essay from the dry tone that has resulted from Wells's recitation of diameters and distances from the sun.

[11] The humorous, sarcastic tone is lost. Although he is discussing the matter on a smaller scale, the recitation of sizes and distances is still dry and factual.

[12] Possibly because this is merely a single chapter in a longer work, there is no apparent conclusion. There is also, however, no apparent transition to the next chapter.

Sample multiple-choice questions:

1. All of the following can be inferred from the opening paragraph EXCEPT

    A. religion no longer considers the world to be a few thousand years old.

    B. the age of the universe might be incalculable.

    C. religion and history are largely matters of speculation.

    D. the Bible is best not interpreted literally.

    E. *the Hebrew Bible is flawed.*

2. All of the following, in the first paragraph, contribute to a mildly humorous tone EXCEPT

    A. "whether this had occurred in the spring or autumn of that year."

    B. "it is universally recognized that the universe in which we live…"

    C. *"What happened before that time was a matter of legend and speculation."*

    D. "fantastically precise misconception."

    E. "may be regarded as an altogether exploded idea."

3. The primary method of development Wells uses in this article is

    A. *comparison/contrast.*

    B. order of magnitude.

    C. thesis/antithesis.

    D. thesis-proof.

    E. point/rebuttal.

4. The final paragraph is significantly different from the rest of the article in that it

    A. no longer cites specific figures.

    B. sheds its comic tone for dry fact.

    C. provides a transition to the next chapter.

    D. *narrows the focus to an earthly scale.*

    E. changes the focus from geology to biology.

5. The shift to direct address that begins in the fourth paragraph helps Wells to

    A. replace humor with intimacy.

    B. transition from discussing space to discussing earth.

    C. enhance reader interest.

    D. *discuss astronomical distances on a scale the reader can understand.*

    E. explain the vastness of space.

Answers and Explanations:

1. (A) is eliminated by: "Such ideas have long since been abandoned by religious teachers…" (B) is eliminated by: "it is universally recognized that the universe in which we live has to all appearances existed for an enormous period of time and possibly for endless time.." (C) is eliminated by: "What happened before that time was a matter of legend and speculation." (D) is eliminated by: "a too literal interpretation of the Hebrew Bible." **(E), however, reflects a misread of the same paragraph. The fact that a source should not be interpreted "too literally" does not necessarily mean that the source itself is flawed. Thus, (E) is the best answer.**

2. The notion of wondering about the actual *season* of creation (not to mention the logical fact that there would be no seasons before the existence of the sun and the earth on a tilted axis) eliminate (A). The tone, and near pun, created by the repetition of "universe" in paragraph 1 eliminates (B). (D) is eliminated by the hyperbole, which implies a tongue-in-cheek tone. Likewise, (E) is more tongue-in-cheek than academic. **Only (C) is a literal statement that can be read at face value. Thus, (C) is the best answer.**

3. (B) might be tempting, as Wells does try to present astronomical distances on a human scale, but his discussion of the various distances of planets to the sun is governed by spatial order. As the article is informative with a mildly entertaining tone, Wells does not have an argument or thesis that he sets out to prove (D), nor does he present an argument and counterargument (C) and (E). Once he establishes with the reader, however, that he will attempt to describe the vast distances between the bodies in space, he develops all of the rest by comparing the sizes of the bodies to earthly objects and the distances between those objects with earth-scaled distances. **Thus, (A) is the correct answer.**

4. (A) is easily eliminated by the fact that this paragraph does, in fact, cite the altitude of the breathable atmosphere and the depth of the oceans. (B) actually occurs much earlier in the article. A possible transition to a discussion of life on earth begins in the fifth paragraph, but there is no sense of closure or transition (C) in this final paragraph. (E) is similarly eliminated, as the transition from space to life begin in the fifth paragraph. This paragraph does, however, cite only earthly distance, the altitude of the atmosphere and the depth of the ocean. The rest of the article cites sizes and distances in space. **Thus, (D) is the correct answer.**

5. (A) is tempting, but the humor has been, at best, mild; and the direct address can really not be described as "intimate." (B) is eliminated by the fact that, although the sizes and distance are all described on an earthly scale, the discussion is still about space. (C) is probably true but is too vague and general to be the best answer. (E) is eliminated

as Wells has been describing the vastness of space even before the switch to first person. The shift to first person, however, coincides with Wells's intention to make the astronomical scale more comprehensible, more meaningful to his reader, to whom he now turns directly. **Thus, (D) is the best answer.**

Sample free-response item:

Carefully read the first chapter of H. G. Wells's *A Short History of the World*. Then, write a well-supported essay in which you analyze the techniques Wells uses to establish the entertainment value of what could be read as a purely informational piece.

Sample Student Essay

H. G. Wells's "The World in Space," which is the first chapter of Wells's longer <u>A Short History of the World</u>, is an enormously informative article that attempts to place the planet earth in it celestial context, along with the sun, the moon, and the other planets. Because it necessarily deals with sizes and distances almost beyond the comprehension of the average reader, Wells strives to achieve a balance between raw information and appealing to his readership; he attempts to make the article entertaining, even as it is instructive. To create this entertaining aspect, Wells uses a number of narrative conventions, specifically direct address to the reader, hyperbole, and informal or colloquial diction.

The first word in the article is "our." From the very start, Wells wants to engage his readers in a conversation. It is not his goal merely to cite facts such as the size of the earth or the distance of the earth from the sun; he wants, from the first word, to impress upon his readers that he is writing of "our world."

Wells's desire to converse with the reader becomes even more apparent in the third and fourth paragraphs when Wells begins to describe the sizes of the planets and the distances between them in earthly terms. Whereas before, the distances were cited objectively, almost dryly" "...there are Mars, Jupiter, Saturn, Uranus and Neptune at mean distances of 141, 483, 886, 1,782, and 1,793 millions of miles respectively....," now, Wells includes himself with his reader in virtually every sentence: "If, then, we represent our earth as a little ball [...] there would be emptiness until you came to Mars..."

The use of first person and direct address is clearly Wells's attempt at presenting potentially dull and incomprehensible information in a manner that will allow his readers to understand it and appreciate its significance. Narrative address, however, is not the only technique Wells employs in his attempt to make his article, not only informative, but entertaining as well.

In the first several paragraphs Wells actually attempts to achieve a mildly humorous or tongue-in-cheek tone. While acknowledging humanity's ignorance of the history of the world of "little more than the last three thousand years," he describes some of the speculation that filled in gaps in human knowledge with an almost laughable specificity: "the world had been created suddenly in 4004 B.C., though authorities differed as to whether this had occurred in the spring or autumn of that year." Specifying 4004, as opposed to 4003 or 4005, or simply estimating—as Wells admits that the date is speculation or theory—"approximately 4000 B.C.," is comic. It may not cause the reader to fall into hysterical laughter, but it should at least make the reader smile. The admission that it is not known whether the creation occurred in the spring or fall is even more laughable. Narrowing the "date" of creation to a matter of months is much more unlikely than being able to determine the specific year, and there remains the illogic of asserting that there were seasons before the existence of the earth on a tilted axis.

Wells himself calls the estimated date of creation a "fantastically precise misconception." The words "fantastically precise" are also arguably intended to bring a smile.

To continue the humorous tone, Wells peppers the first several paragraphs with additional informal diction, insisting that the 4004 B.C., date for creation is an "altogether exploded idea"—not "discredited," not "obsolete," but "altogether exploded." In the next paragraph, Wells refers to his contemporaneous time period informally as "nowadays," and he suggests the universality of contemporaneous belief with the almost dismissive "everybody knows." The intent is clear: While he is about to present numerical facts that might be overwhelming at best and stupefying at worst, Wells first desires to informalize, humorize, and entertain.

There are, of course, other blatant attempts to maintain reader interest and understanding. Comparing the planets to peas and oranges, and describing the distance of the earth to the sun in terms of "four or five minutes' walking" renders the article, in addition to informational, enjoyable to read—in short, entertaining.

"The World in Space," then, while clearly written to inform and to explain the vastness of the universe, is also written to attract a popular readership and meets its needs for both information and entertainment. ❦

Exercise Three:

Questions 11-15. Read the following passage carefully before you choose your answers.

Don Marquis (his name is pronounced "Mark-wiss") was born in Illinois in 1878, and did newspaper work in Philadelphia and Atlanta before writing a column called "The Sun Dial" for the New York Evening Sun. His humorous columns have been likened to Mark Twain's writings.

The Almost Perfect State

DON MARQUIS

I

1 NO MATTER HOW NEARLY PERFECT an Almost Perfect State may be, it is not nearly enough perfect unless the individuals who compose it can, somewhere between death and birth, have a perfectly corking time for a few years. The most wonderful governmental

system in the world does not attract us, as a system; we are after a system that scarcely knows it is a system; the great thing is to have the largest number of individuals as happy as may be, for a little while at least, some time before they die.

2   Infancy is not what it is cracked up to be. The child seems happy all the time to the adult, because the adult knows that the child is untouched by the real problems of life; if the adult were similarly untouched he is sure that he would be happy. But children, not knowing that they are having an easy time, have a good many hard times. Growing and learning and obeying the rules of their elders, of fighting against them, are not easy things to do. Adolescence is certainly far from a uniformly pleasant period. Early manhood might be the most glorious time of all were it not that the sheer excess of life and vigor gets a fellow into continual scrapes. Of middle age the best that can be said is that a middle aged person has likely learned how to have a little fun in spite of his troubles.

3   It is to old age that we look for reimbursement, the most of us. And most of us look in vain. For the most of us have been wrenched and racked, in one way or another, until old age is the most trying time of all.

4   In the Almost Perfect State every person shall have at least ten years before he dies of easy, carefree, happy living...things will be so arranged economically that this will be possible for each individual.

5   Personally we look forward to an old age of dissipation and indolence and unreverend disrepute. In fifty years we shall be ninety-two years old. We intend to work rather hard during those fifty years and accumulate enough to live on without working any more for the next ten years, for we have determined to die at the age of one hundred two.

6   During the last ten years we shall indulge ourself in many things that we have been forced by circumstances to forego. We have always been compelled, and we shall be compelled for many years to come, to be prudent, cautious, staid, sober, conservative, industrious, respectful of established institutions, a model citizen. We have not liked it, but we have been unable to escape it. Our mind, our logical faculties, our observation, inform us that the conservatives have the right side of the argument in all human affairs. But the people whom we really prefer as associates, though we do not approve their ideas, are the rebels, the radicals, the wastrels, the vicious, the poets, the Bolshevists, the idealists, the nuts, the Lucifers, the agreeable good-for-nothings, the sentimentalists, the prophets, the freaks. We have never dared to know any of them, far less become intimate with them.

7   Between the years of ninety-two and a hundred and two, however, we shall be the ribald, useless, drunken outcast person we have always wished to be. We shall have a long white beard and long white hair; we shall not walk at all, but recline in a wheel chair and bellow for alcoholic beverages; in the winter we shall sit before the fire with our feet in a bucket of hot water, with a decanter of corn whiskey near at hand, and write ribald songs against organized society; strapped to one arm of our chair will be a forty-five caliber revolver, and we shall shoot out the lights when we want to go to sleep, instead of turning them off; when we want air we shall throw a silver candlestick through the front window and be damned to it; we shall address public meetings to which we have been invited because of our wisdom in a vein of jocund malice. We shall...but we don't wish to make any one envious of the good time that is coming to us...we look forward to a disreputable, vigorous, unhonored and disorderly old age.

8   (In the meantime, of course, you understand you can't have us pinched and deported for our yearnings.)

9   We shall know that the Almost Perfect State is here when the kind of old age each person wants is possible to him. Of course, all of you may not want the kind we want… some of you may prefer prunes and morality to the bitter end. Some of you may be dissolute now and may look forward to becoming like one of the nice old fellows in a Wordsworth poem. But for our part we have always been a hypocrite and we shall have to continue being a hypocrite for a good many years yet, and we yearn to come out in our true colors at last. The point is, that no matter what you want to be, during those last ten years, that you may be, in the Almost Perfect State.

10   Any system of government under which the individual does all the sacrificing for the sake of the general good, for the sake of the community, the State, gets off on its wrong foot. We don't want things that cost us too much. We don't want too much strain all the time.

11   The best good that you can possibly achieve is not good enough if you have to strain yourself all the time to reach it. A thing is only worth doing, and doing again and again, if you can do it rather easily, and get some joy out of it.

12   Do the best you can, without straining yourself too much and too continuously, and leave the rest to God. If you strain yourself too much you'll have to ask God to patch you up. And for all you know, patching you up may take time that it was planned to use some other way.

13   BUT…overstrain yourself now and then. For this reason: The things you create easily and joyously will not continue to come easily and joyously unless you yourself are getting bigger all the time. And when you overstrain yourself you are assisting in the creation of a new self—if you get what we mean. And if you should ask us suddenly just what this has to do with the picture of the old guy in the wheel chair we should answer: Hanged if we know, but we seemed to sort o' run into it, somehow.

II

14   INTERPLANETARY COMMUNICATION IS ONE of the persistent dreams of the inhabitants of this oblate spheroid on which we move, breathe and suffer for lack of beer. There seems to be a feeling in many quarters that if we could get speech with the Martians, let us say, we might learn from them something to our advantage. There is a disposition to concede the superiority of the fellows Out There…just as some Americans capitulate without a struggle to poets from England, rugs from Constantinople, song and sausage from Germany, religious enthusiasts from Hindustan and cheese from Switzerland, although they have not tested the goods offered and really lack the discrimination to determine their quality. Almost the only foreign importations that were ever sneezed at in this country were Swedish matches and Spanish influenza.

15   But are the Martians…if Martians there be…any more capable than the persons dwelling between the Woolworth Building and the Golden Horn, between Shwe Dagon and the First Church, Scientist, in Boston, Mass.? Perhaps the Martians yearn toward earth, romantically, poetically, the Romeos swearing by its light to the Juliets; the idealists

and philosophers fabling that already there exists upon it an ALMOST PERFECT STATE—and now and then a wan prophet lifting his heart to its gleams, as a cup to be filled from Heaven with fresh waters of hope and courage. For this earth, it is also a star.

16   We know they are wrong about us, the lovers in the far stars, the philosophers, poets, the prophets...or are they wrong?

17   They are both right and wrong, as we are probably both right and wrong about them. If we tumbled into Mars or Arcturus of Sirius this evening we should find the people there discussing the shimmy, the jazz, the inconstancy of cooks and the iniquity of retail butchers, no doubt...and they would be equally disappointed by the way we flitter, frivol, flutter and flivver.

18   And yet, that other thing would be there too...that thing that made them look at our star as a symbol of grace and beauty.

19   Men could not think of THE ALMOST PERFECT STATE if they did not have it in them ultimately to create THE ALMOST PERFECT STATE.

20   We used sometimes to walk over the Brooklyn Bridge, that song in stone and steel of an engineer who was also a great artist, at dusk, when the tides of shadow flood in from the lower bay to break in a surf of glory and mystery and illusion against the tall towers of Manhattan. Seen from the middle arch of the bridge at twilight, New York with its girdle of shifting waters and its drift of purple cloud and its quick pulsations of unstable light is a miracle of splendor and beauty that lights up the heart like the laughter of a god.

21   But, descend. Go down into the city. Mingle with the details. The dirty old shed from which the "L" trains and trolleys put out with their jammed and mangled thousands for flattest Flatbush and the unknown bourne of ulterior Brooklyn is still the same dirty old shed; on a hot, damp night the pasty streets stink like a paperhanger's overalls; you are trodden and over-ridden by greasy little profiteers and their hopping victims; you are encompassed round about by the ugly and the sordid, and the objectionable is exuded upon you from a myriad candid pores; your elation and your illusion vanish like ingenuous snowflakes that have kissed a hot dog sandwich on its fiery brow, and you say: "Beauty? Aw, h—l! What's the use?"

22   And yet you have seen beauty. And beauty that was created by these people and people like these....You have seen the tall towers of Manhattan, wonderful under the stars. How did it come about that such growths came from such soil—that a breed lawless and sordid and prosaic has written such a mighty hieroglyphic against the sky? This glamor out of a pigsty...how come? How is it that this hideous, half-brute city is also beautiful and a fit habitation for demi-gods? How come?

23   It comes about because the wise and subtle deities permit nothing worthy to be lost. It was with no thought of beauty that the builders labored; no conscious thought; they were masters or slaves in the bitter wars of commerce, and they never saw as a whole what they were making; no one of them did. But each one had had his dream. And the baffled dreams and the broken visions and the ruined hopes and the secret desires of each one labored with him as he labored; the things that were lost and beaten and trampled down went into the stone and steel and gave it soul; the aspiration denied and the hope abandoned and the vision defeated were the things that lived, and not the apparent purpose for which each one of all the millions sweat and toiled or cheated; the

hidden things, the silent things, the winged things, so weak they are easily killed, the unacknowledged things, the rejected beauty, the strangled appreciation, the inchoate art, the submerged spirit—these groped and found each other and gathered themselves together and worked themselves into the tiles and mortar of the edifice and made a town that is a worthy fellow of the sunrise and the sea winds.

24   Humanity triumphs over its details.

25   The individual aspiration is always defeated of its perfect fruition and expression, but it is never lost; it passes into the conglomerate being of the race.

26   The way to encourage yourself about the human race is to look at it first from a distance; look at the lights on the high spots. Coming closer, you will be profoundly discouraged at the number of low spots, not to say two-spots. Coming still closer, you will become discouraged once more by the reflection that the same stuff that is in the high spots is also in the two-spots. ❦

Multiple-choice questions:

11. As it is used in the first paragraph, the word *corking* most likely means all of the following EXCEPT

A. free of responsibility.

B. licentious.

C. thoroughly enjoyable.

D. extravagant.

E. easily attained.

12. Marquis's use of first person plural throughout the essay is an example of

A. appeal to the reader.

B. authorial intrusion.

C. limited omniscience.

D. the editorial "we."

E. the patronizing "we."

13. The basis of Marquis's comparison of humans and Martians is that

A. each most likely idealizes the other.

B. both are godlike, though flawed.

C. Martians probably misunderstand humans.

D. humans probably misunderstand Martians.

E. Martians and humans are essentially the same.

14. The tone of this essay can best be described as
   A. formal.
   B. academic.
   C. cordial.
   D. aloof.
   E. colloquial.

15. The overall contribution of the metaphors in the second portion of this essay is to
   A. deify human achievement.
   B. exaggerate human achievement.
   C. brutalize human failings.
   D. contrast alien and human culture.
   E. stress the potential achievement of a perfect state.

Free Response Item:

Carefully read Don Marquis's two-part column "The Almost Perfect State." Then, write a well-organized and well-supported essay in which you analyze Marquis's language and how it contributes to the overall entertainment value of the column. Avoid summary.

Analyzing Language Conventions

CHAPTER 2

🧩 Diction and Syntax

The word and the sentence are, clearly, the writer's most basic tools, and it almost is unnecessary to say that an author must carefully choose the word or words that will most powerfully establish the main points and create the effect he or she hopes to create on the reader.

What is the difference between the weather's being *cold*, and its being *frigid*? Did the writer experience a *storm*, a *cloudburst*, or a *tempest*? (What is the difference in those three synonyms?)

No analysis of a writer's language would be complete without examining that author's word choice. What denotations is the author being careful to establish? What connotations is he or she hinting at? What emotional impact is suggested?

Consider the brief passage below, a speech made by the famous women's suffragist, Susan B. Anthony, on the occasion of her arrest and $100 fine for attempting to vote in the 1872 presidential election. After you examine the text of the speech and the notes pointing out Anthony's careful and effective word choice, look at how a student taking the AP Language exam might respond to multiple-choice questions and a free-response item dealing with Anthony's diction in her speech.

On Woman's Right to the Suffrage (1873)

SUSAN BROWNELL ANTHONY (1820-1906)

1 FRIENDS AND FELLOW CITIZENS[1]:—I stand before you to-night under indictment for the alleged crime[2] of having voted at the last presidential election, without having a lawful[3] right to vote. It shall be my work this evening to prove to you that in thus voting, I not only committed no crime, but, instead, simply exercised my *citizen's* rights[4], guaranteed to me and all United States citizens by the National Constitution[5], beyond the power of any State to deny....The preamble of the Federal Constitution says:

2 "We, the people of the United States, in order to form a more perfect union, establish justice, insure *domestic* tranquility, provide for the common defense, promote the general welfare, and secure the blessings of liberty to ourselves and our posterity, do ordain and establish this Constitution for the United States of America."

3 It was we, the people; not we, the white male citizens; nor yet we, the male citizens[6]; but we, the whole people[7], who formed the Union. And we formed it, not to give the blessings of liberty, but to secure[8] them; not to the half of ourselves and the half of our posterity, but to the whole people—women as well as men. And it is a downright mockery[9] to talk to women of their enjoyment of the blessings of liberty while they are denied the use of the only means of securing them provided by this democratic-republican government—the ballot.

4 For any State to make sex a qualification that must ever result in the disfranchisement of one entire half[10] of the people is to pass a bill of attainder, or an *ex post facto* law, and is therefore a violation of the supreme law of the land. By it the blessings of liberty are for ever withheld from women and their female posterity. To them this government has no just powers derived from the consent of the governed[11]. To them this government is not a democracy. It is not a republic. It is an odious aristocracy; a hateful oligarchy of sex[12]; the most hateful aristocracy ever established on the face of the

---

Sample Student Commentary

[1] Anthony's address is a common beginning for a speech, but she is addressing a broad crowd, not only women, whom she addresses as "citizens." She will use this term several times in her speech.

[2] Another careful use of words. There is no doubt what she did. The allegation is that her voting was a crime.

[3] Not "legal," not "legitimate," both of which are synonyms. "Lawful" anticipates Anthony's later appeal to the law in the Constitution.

[4] Second use of the word "citizen."

[5] The "law" to which she referred earlier and another reference to "citizen."

[6] Two more uses of "citizens." Notice how she broadens her appeal, also through word choice: "not white male... not male..."

[7] See the next paragraph in which Anthony will contrast this "whole" with an "entire half."

[8] Notice how she contrasts "give" with "secure." The implication is that the "blessings of liberty" hold primacy over the Constitution.

[9] Strong and direct. No attempt at euphemism or implication.

[10] The oxymoron "entire half" is surely intentional in order for Anthony to emphasize the magnitude of the injustice. "Entire half" echoes the sentiment expressed in the previous paragraph—the "whole people."

[11] This is not a reference to the Constitution, but a quotation from and paraphrase of The Declaration of Independence.

[12] Again, no attempt at euphemism.

globe[13]; an <u>oligarchy</u> of wealth, where the rich govern the poor. An <u>oligarchy</u> of learning, where the educated govern the ignorant, or even an <u>oligarchy</u> of race, where the Saxon rules the African, might be endured; but this <u>oligarchy</u> of sex, which makes father, brothers, husband, sons, the <u>oligarchs</u>[14] over the mother and sisters, the wife and daughters of every household—which ordains all men sovereigns, all women subjects, carries dissension, discord and rebellion into every home of the nation.

5   Webster, Worcester and Bouvier all define a <u>citizen to be a person</u>[15] in the United States, entitled to vote and hold office.

6   The only question left to be settled now is: Are women <u>persons</u>?[16] And I hardly believe any of our opponents will have the hardihood to say they are not. Being persons, then, women are citizens; and <u>no State has a right to make any law, or to enforce any old law, that shall abridge their privileges or immunities</u>.[17] Hence, every discrimination against women in the constitutions and laws of the several States is to-day null and void, precisely as in every one against Negroes. ❧

Sample Student Commentary

[13] Perhaps hyperbole here.

[14] Notice the repetition of "oligarchy" and "oligarchs."

[15] Citing these authorities, Anthony is able to return to the term "citizen" and broaden it to mean "person."

[16] Building on the definition in the previous passage, Anthony now establishes that women, being persons, are citizens.

[17] Amendment XIV, Section 1, Clause 2 (Privileges or Immunities) of the United States Constitution reads: "No State shall make or enforce any law which shall abridge the privileges or immunities of citizens of the United States." Anthony's paraphrase emphasizes that no law, either old or new, can deny female citizens their right to vote.

Sample multiple-choice questions:

1. Which of the following best describes the principle governing Anthony's diction?
   A. euphemistic and synonymic
   B. blunt and direct
   C. repetitive and ambiguous
   D. emotive and balanced
   E. tentative and apologetic

2. Which of the following phrases does Anthony use to illustrate the unlawful nature of the status quo?
   A. "alleged crime" (paragraph 1)
   B. "lawful right" (paragraph 1)
   C. "downright mockery" (paragraph 3)
   D. "most hateful oligarchy" (paragraph 4)
   E. "null and void" (paragraph 6)

3. Anthony appeals to a broader audience by equating

    A. Saxons and Africans.

    B. women and persons.

    C. women and negroes.

    D. citizens and persons.

    E. citizens and women.

4. In context, the word "odious" (paragraph 4) is best interpreted to mean

    A. hateful.

    B. unpleasant.

    C. unyielding.

    D. absolute.

    E. strong.

5. Throughout her speech, Antony employs all of the following EXCEPT

    A. concrete diction.

    B. hyperbole.

    C. quotation and paraphrase.

    D. understatement.

    E. oxymoron.

Answers and Explanations:

1. (A) is clearly eliminated by the use of such phrases as "outright mockery" and "odious aristocracy," which are clearly not euphemisms. (C) is tempting, as Anthony does employ a good deal of repetition, but her word choice is certainly not ambiguous. (D) is likewise tempting, as certainly her words are chosen for their emotional impact, but there is no attempt to "balance" positive feelings with the indignation she is obviously trying to raise. And she is certainly neither "tentative" in her word choice, nor "apologetic." Thus, (E) is eliminated. Phrases like "outright mockery" and "hateful oligarchy," however, are nothing if not **blunt and direct. Thus, (B) is the correct answer**.

2. (B) incorporates the word "lawful," but as a phrase, does not suggest any unlawfulness. (C) suggests neither law nor lack of law. (D), likewise, establishes the unpopularity of a form of law, but not necessarily its unlawfulness. The terms in (E), while perhaps sounding like legal terms and clearly establishing a negation of something, do not suggest unlawfulness. The phrase "alleged crime" (A), however, clearly suggests that the "crime" for which Anthony was fined was no real crime. That it might be viewed as a crime points to a flaw in the society and its government. **Thus, (A) is the best answer**.

3. (A) is excluded by the fact that Anthony posits an oligarchy that sets Saxons *above* Africans. (B) is tempting, but this equation does not broaden Anthony's appeal to include men. (C) is excluded because, as in (A), Anthony seems to be setting women above negroes by saying a "racial oligarchy" could be endured, but a gender oligarchy cannot. (D) might also tempt some students, but there is no direct appeal to any segment of Anthony's audience here. (E), however, appeals to both "citizens," which includes men, and "women," Anthony's obvious target audience. **Thus, (E) is the correct answer.**

4. All of the choices would "fill in the blank" with the correct form of the correct part of speech. (C), (D), and (E) all might be used to describe a type of government (as in *absolute monarchy*). But only (B) and (A) are supported by the context, in which the word "odious" is amplified by Anthony's twice using "hateful" in the remainder of the same sentence. (A) is more clearly and strongly supported than (B), so **(A) is the best answer**.

5. (A) is excluded by such phrases as "downright mockery." (B) is eliminated by Anthony's description of her state's government as, "the most hateful aristocracy ever established on the face of the globe." (C) is eliminated by Anthony's references to the Constitution, the Fourteenth Amendment, and the Declaration of Independence. (E) is eliminated by her use of the phrase "entire half." **There are, however, no understatements in the speech. Thus, (D) is the correct answer.**

Sample free-response item:

Carefully read the text of a famous speech delivered in 1873 by the famous women's suffragist Susan B. Anthony. In this speech, Anthony explains that female suffrage already is the law and that those who attempt to deny women their right are operating illegally. After reading the passage, write an essay in which you analyze Anthony's diction and how it contributes to the overall impact of the speech.

Sample Student Essay

In her famous 1873 speech, following her arrest for the "crime" of voting, Susan B. Anthony is precise in her word choice, while alienating as few listeners as possible, so that she can clearly establish her argument that female suffrage falls within the already-existing law of the United States. Specifically, Anthony adheres to a strict denotative use of many forceful key words. She borrows carefully from America's two most significant documents, offering quotations and paraphrases that will ring familiar in the ears of her listeners, while clearly suggesting the legitimacy of her claim. Finally, Anthony employs several word groupings, which further help her define the terms of her argument, either by association or by contrast. The short speech is moving, not only because of the rightness of its ideas, but because of the absolute meticulousness with which Anthony selects and uses the words with which to convey those ideas.

The key word in Anthony's oration is "citizen." The speech is addressed to "Friends and fellow citizens," and that one word appears seven times—quite a lot for a text that is only 536 words in total. By first addressing her audience as "fellow citizens," Anthony is establishing, not only her listeners' role, but her own as well. She is a "citizen" speaking to other "citizens." This relationship adds the necessary force to her assertion that, when she appeared to vote, she was merely invoking her "citizen's right." Anthony continues to hammer the concept of "citizen" home to her reader as she explores whether "white male citizens," or, even more generally, "male citizens" can and should enjoy benefits denied to others. Finally, Anthony is able to establish that a "citizen" is a "person," and she is, therefore, by virtue of her personhood, a citizen. Anthony's process has been a very careful establishment of the word's denotation, not an experiment with a connotation her audience might not accept. She employs a similar respect for denotation when, in the first paragraph, she describes her act as "lawful." While "lawful" and "legal" might, on the surface, appear to be synonyms, only "lawful" carries with it the authority of the Law. "Legal" denotes an interpretation or application, a mere technicality. By describing her act as "lawful," Anthony is insisting that her voting in the 1872 election was fully sanctioned and justified by the law—and the law she appeals to is no less than the Constitution of the United States of America. The choice of a word like "lawful" might seem insignificant, but Anthony clearly understands the importance of that choice.

Relying on denotation, Anthony is also careful to select the most powerful words available. It is not an "inconsistency" or a mere "injustice" to deny women their right to vote, it is "downright mockery." As the government currently functions, it is both "odious" and "hateful." Such forceful words leave no room in the listener's mind to wonder what connotation Anthony might have intended. These words are absolutely unambiguous.

Where her own words might fall short, Anthony also employs careful quotation and paraphrase from the Constitution itself, including a key amendment, and from The Declaration of Independence. Quoting the Preamble to the Constitution, Anthony emphasizes that the law is not established to "give" what the founders called "the blessings of liberty," but to "secure" them. Thus, according to Anthony—and she has the text of the Constitution to support her—female suffrage, one of the "blessings of liberty," is not the government's to give, but has already been given. It is the role of the government only to secure that blessing for her. She again quotes, with some judicious paraphrase, from the Fourteenth Amendment, specifically the "Privileges or Immunities Clause." The clause itself reads, "No State shall make or enforce any law" that would abridge any right or benefit of citizenship bestowed by the Constitution. Anthony inserts the words "No State has the right to make any law or to enforce any old law..." The additions emphasize the purpose of the amendment—no law can exist, and if any ever did, it could not be enforced—that would deprive a United States citizen of her rights. To rally further support for her argument that female suffrage is already the law, Anthony quotes *The Declaration of Independence*, which asserts that a just government can rule only with the "consent of the governed." However, as the "governed" include women, and women are not permitted to express or withhold their "consent," then the government is not "just." Thus, a few well-chosen words from an easily recognized document bolster Anthony's claim of the lawfulness of female suffrage.

Anthony's diction isn't limited to quotations from famous documents, however. To deliver her point with resonance and force, Anthony devises her own phrasings and repetitions to hammer her message home. In establishing the extent of the injustice of denying female suffrage, Anthony employs the oxymoron "entire half." An "entire half" of the population is disenfranchised. This injustice affects an "entire half" of the citizenry of the United States. The phrase "entire half" not only conveys the numbers of those denied their rights, it stands in direct contrast to the "whole people" referred to earlier in the same paragraph. The "union" is formed by the "whole people," while an "entire half" of that population is denied the right to vote. It's not just the rightness of Anthony's thesis that impresses the reader or listener, but the powerful word choice with which she expresses it.

Other powerful contrasts and juxtapositions allow her to condemn the government that would deny its citizens their lawful rights. In the fourth paragraph, for example, she uses the word "oligarchy" five times (and "oligarch" once). Each time, she modifies the term in a pattern of clearly increasing intolerability—"hateful oligarchy of sex," "oligarchy of wealth," "oligarchy of learning," "oligarchy of race," climaxing where she began, with the unendurable "oligarchy of sex." Twice in the same paragraph, she employs "aristocracy," also amplifying it to the point of hyperbole: "odious aristocracy," "the most hateful aristocracy ever established on the face of the globe."

It is difficult to imagine, nearly a century and a half after the fact, that something as basic as the right to vote could have been denied to women and had to be fought for. To arrest and fine a person simply for attempting to cast a vote in an election is, by our standards, unthinkable. The sheer rightness of Susan B. Anthony's cause would make for a powerful speech, but Anthony knew (as writers and orators still know today) that a powerful message alone is not usually sufficient. One must employ powerful language in expressing that message, and this famous 1873 speech is a fitting example of the capacity of careful word choice and phrasing to drive a message home. 🍎

Exercise One:

Questions 1-5. Carefully read the address and then select the best answers to the multiple-choice questions that follow.

Patrick Henry delivered this, his most famous speech, before the Second Virginia Convention on 23 March 1775. In it, he argues for the arming of a Virginia militia, both to defend Virginia from the increasing British military presence and to, perhaps, stage attacks against the British. The following account was recorded by Patrick Henry's first biographer William Wirt. According to Wirt's account, at the end of the speech, members of the Convention jumped up and shouted "To Arms! To Arms!"

Other historians, however, allege that Henry preyed upon his listeners' fear of Indian raids and slave revolts to build his case for arming against the British. The only written first-hand account further criticizes Henry for stooping to vitriolic name-calling.

Henry refused to participate in the Constitutional Convention of 1787, saying that he "smelt a rat...tending toward the monarchy." He did serve as a representative to the 1788 Virginia convention that ratified the Constitution, voting against ratification.

He was offered the position of President Washington's Secretary of State, but he declined, still suspecting the new Federal Government's potential threat to states' rights. It was not until the Reign of Terror of the French Revolution that Henry realized the potential of near-anarchy to break loose in the United States, and he came to support a strong Federal Government. His new Federal leanings were so strong that he publicly denounced the Virginia and Kentucky Resolutions, which tried to assert the right of any state's legislature to declare an act of Congress null and void.

In March 1799, in his last public address, Henry warned that the Resolutions threatened civil war, and he expressed deep regret that his native Virginia had fallen from the birth-mother of the Federal Government to the petulant stepson who desired to see the union's downfall.

Patrick Henry's
Speech to the Second Virginia Convention
St. John's Church, Richmond
23 March 1775

Mr. President:

1   No man thinks more highly than I do of the patriotism, as well as abilities, of the very worthy gentlemen who have just addressed the House. But different men often see the same subject in different lights; and, therefore, I hope it will not be thought disrespectful to those gentlemen if, entertaining as I do, opinions of a character very opposite to theirs, I shall speak forth my sentiments freely, and without reserve.

2   This is no time for ceremony. The question before the House is one of awful moment to this country. For my own part, I consider it as nothing less than a question of freedom or slavery; and in proportion to the magnitude of the subject ought to be the freedom of

the debate. It is only in this way that we can hope to arrive at truth, and fulfill the great responsibility which we hold to God and our country. Should I keep back my opinions at such a time, through fear of giving offence, I should consider myself as guilty of treason towards my country, and of an act of disloyalty toward the majesty of heaven, which I revere above all earthly kings.

3   Mr. President, it is natural to man to indulge in the illusions of hope. We are apt to shut our eyes against a painful truth, and listen to the song of that siren till she transforms us into beasts. Is this the part of wise men, engaged in a great and arduous struggle for liberty? Are we disposed to be of the number of those who, having eyes, see not, and, having ears, hear not, the things which so nearly concern their temporal salvation? For my part, whatever anguish of spirit it may cost, I am willing to know the whole truth; to know the worst, and to provide for it.

4   I have but one lamp by which my feet are guided; and that is the lamp of experience. I know of no way of judging of the future but by the past. And judging by the past, I wish to know what there has been in the conduct of the British ministry for the last ten years, to justify those hopes with which gentlemen have been pleased to solace themselves, and the House? Is it that insidious smile with which our petition has been lately received? Trust it not, sir; it will prove a snare to your feet. Suffer not yourselves to be betrayed with a kiss. Ask yourselves how this gracious reception of our petition comports with these war-like preparations which cover our waters and darken our land.

5   Are fleets and armies necessary to a work of love and reconciliation? Have we shown ourselves so unwilling to be reconciled, that force must be called in to win back our love? Let us not deceive ourselves, sir. These are the implements of war and subjugation; the last arguments to which kings resort. I ask, gentlemen, sir, what means this martial array, if its purpose be not to force us to submission? Can gentlemen assign any other possible motive for it? Has Great Britain any enemy, in this quarter of the world, to call for all this accumulation of navies and armies? No, sir, she has none. They are meant for us; they can be meant for no other. They are sent over to bind and rivet upon us those chains which the British ministry have been so long forging.

6   And what have we to oppose to them? Shall we try argument? Sir, we have been trying that for the last ten years. Have we anything new to offer upon the subject? Nothing. We have held the subject up in every light of which it is capable; but it has been all in vain. Shall we resort to entreaty and humble supplication? What terms shall we find which have not been already exhausted? Let us not, I beseech you, sir, deceive ourselves. Sir, we have done everything that could be done, to avert the storm which is now coming on. We have petitioned; we have remonstrated; we have supplicated; we have prostrated ourselves before the throne, and have implored its interposition to arrest the tyrannical hands of the ministry and Parliament. Our petitions have been slighted; our remonstrances have produced additional violence and insult; our supplications have been disregarded; and we have been spurned, with contempt, from the foot of the throne.

7   In vain, after these things, may we indulge the fond hope of peace and reconciliation. There is no longer any room for hope. If we wish to be free, if we mean to preserve inviolate those inestimable privileges for which we have been so long contending, if we mean not basely to abandon the noble struggle in which we have been so long engaged,

and which we have pledged ourselves never to abandon until the glorious object of our contest shall be obtained, we must fight! I repeat it, sir, we must fight! An appeal to arms and to the God of Hosts is all that is left us!

8   They tell us, sir, that we are weak; unable to cope with so formidable an adversary. But when shall we be stronger? Will it be the next week, or the next year? Will it be when we are totally disarmed, and when a British guard shall be stationed in every house? Shall we gather strength by irresolution and inaction? Shall we acquire the means of effectual resistance, by lying supinely on our backs, and hugging the delusive phantom of hope, until our enemies shall have bound us hand and foot? Sir, we are not weak if we make a proper use of those means which the God of nature hath placed in our power. Three millions of people, armed in the holy cause of liberty, and in such a country as that which we possess, are invincible by any force which our enemy can send against us. Besides, sir, we shall not fight our battles alone. There is a just God who presides over the destinies of nations; and who will raise up friends to fight our battles for us. The battle, sir, is not to the strong alone; it is to the vigilant, the active, the brave.

9   Besides, sir, we have no election. If we were base enough to desire it, it is now too late to retire from the contest. There is no retreat but in submission and slavery! Our chains are forged! Their clanking may be heard on the plains of Boston! The war is inevitable and let it come! I repeat it, sir, let it come.

10   It is in vain, sir, to extenuate the matter. Gentlemen may cry, Peace! Peace! But there is no peace. The war is actually begun! The next gale that sweeps from the north will bring to our ears the clash of resounding arms! Our brethren are already in the field! Why stand we here idle? What is it that gentlemen wish? What would they have? Is life so dear, or peace so sweet, as to be purchased at the price of chains and slavery? Forbid it, Almighty God! I know not what course others may take; but as for me, give me liberty, or give me death! ❦

Source: Wirt, William. *Sketches of the Life and Character of Patrick Henry.* (Philadelphia) 1836.

Multiple-choice questions:

1. Given the context of the rest of the speech, the word *patriotism*, as used in the first sentence, most likely means loyalty to the
   A. British Parliament.
   B. United States.
   C. state of Virginia.
   D. American people.
   E. English king.

2. Throughout his speech, Patrick Henry alludes to each of the following EXCEPT the

A. mythology of ancient Greece.

B. Judeo-Christian Old Testament.

C. Christian New Testament.

D. 1774 petition to King George III.

E. Magna Carta.

3. Patrick Henry's use of the word *treason* (paragraph 2) can best be described as

A. sarcastic.

B. fervent.

C. connotative.

D. ambiguous.

E. understated.

4. Henry's frequent uses of first person serve to make his address

A. personally revealing.

B. universally appealing.

C. antagonistic.

D. conciliatory.

E. broadly accusatory.

5. Which of the following most nearly approaches a propagandistic appeal?

A. "...judging by the past, I wish to know what there has been in the conduct of the British ministry for the last ten years, to justify those hope..." (paragraph 4)

B. "Suffer not yourselves to be betrayed with a kiss." (paragraph 4)

C. "Are fleets and armies necessary to a work of love and reconciliation? Have we shown ourselves so unwilling to be reconciled, that force must be called in to win back our love?" (paragraph 5)

D. "We have petitioned; we have remonstrated; we have supplicated; we have prostrated ourselves before the throne." (paragraph 6)

E. "There is no retreat but in submission and slavery!" (paragraph 9)

Free Response Item:

Carefully read Patrick Henry's 1775 Speech to the Second Virginia Convention, paying close attention to the speaker's word choice and sentence structure. Then, write a well-supported essay in which you support, refute, or qualify modern historians' charges that Patrick Henry tended toward demagoguery and propaganda in this address. Do not merely summarize the speech.

✄ Figurative and Rhetorical Devices

For nearly three decades, *rhetoric* has been cast aside as the ugly stepsister of writing instruction [METAPHOR and ALLUSION]. The fact remains, however, that the most effective communicators throughout history have intentionally, knowingly, and skillfully [PARALLELISM] employed an extensive toolkit [METAPHOR] of rhetorical devices, a toolkit that includes not only the standard simile and metaphor, but also such effective yet undervalued devices as anaphora, polysyndeton, and enumeration [AMPLIFICATION].

Modern linguists might argue that the formal study of rhetoric is *passé*, that student writers need only listen and read to "pick up" whatever language skills they need, but the truth is that [PROCATALEPSIS] the writer who *knows* what he or she is doing and can talk about his or her writing has a vast advantage over the writer who has only instincts to rely on.

To memorize terms and definitions is, of course, tedious and pointless; to learn how to build a strong and convincing argument, however, is the beginning of success [ANTITHESIS]. Just as important is a reader's ability to analyze other writers' deliberate and skillful use of language. What subtle distinctions are suggested by the two terms of a metaphor? What shade of meaning does that particular allusion contribute? What points are being emphasized, or glossed over? [RHETORICAL QUESTIONS]

There is probably no need to mention in a book of this nature that a sound knowledge of rhetoric, including the names and appropriate uses of at least the most common rhetorical devices, will serve you well on your Advanced Placement Exam [APOPHASIS]. Still, the benefits of some attention to language use beyond mere grammar and mechanics are undeniable.

The passage below is an account of two public gatherings that the American-born Henry James encountered on a trip to London. Closely read James's description of the two events and consider the notes pointing out his careful use of a number of literary and rhetorical devices. Then, look at how a student taking the AP Language exam might respond to multiple-choice questions and a free-response item dealing with James's use of rhetoric.

from:

Henry James, *Portraits of Places, Second Edition,* 1883.

1 I HAVE IT AT HEART to add that <u>if the English are handsomer than ourselves, they are also very much uglier.</u>[1] Indeed I think that all the European peoples are uglier than the American; we are far from producing those <u>magnificent types of facial eccentricity</u>[2] which flourish among older civilisations. American ugliness is on the side of physical poverty and meanness; English on that of redundancy and monstrosity. <u>In America there are few grotesques; in England there are many</u>[3] and some of them have a high <u>pictorial</u> value.

2 The element of the <u>grotesque</u> was very noticeable to me in the most <u>striking</u> collection of the <u>shabbier</u>[4] English types that I had seen since I came to London. The occasion of my seeing them was the funeral of Mr. George Odger, which befell some four or five weeks before the Easter period. Mr. George Odger, it will be remembered,[5] was an English <u>radical</u> agitator of <u>humble</u> origin, who had <u>distinguished</u> himself by a <u>perverse</u>[6] desire to get into Parliament. He exercised, <u>I believe</u>,[7] the useful profession of shoemaker, and he knocked in vain at the door that opens but to the refined. But he was a useful and honourable man, and his own people gave him an honourable burial.[8] I emerged accidentally into Piccadilly at the moment they were so engaged, and the <u>spectacle</u>[9] was one I should have been sorry to miss. The crowd was enormous, but I managed to squeeze through it and to get into a hansom cab that was drawn up beside the pavement, and here I looked on <u>as from a box at the play.</u>[10]

3 Though it was a funeral that was going on I will not call it a tragedy; but it was a very serious comedy. The day happened to be magnificent the finest of the year. The funeral had been taken in hand by the classes who are socially unrepresented in Parliament, and it had the character of a great popular "manifestation." The hearse was followed by very few carriages, but the cortege of pedestrians stretched away in the sunshine, up and

---

Sample Student Commentary

[1] James's thesis employs ANTITHESIS, contrasting the ideas of "handsomer" and "uglier." As the "handsomer" aspect of the pair appears in the subordinate clause, it is likely that this essay will elaborate on the "uglier" aspect.

[2] James's careful choice of the words magnificent and eccentricity establish that he does not mean offense when he calls Europeans "ugly." Further clarification of his use of the term will probably follow.

[3] Here James employs a clever combination of PARALLELISM and ANTITHESIS. He also introduces the term grotesques, which echoes his earlier use of eccentricity when defining "ugly."

[4] Before he describes the crowd as "shabby," James uses the words pictorial, grotesque, and striking, thus emphasizing that he does not intend to use "ugly" and "shabby" to insult the subjects of his essay.

[5] The SENTENTIAL ADVERB, "it will be remembered," neither provides new information, nor clarifies anything. James uses it here simply to establish tone.

[6] Does James's word choice suggest sarcasm? These antithetical words, and the frequent use of SENTENTIAL ADVERBS suggest at least condescension toward Odger and his aspiration.

[7] Here is another SENTENTIAL ADVERB.

[8] James makes the ALLUSION to Shakespeare's Julius Caesar, in which Marc Antony refers to the conspirators as "all honourable men."

[9] Remember that James is describing a man's funeral. "Spectacle" clearly does not connote a serious display.

[10] Here is a basic SIMILE. James's comparing his vantage point to a box in a theater emphasizes the amusement evident in his earlier reference to the funeral as a "spectacle."

down the classic gentility of Piccadilly, on a scale that was highly impressive. Here and there the line was broken by a small brass band apparently one of those bands of itinerant Germans that play for coppers beneath lodging-house windows; but for the rest it was compactly made up of <u>what the newspapers call the dregs of the population</u>.[11] It was the <u>London rabble, the metropolitan mob, men and women, boys and girls, the decent poor and the indecent</u>,[12] who had scrambled into the ranks as they gathered them up on their passage, and were making a sort of solemn "lark" of it. Very solemn it all was perfectly proper and undemonstrative. They shuffled along in an interminable line, and as I looked at them out of the front of my hansom I seemed to be having a sort of panoramic view of <u>the under side, the wrong side, of the London world</u>.[13] The procession was filled with figures which seemed never to have "shown out," as the English say, before; of strange, pale, mouldy paupers who blinked and stumbled in the Piccadilly sunshine.

4   I have no space to describe them more minutely, but I found the whole affair rather suggestive. My impression rose not simply from the radical, or, as I may say for the sake of colour, the revolutionary, emanation of this dingy concourse, lighted up by the ironical sky; <u>but from the same causes that I had observed a short time before</u>,[14] on the day the Queen went to open Parliament, when in Trafalgar Square, looking straight down into Westminster and over the royal procession, were gathered a group of banners and festoons inscribed in big staring letters with mottoes and sentiments which a sensitive police department might easily have found seditious. They were mostly in allusion to the Tichborne claimant*, whose release from his dungeon they peremptorily demanded, and whose cruel fate was taken as a pretext for several sweeping reflections on the social arrangements of the time and country. These impertinent standards were allowed to sun themselves <u>as freely as if they had</u> been the manifestoes of the Irish Giant† or the Oriental Dwarf‡ at a fair.[16]

5   I had lately come from Paris, where the police-department is more sensitive, and where revolutionary placards are not observed to adorn the base of the obelisk in the *Place de la Concorde*. I was, therefore, the more struck on both of the occasions I speak of with

---

* This refers to a case in the nineteenth century, in which an Arthur Orton claimed to be the missing Sir Roger Tichborne and extorted exorbitant sums of money from Tichborne's bereaved mother. Finally, Orton was tried on both civil and criminal charges, fined, and imprisoned. Those who believed Orton's claim protested and claimed that he had been unjustly persecuted.

† Charles Byrne (1761-1783) popularly known as "The Irish Giant," was a "human curiosity" in 1780s London. While his exact height is unknown, skeletal evidence suggests he stood at approximately 7ft, 7in tall.

‡ This is possibly a reference to the Oriental Dwarf Kingfisher, a small and beautiful bird indigenous to southeast Asia. In the nineteenth century, rare and exotic species of plants and animals were often put on display in museums and other public venues and were popular attractions.

Sample Student Commentary

[11] "What the newspapers call..." not what James would call...

[12] The technique of SCESIS ONOMATON adds emphasis by repeating and rephrasing. It may help to clarify, but does not further develop, the idea being communicated.

[13] Here is another example of SCESIS ONOMATON.

[14] While there is nothing rhetorically notable in this portion, it is important not to miss that James is shifting his focus and transitioning from the funeral of George Odger to a demonstration he witnessed a few days earlier.

[15] Here is another example of SCESIS ONOMATON.

[16] Another basic SIMILE that simply reinforces James's point that the crowds at both gatherings he has described drew no more attention than would patrons of a museum.

the admirable English practice of letting people alone with <u>the good sense and the good humour and even the good taste</u>[17] of it. It was this that I found impressive, as I watched the "manifestation" of Mr. Odger's under-fed partisans the fact that the mighty mob could march along and do its errand, while the excellent quiet policemen stood by simply to see that the channel was kept clear and comfortable. ॐ

Sample Student Commentary

[17] The repetition of the word "good" in this series of phrases is an example of ANAPHORA and adds both lyrical rhythm and emphasis to the wisdom of the English authorities who allow crowds like the two described in this essay to gather without molestation.

Sample multiple-choice questions:

1. The overall tone of this passage can best be described as

A. mocking.

B. condemning.

C. incredulous.

D. dismissive.

E. condescending.

2. The primary effect of the simile *as from a box at the play* (paragraph 2) is

A. emphasis.

B. contradiction.

C. irony.

D. comedy.

E. clarification.

3. The paragraph containing the final anaphora (paragraph 5) suggests all of the following EXCEPT

A. England has a classless, egalitarian society.

B. the English value taste above other traits.

C. the English police are generally decent people.

D. Londoners are people of good will.

E. all citizens expect the right of assembly.

4. By the end of the passage, the word "grotesque" (paragraphs 1,2) is best interpreted to mean

A. ugly.

B. shabby.

C. eccentric.

D. perverse

E. radical.

5. All of the following contribute to the overall tone of the passage EXCEPT
   A. scesis onomaton.
   B. sentential adverb.
   C. simile.
   D. antithesis.
   E. allusion.

Answers and Explanations:

1. (A) is tempting, but James's use of words like "useful" and "honourable" when describing Odger, and the final anaphora emphasizing the *good* soften the sarcasm so that "mockery" is too strong a word. (B), likewise, is too strong a description, and is not supported by James's obvious enjoyment of the scene. (C) is completely unfounded. (D) might tempt some, but, while James clearly does not consider the funeral to be a solemn occasion, he does acknowledge the worth of such a demonstration. **Thus, (E) is the best answer. James's word choice and rhetorical devices clearly show him to be above the masses, distant, watching the funeral as from a theater box. While the scene is a source of amusement to him, he is more condescending than condemning or mocking.**

2. (A) is tempting since the comparison of James's vantage point does emphasize his comparison of the funeral to an entertainment; the simile adds the new element of spectator in theater box. Clearly James uses it for more than mere emphasis. (B) suggests the simile's role of juxtaposing two *different* elements, but a simile also *likens* the two elements. Contradiction is not a purpose of simile. (D) is tempting, but while the passage suggests James's amusement, this amusement is not strong enough to be considered comic. (E) is also tempting, as similes are used to explain an unknown by comparing it to the known. **This simile, however, adds a new element to the passage. The simile picks up a motif already established by James—the funeral as spectacle or entertainment—and adds to it the narrative perspective of the upper-class theater patron in a box. In the single simile, James specifically articulates the irony of regarding the funeral like an entertainment, a play. Thus, (C) is the best answer**.

3. (B) is suggested by the fact that "taste" is placed third in the progression of three, clearly emphasizing it as the most important or notable. (C) is suggested by the "good humor" element of the anaphora as well as the later description of the policemen as "excellent quiet." (D) and (E) are excluded by the same elements, as James is clearly talking about the people in general as well as the police specifically, and the right of assembly is discussed in terms of "sense, humor, and taste" and not law. **Only (A) cannot be inferred from the paragraph, as James clearly describes these demonstrators as "Mr. Odger's under-fed partisans," thus establishing that there is, indeed, class consciousness in this society.**

4. All of the choices appear in one form or another in the passage, and some are denotative synonyms for "grotesque." (A) is eliminated, however, by the fact that, even in the first paragraph, James suggests a distinction between ugly and grotesque. He also introduces the Odger's funeral as "grotesque," but does not develop any sense of its being ugly. (B) is eliminated for similar reasons. While James does reiterate the shabbiness of the mourners at the funeral, he again does not depict the funeral or its participants as ugly. (D) is tempting, as there is some equation of the grotesqueness of the funeral and the perversity of Odger's Parliamentary aspiration, but the overall tone of the passage does not support the inference that James finds the entire experience perverse. (E) is probably the least tempting choice, as the radical nature of the participants might be an element of the experience's grotesqueness, but they are not synonymous. **The best answer is (C). In the first paragraph, James begins to relate the eccentric and the grotesque. Throughout the passage, beginning in the second paragraph, it becomes clear that what James finds grotesque in the funeral experience are its eccentricities—the incongruous blend of funeral and spectacle, the rabble's sincere attempt at a stately occasion.**

5. (A) is excluded by the two occasions on which James claims to find the mourners at the funeral worthy and admirable, while emphasizing their poverty and unruliness. (B) is eliminated by James's conversational pauses—"it will be remembered" and "I believe." One key simile (C) likens his observing the funeral from a coach to watching a play from a box. (E) is eliminated by the allusion to the Tichborne Affair, suggesting the protestors' lack of sophistication and willingness to gather at any excuse. **The antithesis (D) in the first paragraph, however, introduces James's thesis, but does not begin to establish the mocking, condescending tone he will adopt beginning in the second paragraph.**

Sample free-response item:

Carefully read the excerpt from Henry James's 1883 travelogue, *Portraits of Places*, in which the author recounts two public demonstrations he witnessed. After reading the passage, write an essay in which you analyze how James's diction and his use of literary and rhetorical devices help to convey his attitude toward the participants in the demonstrations.

Sample Student Essay

It is clear from his depiction of a working class funeral in his 1883 travelogue, *Portraits of Places*, that Henry James was something of a snob who looked down upon those he considered to be below him in social class. While his thesis at the beginning of his description of George Odger's funeral ostensibly praises the unique and the eccentric that might be dismissed as ugly, James's choice of words and the rhetorical devices he uses in developing that thesis combine to create a passage that is, at best, condescending in tone.

James introduces his account by saying he found the funeral to be "grotesque." He attempts to clarify that, by "grotesque," he means "eccentric" and "striking." These terms do not necessarily denote negative criticism, so James avoids the condescending mockery into which he will fall in the body of his essay. Once he begins his description of the funeral itself, however, his word choice and rhetorical decisions reveal an underlying air of superiority. From the beginning, "grotesque" and "striking" become "shabbier." A "humble" man's aspiration to rise in status is "perverse," and the "honourable burial" for an "honourable man" is reduced to a "spectacle," not a "tragedy," but a "serious comedy," a procession of "mouldy paupers who blinked and stumbled" in the sunshine.

While there is no sense of criticism in James's word choice, certainly there is nothing positive in the adjectives with which he describes the mourners ("shabbier," "humble," "perverse," "mouldy") or in the noun he uses to name them, ("paupers"). Eventually, he will become more blatantly critical, calling the mourners a "mob," comprising the "indecent" poor and "the wrong side" of London society. The words clearly reveal an attitude that is, at best, condescending.

The similes with which James clarifies and enlivens his account also reveal James's superior air. His vantage point, from inside a hansom cab, does not merely render him an outsider, a mere observer; it evokes in James the sense of watching the spectacle "as from a box at the play." Now he is not spectator; he is audience. Similarly, James compares the mob he observes protesting the treatment of Arthur Orton in the Tichborne Affair to a crowd of curiosity-seekers looking at circus freaks like "the Irish Giant" and rare birds, such as the "Oriental Dwarf." Again, there is no criticism here, but clearly James chooses terms that dismiss the concerns of the masses, their desire for social justice and political equality, as trivial.

Other devices contribute to James's condescending tone as well. While the sentential adverb can be used to establish intimacy between author and reader or to emphasize the author's credibility, James's conversational insertions—"it will be remembered" and "I believe"—suggest that he is addressing members of his own class who share his classist views. The emphasis that James strives for in the scesis onamaton further shows his superior attitude. He describes the crowd at the funeral as, "the London rabble, the metropolitan mob...the decent poor and the indecent." The words, of course, leave little room for interpretation, but the progression also points to James's disregard for the mourners. The second occurrence of scesis onamaton advances this evaluation. Here, James admits that he is observing "the under side, the wrong side, of the London world." Again, both word choice and the progression of terms make it clear what James's attitude toward those at the "wrong side of the London world" is.

Thus, it is interesting to note that, while James may begin and end his observation with apparent praise for the character of the English, the word choice and rhetorical forms in the body of the essay reveal that James considers himself above the rabble and finds their concerns, including their grief and social indignation, amusing. His tone through the bulk of the essay is condescending at best, mocking at worst. 🐚

Exercise Two:

Questions 6-10. Carefully read the address and then select the best answers to the multiple-choice questions that follow.

The following passage is the inaugural address presented by President Barack Obama on Tuesday, January 20, 2009. Read it carefully, paying close attention, not only to the President's arguments, but to the rhetorical devices he uses to communicate those arguments. Then, select the best answers to the multiple-choice questions that follow.

My fellow citizens:

1   I stand here today humbled by the task before us, grateful for the trust you have bestowed, mindful of the sacrifices borne by our ancestors. I thank President Bush for his service to our nation, as well as the generosity and cooperation he has shown throughout this transition.

2   Forty-four Americans have now taken the presidential oath. The words have been spoken during rising tides of prosperity and the still waters of peace. Yet, every so often the oath is taken amidst gathering clouds and raging storms. At these moments, America has carried on not simply because of the skill or vision of those in high office, but because We the People have remained faithful to the ideals of our forbearers, and true to our founding documents.

3   So it has been. So it must be with this generation of Americans.

4   That we are in the midst of crisis is now well understood. Our nation is at war, against a far-reaching network of violence and hatred. Our economy is badly weakened, a consequence of greed and irresponsibility on the part of some, but also our collective failure to make hard choices and prepare the nation for a new age. Homes have been lost; jobs shed; businesses shuttered. Our health care is too costly; our schools fail too many; and each day brings further evidence that the ways we use energy strengthen our adversaries and threaten our planet.

5   These are the indicators of crisis, subject to data and statistics. Less measurable but no less profound is a sapping of confidence across our land—a nagging fear that America's decline is inevitable, that the next generation must lower its sights.

6   Today I say to you that the challenges we face are real. They are serious and they are many. They will not be met easily or in a short span of time. But know this, America—they will be met.

7   On this day, we gather because we have chosen hope over fear, unity of purpose over conflict and discord.

8   On this day, we come to proclaim an end to the petty grievances and false promises, the recriminations and worn-out dogmas that for far too long have strangled our politics.

9   We remain a young nation, but in the words of Scripture, the time has come to set aside childish things. The time has come to reaffirm our enduring spirit; to choose our better history; to carry forward that precious gift, that noble idea, passed on from generation to generation: the God-given promise that all are equal, all are free, and all deserve a chance to pursue their full measure of happiness.

10   In reaffirming the greatness of our nation, we understand that greatness is never a given. It must be earned. Our journey has never been one of shortcuts or settling for less. It has not been the path for the faint-hearted—for those who prefer leisure over work, or seek only the pleasures of riches and fame. Rather, it has been the risk-takers, the doers, the makers of things—some celebrated but more often men and women obscure in their labor, who have carried us up the long, rugged path towards prosperity and freedom.

11   For us, they packed up their few worldly possessions and traveled across oceans in search of a new life.

12   For us, they toiled in sweatshops and settled the West; endured the lash of the whip and plowed the hard earth.

13   For us, they fought and died, in places like Concord and Gettysburg; Normandy and Khe Sahn.

14   Time and again these men and women struggled and sacrificed and worked till their hands were raw so that we might live a better life. They saw America as bigger than the sum of our individual ambitions; greater than all the differences of birth or wealth or faction.

15   This is the journey we continue today. We remain the most prosperous, powerful nation on Earth. Our workers are no less productive than when this crisis began. Our minds are no less inventive, our goods and services no less needed than they were last week or last month or last year. Our capacity remains undiminished. But our time of standing pat, of protecting narrow interests and putting off unpleasant decisions—that time has surely passed. Starting today, we must pick ourselves up, dust ourselves off, and begin again the work of remaking America.

16   For everywhere we look, there is work to be done. The state of our economy calls for action, bold and swift, and we will act—not only to create new jobs, but to lay a new foundation for growth. We will build the roads and bridges, the electric grids and digital lines that feed our commerce and bind us together. We will restore science to its rightful place, and wield technology's wonders to raise health care's quality and lower its cost. We will harness the sun and the winds and the soil to fuel our cars and run our factories. And we will transform our schools and colleges and universities to meet the demands of a new age. All this we can do. All this we will do.

17   Now, there are some who question the scale of our ambitions—who suggest that our system cannot tolerate too many big plans. Their memories are short. For they have forgotten what this country has already done; what free men and women can achieve when imagination is joined to common purpose, and necessity to courage.

18   What the cynics fail to understand is that the ground has shifted beneath them—that the stale political arguments that have consumed us for so long no longer apply. The question we ask today is not whether our government is too big or too small, but whether it works—whether it helps families find jobs at a decent wage, care they can afford, a retirement that is dignified. Where the answer is yes, we intend to move forward. Where the answer is no, programs will end. And those of us who manage the public's dollars will be held to account—to spend wisely, reform bad habits, and do our business in the light of day—because only then can we restore the vital trust between a people and their government.

19   Nor is the question before us whether the market is a force for good or ill. Its power to generate wealth and expand freedom is unmatched, but this crisis has reminded us that without a watchful eye, the market can spin out of control—the nation cannot prosper long when it favors only the prosperous. The success of our economy has always depended not just on the size of our Gross Domestic Product, but on the reach of our prosperity; on the ability to extend opportunity to every willing heart—not out of charity, but because it is the surest route to our common good.

20   As for our common defense, we reject as false the choice between our safety and our ideals. Our Founding Fathers, faced with perils that we can scarcely imagine, drafted a charter to assure the rule of law and the rights of man, a charter expanded by the blood of generations. Those ideals still light the world, and we will not give them up for expedience's sake. And so to all the other peoples and governments who are watching today, from the grandest capitals to the small village where my father was born: know that America is a friend of each nation and every man, woman, and child who seeks a future of peace and dignity, and we are ready to lead once more.

21   Recall that earlier generations faced down fascism and communism not just with missiles and tanks, but with the sturdy alliances and enduring convictions. They understood that our power alone cannot protect us, nor does it entitle us to do as we please. Instead, they knew that our power grows through its prudent use; our security emanates from the justness of our cause, the force of our example, the tempering qualities of humility and restraint.

22   We are the keepers of this legacy. Guided by these principles once more, we can meet those new threats that demand even greater effort—even greater cooperation and understanding between nations. We will begin to responsibly leave Iraq to its people, and forge a hard-earned peace in Afghanistan. With old friends and former foes, we will work tirelessly to lessen the nuclear threat, and roll back the specter of a warming planet. We will not apologize for our way of life, nor will we waver in its defense, and for those who seek to advance their aims by inducing terror and slaughtering innocents, we say to you now that our spirit is stronger and cannot be broken; you cannot outlast us, and we will defeat you.

23   For we know that our patchwork heritage is a strength, not a weakness. We are a nation of Christians and Muslims, Jews and Hindus—and non-believers. We are shaped by every language and culture, drawn from every end of this Earth; and because we have tasted the bitter swill of civil war and segregation, and emerged from that dark chapter stronger and more united, we cannot help but believe that the old hatreds shall someday pass; that the lines of tribe shall soon dissolve; that as the world grows smaller, our common humanity shall reveal itself; and that America must play its role in ushering in a new era of peace.

24   To the Muslim world, we seek a new way forward, based on mutual interest and mutual respect. To those leaders around the globe who seek to sow conflict, or blame their society's ills on the West—know that your people will judge you on what you can build, not what you destroy. To those who cling to power through corruption and deceit and the silencing of dissent, know that you are on the wrong side of history; but that we will extend a hand if you are willing to unclench your fist.

25   To the people of poor nations, we pledge to work alongside you to make your farms flourish and let clean waters flow; to nourish starved bodies and feed hungry minds. And to those nations like ours that enjoy relative plenty, we say we can no longer afford indifference to the suffering outside our borders; nor can we consume the world's resources without regard to effect. For the world has changed, and we must change with it.

26   As we consider the road that unfolds before us, we remember with humble gratitude those brave Americans who, at this very hour, patrol far-off deserts and distant mountains. They have something to tell us, just as the fallen heroes who lie in Arlington whisper through the ages. We honor them not only because they are the guardians of our liberty, but because they embody the spirit of service; a willingness to find meaning in something greater than themselves. And yet, at this moment—a moment that will define a generation—it is precisely this spirit that must inhabit us all.

27   For as much as government can do and must do, it is ultimately the faith and determination of the American people upon which this nation relies. It is the kindness to take in a stranger when the levees break, the selflessness of workers who would rather cut their hours than see a friend lose their job which sees us through our darkest hours. It is the firefighter's courage to storm a stairway filled with smoke, but also a parent's willingness to nurture a child, that finally decides our fate.

28   Our challenges may be new. The instruments with which we meet them may be new. But those values upon which our success depends—honesty and hard work, courage and fair play, tolerance and curiosity, loyalty and patriotism—these things are old. These things are true. They have been the quiet force of progress throughout our history. What is demanded then is a return to these truths. What is required of us now is a new era of responsibility—a recognition, on the part of every American, that we have duties to ourselves, our nation, and the world, duties that we do not grudgingly accept but rather seize gladly, firm in the knowledge that there is nothing so satisfying to the spirit, so defining of our character, than giving our all to a difficult task.

29   This is the price and the promise of citizenship.

30   This is the source of our confidence—the knowledge that God calls on us to shape an uncertain destiny.

31   This is the meaning of our liberty and our creed—why men and women and children of every race and every faith can join in celebration across this magnificent mall, and why a man whose father less than sixty years ago might not have been served at a local restaurant can now stand before you to take a most sacred oath.

31   So let us mark this day with remembrance, of who we are and how far we have traveled. In the year of America's birth, in the coldest of months, a small band of patriots huddled by dying campfires on the shores of an icy river. The capital was abandoned. The enemy was advancing. The snow was stained with blood. At a moment when the outcome of our revolution was most in doubt, the father of our nation ordered these words be read to the people:

32   "Let it be told to the future world...that in the depth of winter, when nothing but hope and virtue could survive...that the city and the country, alarmed at one common danger, came forth to meet...it."

33   America! In the face of our common dangers, in this winter of our hardship, let us remember these timeless words. With hope and virtue, let us brave once more the icy currents, and endure what storms may come. Let it be said by our children's children that when we were tested we refused to let this journey end, that we did not turn back nor did we falter; and with eyes fixed on the horizon and God's grace upon us, we carried forth that great gift of freedom and delivered it safely to future generations.

34   Thank you. God bless you. And God bless the United States of America. ❧

Multiple-choice questions:

6. The controlling device of the last full paragraph of this speech is
   A. apostrophe.
   B. hyperbole.
   C. metaphor.
   D. allusion.
   E. anaphora.

7. Paragraphs 11-13 are connected by which of the following rhetorical devices?
   A. allusion
   B. metaphor
   C. climax
   D. anaphora
   E. polysyndeton

8. Which of the following is most likely a deliberate hyperbole?
   A. "mindful of the sacrifices borne by our ancestors" (paragraph 1)
   B. "that precious gift, that noble idea" (paragraph 9)
   C. "endured the lash of the whip and plowed the hard earth" (paragraph 12)
   D. "we understand that greatness is never a given" (paragraph 10)
   E. "let us brave the icy currents, and endure what storms may come" (paragraph 33)

9. The consonance in paragraph 29 achieves all of the following EXCEPT to
   A. link contrasting concepts.
   B. accentuate a contradiction.
   C. create audial harmony.
   D. suggest verbal tension.
   E. emphasize a paradox.

10. The primary rhetorical purpose for the quotation in paragraph 32 is to
   A. reinforce the speech's optimistic tone.
   B. allude to a key historical figure.
   C. connect the future with the past.
   D. clarify the allusion in the next paragraph.
   E. begin the transition to the end of the speech.

Free Response Item:

Carefully read Barack Obama's January 20, 2009, Presidential *Inaugural Address* paying close attention, not only to the President's arguments, but to the rhetorical devices he uses to communicate those arguments. Then, write a thoughtful and well-supported essay in which you evaluate the impact of the President's use of rhetoric on the strength of his message and his appeal to his audience.

Unusual or unconventional usages

Every writer must know, and for the most part adhere to, the conventions of the language and genre in which he or she is writing. Without conventions such as mutually agreed-upon word orders (sentence structure and syntax), word meanings (connotation and denotation), and signposts and direction signals (capitalization and punctuation), written communication is virtually impossible.

Of course, for that matter, the reader also needs to know the same conventions. If Josh knows that a *dolly* is a human-propelled, two- or four-wheeled device used to move heavy objects; and Jen knows that a *dolly* is a plaything that usually resembles a miniature person, one of them is going to misunderstand the sentence, *The movers used the dolly to load the refrigerator into the van.*

The writer must know to put a period at the end of a sentence, and the reader must know what the period means. The writer must know to use capital letters when writing about the White House where the president lives, but small letters when describing the white house in which he or she grew up. And the reader needs to know how to tell the difference.

The writer needs to know how to cue his reader when he's making a statement:
   You're tired.
or asking a question:
   You're tired?
And the reader needs to know the difference as well.

There might be times, however, when a skilful writer may choose to stray from a conventional use—to break the rule, as it were. Keep in mind that a grammatical or mechanical *error* is not the same thing as an *unconventional use*. The latter assumes the writer knows how to "do it right" and can articulate his or her reasons for violating the convention. The unconventional use is intentional and, at least in theory, effective. An *error* is simply the writer's wrong use. He or she may not even know that the use is wrong or may not know how to do it correctly; the most likely effect on a careful reader is confusion.

Still, there might be times when the author intentionally violates conventions.

Stylistic sentence fragments, for instance. Perhaps the author may choose to capitalize IMPORTANT WORDS for emphasis. Or he might even choose to begin a sentence with a coordinating conjunction, be gender specific, and end it with an ellipsis...

For the most part writers will use Standard Edited American English (SEAE) in their published works. When they want to achieve emphasis or a comic effect or an endearing or sarcastic tone—when they hope to achieve a specific and identifiable effect—they may elect to violate the conventions. Part of reading and understanding their work, then, is recognizing their unconventional usage and analyzing its function in the work.

Consider the following passage, the introduction to a well-respected book on literary theory. In it, the author reflects on the linguistic, social, and psychological aspects of determining a work's "literary value." The passage has been annotated to point out to you the types of issues—word choice, sentence structure, use of figurative devices—that a careful reader would need to examine in a close reading, an analysis, or an evaluation of the author's argument and how it is presented.

After you examine the passage and the accompanying notes, look at how a student taking the AP Language exam might respond to multiple-choice questions and a free-response item dealing with how Professor Eagelton discusses the nature of "the literary" and how one might arrive at a definition of "literature."

What is Literature?

TERRY EAGLETON

1 IF THERE IS SUCH a thing as literary theory, then it would seem obvious that there is something called literature which it is the theory of. We can begin, then, by raising the question: what is literature?[1]

2 There have been various attempts to define literature. You can define it, for example,

---

Sample Student Commentary

[1] Notice that the premise of this essay is a hypothesis: if A then B.

as "imaginative"[2] writing in the sense of fiction-writing, which is not literally true. But even the briefest reflection on what people commonly include under the heading of literature suggests that this will not do. Seventeenth-century English literature includes Shakespeare, Webster, Marvell, and Milton; but it also stretches to the essays of Francis Bacon, the sermons of John Donne, Bunyan's spiritual autobiography, and whatever it was that Sir Thomas Browne wrote.[3] It might even at a pinch be taken to encompass Hobbes's *Leviathan* or Clarendon's *History of the Rebellion*. French seventeenth-century literature contains, along with Comeille and Racine, La Rochefoucauld's maxims, Bossuet's funeral speeches, Boileau's treatise on poetry, Madame de Sevigne's letters to her daughter and the philosophy of Descartes and Pascal. Nineteenth-century English literature usually includes Lamb (though not Bentham), Macaulay (but not Marx), Mill (but not Darwin or Herbert Spencer).

3 A distinction between "fact" and "fiction"; then, seems unlikely to get us very far, not least because the distinction itself is often a questionable one. It has been argued, for instance, that our own opposition between "historical" and "artistic" truth does not apply at all to the early Icelandic sagas. In the English late sixteenth and early seventeenth centuries, the word "novel" seems to have been used about both true and fictional events, and even news reports were hardly to be considered factual. Novels and news reports were neither clearly factual nor clearly fictional: our sharp discriminations between these categories simply did not apply. Gibbon no doubt thought that he was writing historical truth, and so perhaps did the authors of Genesis, but they are now read as" fact" by some and "fiction" by others; Newman certainly thought his theological meditations were true, but they are now for many readers "literature." Moreover, if "literature" includes much "factual" writing, it also excludes quite a lot of fiction. Superman comics and Mills and Boon novels are fiction but not generally regarded as literature, and certainly not Literature.[4] If literature is "creative" or "imaginative" writing, does this imply that history, philosophy, and natural science are uncreative and unimaginative?

4 Perhaps one needs a different kind of approach altogether.[5] Perhaps literature is definable not according to whether it is fictional or "imaginative" but because it uses language in peculiar ways. On this theory, literature is a kind of writing which, in the words of the Russian critic Roman Jacobson, represents an "organized violence committed on ordinary speech." Literature transforms and intensifies ordinary language, deviates systematically from everyday speech. If you approach me at bus stop and murmur, "Thou still unravished bride of quietness," then I am instantly aware that I am in the presence of the literary. I know this because the texture, rhythm, and resonance of your words are in excess of their abstractable meaning—or as the linguists might more technically put

---

Sample Student Commentary

[2] Eagleton uses quotation marks, not because he is quoting any source but to suggest that he is using the words non-literally. Think of what speakers mean when they use "air quotes."

[3] Eagleton has already used direct address to establish a cordiality with his readers. Now, he introduces an element of humorous sarcasm to maintain that casual, conversational tone.

[4] Literature is not a proper noun, but Eagleton capitalizes it here to highlight the term as an ideal or a classification.

[5] The first element of Eagleton's essay has been about the subject matter of literature. Now, he is going to discuss the language of literature.

it, there is disproportion between the signifiers and the signifieds. Your language draws attention to itself, flaunts its material being, as statements like "Don't you know the drivers are on strike?" do not.

5   This, in effect, was the definition of the "literary" advanced by the Russian formalists, who included in their ranks Viktor Shlovsky, Roman Jakobson, Osip Brik, Yury Tynyanov, Boris Eichenbaum and Boris Tomashevsky. The Formalists emerged in Russia in the years before the 1917 Bolshevik revolution and flourished throughout the 1920s, until they were effectively silenced by Stalinism.[6] A militant, polemical group of critics: they rejected the quasi-mystical symbolist doctrines which had influenced literary criticism before them, and in a practical, scientific spirit shifted attention to the material reality of the literary text itself. Criticism should dissociate art from mystery and concern itself with how literary texts actually worked. Literature was not pseudo-religion or psychology or sociology but a particular organization of language. It had its own specific laws, structures and devices, which were to be studied in themselves rather than reduced to something else. The literary work was neither a vehicle for ideas, a reflection of social reality nor the incarnation of some transcendental truth. It was a material fact, whose functioning could be analyzed rather as one could examine a machine. It was made of words, not of objects or feelings, and it was a mistake to see it as the expression of an author's mind. Pushkin's *Eugene Onegin*, Osip Brik once airily remarked, would have been written even if Pushkin had not lived.

6   Formalism was essentially the application of linguistics to the study of literature; and because the linguistics in question were of a formal kind, concerned with the structures of language rather than with what one might actually say, the Formalists passed over the analysis of literary "content" (where one might always be tempted into psychology or sociology) for the study of literary form.[7] Far from seeing form as the expression of content, they stood the relationship on its head: content was merely the "motivation" of form, an occasion or convenience for a particular kind of formal exercise. Don Quixote is not "about" the character of that name: the character is just a device for holding together different kinds of narrative technique. *Animal Farm* for the Formalists would not be an allegory of Stalinism; on the contrary, Stalinism would simply provide a useful opportunity for the construction of an allegory.[8] It was this perverse insistence which won for the Formalists their derogatory name from their antagonists; and though they did not deny that art had a relation to social reality—indeed some of them were closely associated with the Bolsheviks—they provocatively claimed that this relation was not the critic's business.

7   The Formalists started out by seeing the literary work as a more or less arbitrary assemblage of "devices," and only later came to see these devices as interrelated elements

---

Sample Student Commentary

[6] This is not a digression. Eagleton knows that his readers are probably unfamiliar with the Russian formalists, so he provides a little factual background. It is not unlike plot exposition in fiction.

[7] Thus, Formalism derives its name from the fact that it studies literary form, not from a suggestion that it is a formal (as opposed to a casual) study.

[8] Eagleton is clearly describing an extreme, exclusive kind of Formalism that completely disregards the role of content or subject matter.

or "functions" within a total textual system.[9] "Devices" included sound, imagery, rhythm, syntax, metre, rhyme, narrative techniques, in fact the whole stock of formal literary elements; and what all of these elements had in common was their "estrangement;" or "defamiliarizing" effect. What was specific to literary language, what distinguished it from other forms of discourse, was that it "deformed" ordinary language in various ways. Under the pressure of literary devices, ordinary language was intensified, condensed, twisted, telescoped, drawn out, turned on its head. It was language "made strange"; and because of this estrangement, the everyday world was also suddenly made unfamiliar. In the routines of everyday speech, our perceptions of and responses to reality become stale, blunted, or, as the Formalists would say, "automatized." Literature, by forcing us into a dramatic awareness of language, refreshes these habitual responses and renders objects more "perceptible." By having to grapple with language in a more strenuous, self-conscious way than usual, the world which that language contains is vividly renewed. The poetry of Gerard Manley Hopkins might provide a particularly graphic example of this. Literary discourse estranges or alienates ordinary speech, but in doing so, paradoxically, brings us into a fuller, more intimate possession of experience.[10] Most of the time we breathe in air without being conscious of it: like language, it is the very medium in which we move. But if the air is suddenly thickened or infected we are forced to attend to our breathing with new vigilance, and the effect of this may be a heightened experience of our bodily life, we read a scribbled note from a friend without paying much attention to its narrative structure; but if a story breaks off and begins again, switches constantly from one narrative level to another and delays its climax to keep us in suspense, we become freshly conscious of how it is constructed at the same time as our engagement with it may be intensified. The story, as the Formalists would argue, uses "impeding" or "retarding" devices to hold our attention; and in literary language, these devices are "laid bare". It was this which moved Viktor Shlovsky to remark mischievously of Laurence Sterne's *Tristram Shandy*, a novel which impedes its own story-line so much that it hardly gets off the ground, that it was "the most typical novel in world literature."

8   The Formalists, then, saw literary language as a set of deviations from a norm, a kind of linguistic violence:[11] literature is a "special" kind of language, in contrast to the "ordinary" language we commonly use. But to spot a deviation implies being able to identify the norm from which it swerves.[12] Though "ordinary language" is a concept beloved of some Oxford philosophers, the ordinary language of Oxford philosophers has little in common with the ordinary language of Glaswegian dockers. The language both social groups use to write love letters usually differs from the way they talk to the local vicar. The idea that there s a single "normal" language, a common currency shared

Sample Student Commentary

[9] The "total textual system" is the novel, play, short story, article, etc., which can be analyzed by examining how the combination of words and devices communicates the subject matter of the text.

[10] It does seem as though the line between strict examination of language and consideration of content or theme is hard to maintain.

[11] Notice how the phrase "linguistic violence" echoes the earlier quotation from Roman Jacobson, that literature is writing that commits an "organized violence...on ordinary speech."

[12] This "but" will mark the beginning of an important transition. Eagleton began this essay with a logical premise, and he will continue to follow logic in his attempt to define literature.

equally by all members of society, is an illusion. Any actual language consists of a highly complex range of discourses, differentiated according to class, region, gender, status and so on, which can by no means be neatly unified into a single, homogeneous linguistic community. One person's norm may be another's deviation: "ginnel" for "alleyway" may be poetic in Brighton but ordinary language in Barnsley. Even the most "prosaic" text of the fifteenth century may sound "poetic" to us today because of its archaism.[13] If we were to stumble across an isolated scrap of writing from some long-vanished civilization, we could not tell whether it was "poetry" or not merely by inspecting it, since we might have no access to that society's "ordinary" discourses; and even if further research were to reveal that it was "deviatory," this would still not prove that it was poetry as not all linguistic deviations are poetic. Slang, for example. We would not be able to tell just by looking at it that it was not a piece of "realist" literature, without much more information about the way it actually functioned as a piece of writing within the society in question.[14]

9   It is not that the Russian Formalists did not realize all this. They recognized that norms and deviations shifted around from one social or historical context to another— that "poetry in this sense depends on where you happen to be standing at the time. The fact that a piece of language was "estranging" did not guarantee that it was always and everywhere so: it was estranging only against a certain normative linguistic background, and if this altered then the writing might cease to be perceptible as literary. If everyone used phrases like "unravished bride of quietness" in ordinary pub conversation, this kind of language might cease to be poetic. For the Formalists, in other words, "literariness" was a function of the differential relations between one sort of discourse and another; it was not an eternally given property. They were not out to define "literature," but "literariness"—special uses of language, which could be found in "literary" texts but also in many places outside them. Anyone who believes that "literature" can be defined by such special uses of language has to face the fact that there is more metaphor in Manchester than there is in Marvell.[15] There is no "literary" device—metonymy, synecdoche, litotes, chiasmus, and so on—which is not quite intensively used in daily discourse.

10   Nevertheless, the Formalists still presumed that "making strange" was the essence of the literary. It was just that they relativized this use of language, saw it as a matter of contrast between one type of speech and another. But what if I were to hear someone at the next pub table remark "This is awfully squiggly handwriting!" Is this "literary" or "non-literary" language? As a matter of fact, it is "literary" language because it comes from Knut Hamsun's novel *Hunger*. But how do I know that it is literary? It doesn't, after all, focus any particular attention on itself as a verbal performance. One answer to the question of how I know that this is literary is that it comes from Knit Hamsun's novel *Hunger*. It is part of a text which I read as "fictional," which announces itself as

---

Sample Student Commentary

[13] Is there any irony in Eagleton's using quotation marks to emphasize an "un-ordinary" use of a word or phrase in the context of his arguing that the accompanying "normal" uses do not really exist?

[14] Thus, according to Eagleton, a reader does need social and historical context in order to evaluate the "literariness" of a text.

[15] Note the alliteration of the "m" sound to add a sense of comedy, perhaps sarcasm or irony, to Eagleton's point.

a "novel," which may be put on university literature syllabuses and so on. The context tells me that it is literary; but the language itself has no inherent properties or qualities which might distinguish it from other kinds of discourse, and someone might well say this in a pub without being admired for their literary dexterity.[16] To think of literature as the Formalists do is really to think of all literature as poetry. Significantly, when the Formalists came to consider prose writing, they often simply extended to it the kinds of technique they had used with poetry. But literature is usually judged to contain much besides poetry—to include, for example, realist or naturalistic writing which is not linguistically self-conscious or self-exhibiting in any striking way.[17] People sometimes call writing "fine" precisely because it doesn't draw undue attention to itself: they admire its laconic plainness or low-keyed sobriety. And what about jokes, football chants and slogans, newspaper headlines, advertisements, which are often verbally flamboyant but not generally classified as literature?

11   Another problem with the "estrangement" case is that there is no kind of writing which cannot, given sufficient ingenuity, be read as estranging. Consider a prosaic, quite unambiguous statement like the one sometimes seen in the London underground system: "Dogs must be carried on the escalator." This is not perhaps quite as unambiguous as it seems at first sight: does it mean that you must carry a dog on the escalator? are you likely to be banned from the escalator unless you can find some stray mongrel to clutch in your arms on the way up? Many apparently straightforward notices contain such ambiguities: "Refuse to be put in this basket," for instance, or the British road-sign "Way Out" as read by a Californian. But even leaving such troubling ambiguities aside, it is surely obvious that the underground notice could be read as literature. One could let oneself be arrested by the abrupt, minatory staccato of the first ponderous monosyllables; find one's mind drifting, by the time it had reached the rich allusiveness of "carried," to suggestive resonances of helping lame dogs through life; and perhaps even detect in the very lilt and inflection of the word "escalator" a miming of the rolling, up-and-down motion of the thing itself. This may well be a fruitless sort of pursuit, but it is NOT significantly more fruitless than claiming to hear the cut and thrust of the rapiers in some poetic description of a duel, and at least has the advantage of suggesting that "literature" may be at least as much a question of what people do to writing as of what writing does to them.[18]

12   But even if someone were to read the notice in this way, it would still be a matter of reading it as poetry, which is only part of what is usually included in literature. Let us therefore consider another way of "misreading" the sign which might move us a little beyond this. Imagine a late-night drunk doubled over the escalator handrail who reads the notice with laborious attentiveness for several minutes and then mutters to himself "How rude!" What kind of mistake is occurring here? What the drunk is doing, in fact,

---

Sample Student Commentary

[16] Eagleton points out a conundrum of sorts: Does "literary phrasing" create a literary text, or does the context of a literary text characterize the phrasing as literary?

[17] The earlier context of the essay, references to "organized violence" against language and the "defamiliarizing" effect of literary devices should prepare the reader to understand what Eagleton means here.

[18] This last phrase is an example of the rhetorical device antimetabole, a reversal in order of repeated words to achieve emphasis and contrast.

is taking the sign as some statement of general, even cosmic significance. By applying certain conventions of reading to its words, he prises them loose from their immediate context and generalizes them beyond their pragmatic purpose to something of wider and probably deeper import.[19] This would certainly seem to be one operation involved in what people call literature. When the poet tells us that his love is like a red rose, we know by the very fact that he puts this statement in metre that we are not supposed to ask whether he actually had a lover, who for some bizarre reason seemed to him to resemble a rose. He is telling us something about women and love in general. Literature, then, we might say, is "non-pragmatic" discourse: unlike biology textbooks and notes to the milkman, it serves no immediate practical purpose, but is to be taken as referring to general state of affairs. Sometimes, though not always, it may employ peculiar language as though to make this fact obvious—to signal that what is at stake is a way of talking about a woman rather than any particular real-life woman. This focusing on the way of talking, rather than on the reality of what is talked about, is sometimes taken to indicate that we mean by literature a kind of self-referential language, a language which talks about itself.[20]

13   There are, however, problems with this way of defining literature too. For one thing, it would probably have come as a surprise to George Orwell to hear that his essays were to be read as though the topics he discussed were less important than the way he discussed them. In much that is classified as literature the truth-value and practical relevance of what is said is considered important to the overall effect But even if treating discourse "non-pragmatically" is part of what is meant by literature," then it follows from this "definition" that literature cannot in fact be "objectively" defined. It leaves the definition of literature up to how somebody decides to read, not to the nature of what is written. There are certain kinds of writing—poems, plays, novels—which are fairly obviously intended to be "non-pragmatic" in this sense, but this does not guarantee that they will actually be read in this way. I might well read Gibbon's account of the Roman empire, not because I am misguided enough to believe that it will be reliably informative about ancient Rome, but because I enjoy Gibbon's prose style, or revel in images of human corruption whatever their historical source. But I might read Robert Burns's poem because it is not clear to me, as a Japanese horticulturalist, whether or not the red rose flourished in eighteenth-century Britain. This, it will be said, is not reading it "as literature"; but am I reading Orwell's essays as literature only if I generalize what he says about the Spanish civil war to some cosmic utterance about human life? It is true that many of the works studied as literature in academic institutions were "constructed" to be read as literature, but it is also true that many of them were not. A piece of writing may start off life as history or philosophy and then come to be ranked as literature; or it may start off as literature and then come to be valued for its archaeological significance. Some texts are born literary, some achieve literariness, and some have literariness thrust

---

Sample Student Commentary

[19] What two meanings might the drunk have inferred from the words on the sign?

[20] Notice that, in this section, as Eagleton begins to address the purpose of literature, he himself stops playing with language.

upon them.[21] Breeding in this respect may count for a good deal more than birth. What matters may not be where you came from but how people treat you. If they decide that you are literature then it seems that you are, irrespective of what you thought you were.

14   In this sense, one can think of literature less as some inherent quality or set of qualities displayed by certain kinds of writing all the way from *Beowulf* to Virginia Woolf, than as a number of ways in which people relate themselves to writing. It would not be easy to isolate, from all that has been variously called "literature," some constant set of inherent features. In fact it would be as impossible as trying to identify the single distinguishing feature which all games have in common. There is no "essence" of literature whatsoever.[22] Any bit of writing may be read "non-pragmatically," if that is what reading a text as literature means, just as any writing may be read "poetically." If I pore over the railway timetable not to discover a train connection but to stimulate in myself general reflections on the speed and complexity of modern existence, then I might be said to be reading it as literature. John M. Ellis has argued that the term "literature" operates rather like the word "weed": weeds are not particular kinds of plant, but just any kind of plant which for some reason or another a gardener does not want around. Perhaps "literature" means something like the opposite: any kind of writing which for some reason or another somebody values highly. As the philosophers might say, "literature" and "weed" are functional rather than ontological[23] terms: they tell us about what we do, not about the fixed being of things. They tell us about the role of a text or a thistle in a social context, its relations with and differences from its surroundings, the ways it behaves, the purposes it may be put to and the human practices clustered around it. "Literature" is in this sense a purely formal, empty sort of definition. Even if we claim that it is a non-pragmatic treatment of language, we have still not arrived at an "essence" of literature because this is also so of other linguistic practices such as jokes. In any case, it is far from clear that we can discriminate neatly between "practical" and "non-practical" ways of relating ourselves to language. Reading a novel for pleasure obviously differs from reading a road sign for information, but how about reading a biology textbook to improve your mind? Is that a "pragmatic" treatment of language or not? In many societies, "literature" has served highly practical functions such as religious ones; distinguishing sharply between "practical" and "non- practical" may only be possible in a society like ours, where literature has ceased to have much practical function at all. We may be offering as a general definition a sense of the "literary" which is in fact historically specific.

15   We have still not discovered the secret, then, of why Lamb, Macaulay, and Mill are literature but not, generally speaking, Bentham, Marx, and Darwin. Perhaps the simple answer is that the first three are examples of "fine writing," whereas the last three are

---

Sample Student Commentary

[21] This is an allusion/paraphrase of Shakespeare's *Twelfth Night*, Act II, scene v: "Some [people] are born great, some achieve greatness, and some have greatness thrust upon them." Note the irony of Eagleton's essentially quoting from a text universally accepted as literary as he tries to establish whether there is any universal and objective standard of literary.

[22] Look back to Eagleton's original hypothesis. If, as he seems to be concluding, there is no "essence" of literature, can there, then, be a "theory of literature"?

[23] Based on the context of this sentence, what would you suppose the word ontological means?

not. This answer has the disadvantage of being largely untrue, at least in my judgment, but it has the advantage of suggesting that by and large people term "literature" writing which they think is good. An obvious objection to this is that if it were entirely true there would be no such thing as "bad literature." I may consider Lamb and Macaulay overrated, but that does not necessarily mean that I stop regarding them as literature. You may consider Raymond Chandler "good of his kind," but not exactly literature.[24] On the other hand, if Macaulay were a really bad writer—if he had no grasp at all of grammar and seemed interested in nothing but white mice—then people might well not call his work literature at all, even bad literature. Value-judgments would certainly seem to have a lot to do with what is judged literature and what isn't—not necessarily in the sense that writing has to be "fine" to be literary, but that it has to be of the kind that is judged fine:[25] it may be an inferior example of a generally valued mode. Nobody would bother to say that a bus ticket was an example of inferior literature, but someone might well say that the poetry of Ernest Dowson was. The term "fine writing", or belles lettres, is in this sense ambiguous: it denotes a sort of writing which is generally highly regarded, while not necessarily committing you to the opinion that a particular specimen of it is "good."

16 With this reservation, the suggestion that "literature" is a highly valued kind of writing is an illuminating one. But it has one fairly devastating consequence. It means that we can drop once and for all the illusion that the category "literature" is "objective,"[26] in the sense of being eternally given and immutable. If anything can be literature, and anything which is regarded as unalterably and unquestionably literature—Shakespeare, for example—can cease to be literature, any belief that the study of literature is the study of a stable, well-definable entity, as entomology is the study of insects, can be abandoned as a chimera. Some kinds of fiction are literature and some are not; some literature is fictional and some is not; some literature is verbally self-regarding, while some highly-wrought rhetoric is not literature. Literature, in the sense of a set of works of assured and unalterable value, distinguished by certain shared inherent properties, does not exist. When I use the words "literary" and "literature" from here on in this book, then, I place them under an invisible crossing-out mark, to indicate that these terms will not really do, but that we have no better ones at the moment.[27]

17 The reason why it follows from the definition of literature as highly valued writing that it is not a stable entity is that value-judgments are notoriously variable. "Times change, values don't," announces an advertisement for a daily newspaper, as though we still believed in killing off infirm infants or putting the mentally ill on public show. Just as people may treat a work as philosophy in one century and as literature in the next, or vice versa, so they may change their minds about what writing they consider valuable. They

---

Sample Student Commentary

[24] Raymond Chandler was the author of very popular detective stories. He created the character Philip Marlowe. Although his novels were international bestsellers and translated into blockbuster films, his body of work is not generally considered "literary."

[25] What is the distinction between writing that is "fine" and writing "of the kind that is judged fine"?

[26] Notice the reintroduction of quotation marks for emphasis and to suggest non-literal uses.

[27] This is a rather unorthodox use of distinctio. Ultimately, Eagleton defines his terms by saying they cannot be defined.

may even change their minds about the sounds they use for judging what is valuable and what is not.[28] This, as I have suggested, does not necessarily mean that they will refuse the title of literature to a work which they have come to deem inferior: they may still call it literature, meaning roughly that it belongs to the type of writing which they generally value. But it does mean that the so-called "literary canon," the unquestioned "great tradition" of the "national literature," has to be recognized as a construct,[29] fashioned by particular people for particular reasons at a certain time. There is no such thing as a literary work or tradition which is valuable in itself, regardless of what anyone might have said or come to say about it. "Value" is a transitive term: it means whatever is valued by certain people in specific situations, according to particular criteria and in the light of given purposes. It is thus quite possible that, given a deep enough transformation of our history, we may in the future produce a society which is unable to get anything at all out of Shakespeare. His works might simply seem desperately alien, full of styles of thought and feeling which such a society found limited or irrelevant. In such a situation, Shakespeare would be no more valuable than much present-day graffiti. And though many people would consider such a social condition tragically impoverished, it seems to me dogmatic not to entertain the possibility that it might arise rather from a general human enrichment. Karl Marx was troubled by the question of why ancient Greek art retained an "eternal charm," even though the social conditions which produced it had long passed; but how do we know that it will remain "eternally" charming, since history has not yet ended?[30] Let us imagine that by dint of some deft archaeological research we discovered a great deal more about what ancient Greek tragedy actually meant to its original audiences, recognized that these concerns were utterly remote from our own, and began to read the plays again in the light of this deepened knowledge. One result might be that we stopped enjoying them. We might come to see that we had enjoyed them previously because we were unwittingly reading them in the light of our own preoccupations; once this became less possible the drama might cease to speak at all significantly to us.[31]

18   The fact that we always interpret literary works to some extent in the light of our own concerns—indeed that in one sense of "our own concerns" we are incapable of doing anything else—might be one reason why certain works of literature seem to retain their value across the centuries. It may be, of course, that we still share many preoccupations with the work itself; but it may also be that people have not actually been valuing the "same" work at all, even though they may think they have. "Our" Homer is not identical with the Homer of the Middle Ages, nor "our" Shakespeare with that of his contemporaries; it is rather that different historical periods have constructed a "different" Homer and Shakespeare for their own purposes, and found in these texts elements to

---

Sample Student Commentary

[28] By "sounds they use," Eagleton means "words." Spoken language is a collection of sounds, and written language is a system of visually representing those sounds.

[29] Construct as a noun, not a verb, means a conceit, an idea.

[30] Inductive reasoning allows for the conclusion—Greek tragedy will always be valued—to be considered tentative as additional evidence is gathered: History has not yet ended, so we do not know that Greek tragedy will "always" be valued.

[31] Here is another hypothesis. If we were to discover...then we might decide...

value or devalue, though, not necessarily the same ones. All literary works, in other words, are "rewritten" if only unconsciously, by the societies which read them; indeed there is no reading of a work which is not also a "re-writing." No work, and no current evaluation of it, can simply be extended to new groups of people without being changed, perhaps almost unrecognizably, in the process; and this is one reason why what counts as literature is a notably unstable affair.[32]

19   I do not mean that it is unstable because value-judgments are "subjective." According to this view , the world is divided between solid facts "out there" like Grand Central station, and arbitrary value-judgments "in here" such as liking bananas or feeling that the tone of a Yeats poem veers from defensive hectoring to grimly resilient resignation. Facts are public and impeachable, values are private and gratuitous.[33] There is an obvious difference between recounting a fact, such as "This cathedral was built in 1612," and registering a value-judgment, as "This cathedral is a magnificent specimen of baroque architecture." But suppose I made the first kind of statement while showing an overseas visitor around England, and found that it puzzled her considerably. Why, she might ask, do you keep telling me the dates of the foundation of all these buildings? Why obsession with origins? In the society I live in, she might go on, we keep no record at all of such events: we classify our buildings instead according to whether they face north-west or south-east. What this might do would be to demonstrate part of the unconscious system of value-judgments which underlies my own descriptive statements. Such value-judgments are not necessarily of the same kind as "This cathedral is a magnificent specimen of baroque architecture," but they are value-judgments nonetheless, and no factual pronouncement I make can escape them. Statements of fact are after all statements, which presumes a number of questionable judgments: that those statements are worth making, perhaps more worth making than certain others, that I am the sort of person entitled to make them and perhaps able to guarantee their truth, that you are the kind of person worth making them to, that something useful will be accomplished by making them, and so on. A pub conversation may well transmit information, but what also bulks large in such dialogue is a strong element of what linguists would call the "phatic," a concern with the act of communication itself. In chatting to you about the weather I am also signaling that I regard conversation with you as valuable, that I consider you a worthwhile person to talk to, that I am not myself anti-social or about to embark on a detailed critique of your personal appearance.[34]

20   In this sense, there is no possibility of a wholly disinterested statement. Of course stating when a cathedral was built is reckoned to be more disinterested in our own culture than passing an opinion about its architecture, but one could also imagine situations in which the former statement would be more "value-laden" than the latter. Perhaps "baroque" and "magnificent" have come to be more or less synonymous, whereas only

---

Sample Student Commentary

[32] Eagleton is basing much of his definition of "literature" on one particular theory of reading: The reader creates part of the meaning of the text he or she is reading.

[33] Combining references to bananas and Yeats in the same sentences maintains (or revives) the mildly humorous tone with which Eagleton started this essay.

[34] This discussion of fact versus value and the psychology involved in an act of communication borders on philosophy. While Eagleton is expressing a view, he is certainly not precluding disagreement of discussion.

a stubborn rump of us cling to the belief that the date when a building was founded is significant, and my statement is taken as a coded way of signaling this partisanship.[35] All of our descriptive statements move within an often invisible network of value-categories, and indeed without such categories we would have nothing to say to each other at all. It is not just as though we have something called factual knowledge which may then be distorted by particular interests and judgments, although this is certainly possible; it is also that without particular interests we would have no knowledge at all, because we would not see the point of bothering to get to know anything. Interests are constitutive of our knowledge, not merely prejudices which imperil it. The claim that knowledge should be "value-free" is itself a value-judgment.[36]

21 It may well be that a liking for bananas is a merely private matter, though this is in fact questionable. A thorough analysis of my tastes in food would probably reveal how deeply relevant they are to certain formative experiences in early childhood, to my relations with my parents and siblings and to a good many other cultural factors which are quite as social and "non-subjective" as railway stations. This is even more true of that fundamental structure of beliefs and interests which I am born into as a member of a particular society, such as the belief that I should try to keep in good health, that differences of sexual role are rooted in human biology or that human beings are more important than crocodiles. We may disagree on this or that, but we can only do so because we share certain "deep" ways of seeing and valuing which are bound up with our social life, and which could not be changed without transforming that life. Nobody will penalize me heavily if I dislike a particular Donne poem, but if I argue that Donne is not literature at all then in certain circumstances I might risk losing my job. I am free to vote Labour or Conservative, but if I try to act on the belief that this choice itself merely masks a deeper prejudice—the prejudice that the meaning of democracy is confined to putting a cross on a ballot paper every few years—then in certain unusual circumstances I might end up in prison.

22 The largely concealed structure of values which informs and underlies our factual statements is part of what is meant by "ideology." By "ideology" I mean,[37] roughly, the ways in which what we say and believe connects with the power-structure and power-relations of the society we live in. It follows from such a rough definition of ideology that not all of our underlying judgments and categories can usefully be said to be ideological. It is deeply ingrained in us to imagine ourselves moving forwards into the future (at least one other society sees itself as moving backwards into it), but though this way of seeing may connect significantly with the power-structure of our society, it need not always and everywhere do so. I do not mean by "ideology" simply the deeply entrenched, often unconscious beliefs which people hold; I mean more particularly those modes of feeling, valuing, perceiving and believing which have some kind of relation to the maintenance and reproduction of social power. The fact that such beliefs are by no means merely

---

Sample Student Commentary

[35] Here he's talking about connotations, socially agreed-upon definitions, and uses.

[36] Here is an excellent example of an oxymoron.

[37] Another distinctio. Eagleton has used quotation marks for emphasis and to suggest unorthodox uses, but here he provides precisely what he means by the word he is using.

private quirks may be illustrated by a literary example.[38]

23 In his famous study *Practical Criticism* (1929), the Cambridge critic I. A. Richards sought to demonstrate just how whimsical and subjective literary value-judgments could actually be by giving his undergraduates a set of poems, withholding from them the titles and authors' names, and asking them to evaluate them. The resulting judgments, notoriously, were highly variable: time-honoured poets were marked down and obscure authors celebrated. To my mind, however, the most interesting aspect of this project, and one apparently quite invisible to Richards himself, is just how tight a consensus of unconscious valuations underlies these particular differences of opinion. Reading Richards's undergraduates' accounts of literary works one is struck by the habits of perception and interpretation which they spontaneously share—what they expect literature to be, what assumptions they bring to a poem and what fulfillments they anticipate they will derive from it. None of this is really surprising: for all the participants in this experiment were, presumably, young, white, upper- or upper middle-class, privately educated English people of the 1920s, and how they responded to a poem depended on a good deal more than purely "literary" factors.[39] Their critical responses were deeply entwined with their broader prejudices and beliefs. This is not a matter of blame: there is no critical response which is not so entwined, and thus no such thing as a "pure" literary critical judgment or interpretation. If anybody is to be blamed it is I. A. Richards himself, who as a young, white, upper-middle-class male Cambridge don was unable to objectify a context of interests which he himself largely shared, and was thus unable to recognize fully that local, "subjective" differences of evaluation work within a particular, socially structured way of perceiving the world.

24 If it will not do to see literature as an "objective," descriptive category, neither will it do to say that literature is just what people whimsically choose to call literature. For there is nothing at all whimsical about such kinds of value-judgment: they have their roots in deeper structures of belief which are as apparently unshakeable as the Empire State building.[40] What we have uncovered so far, then, is not only that literature does not exist in the sense that insects do, and that the value-judgments by which it is constituted are historically variable, but that these value-judgments themselves have a close relation to social ideologies. They refer in the end not simply to private taste, but to the assumptions by which certain social groups exercise and maintain power over others. If this seems a far-fetched assertion, a matter of private prejudice, we may test it out by an account of the rise of "literature" in England.[41] ❦

Sample Student Commentary

[38] Thus, in building toward his conclusion, Eagleton begins to draw the connection between our understanding of what literature is and other ideologies or social constructs.

[39] Eagleton is acknowledging that the students probably do "spontaneously" share their values, but they hold to those values conveyed to them through their educations.

[40] This simile is at least the third time Eagleton has referred to buildings and architecture to illustrate his point.

[41] This essay was written as the introduction to a book. This last sentence, which seems more a transition than a conclusion, invites the reader to continue and examine the literature that will either support or refute Eagleton's thesis.

Reread the first paragraph of this essay. How successfully or satisfactorily has Eagleton followed through on a discussion of his initial hypothesis? Is the end of the essay hypothetical or does he seem to have been arguing a thesis?

Sample multiple-choice questions:

1. The premise of this article can best be classified as
   A. subjunctive.
   B. conditional.
   C. theoretical.
   D. hypothetical.
   E. logical.

2. Through the course of the discussion, Eagleton uses all of the following devices or conventions EXCEPT
   A. exempla.
   B. humor.
   C. connotations.
   D. rhetorical questions.
   E. sententia.

3. The word or phrase that best explains the "disproportion between the signifiers and the signifieds" (paragraph 4) is
   A. excess.
   B. organized violence.
   C. formalism.
   D. organization of language.
   E. resonance.

4. One might infer from Eagleton's discussion of Formalism that the determination of whether a given text is "literary" is the presence of
   A. a sense of estrangement.
   B. devices.
   C. a total textual system.
   D. defamiliarizing effects.
   E. discourse.

5. Eagleton uses slang as an example of
   A. once-current language that has become archaic.
   B. contemporary poetic usage.
   C. unconventional, but not poetic, language usage.
   D. "normal" usage versus "deviatory" usage.
   E. "ordinary" discourse.

Answers and Explanations:

1. Subjunctive is the "if contrary to fact" construction. The suggestion that there is a literary theory is not contrary to fact. Thus, (A) can be eliminated. The *if* statement does not establish a condition (B) for the proposition, but a hypothesis. Many students may confuse a hypothesis with a theory (C), but this is a misapprehension of the meaning of the terms. (E) is likewise tempting, but "logic" is the general discipline, not the specific term of the opening statement of this article. The first sentence follows the form of an *if-then* statement: hypothesis or antecedent (if there is a literary theory), and consequent (then we should be able to define "literature"). **Thus, (D) is the correct answer.**

2. The mention of Hobbes's *Leviathan* and Clarendon's *History of the Rebellion* in the second paragraph eliminates (A). The offhanded way in which Eagleton dismisses "whatever it was that Sir Thomas Browne wrote" eliminated (B). (C) is eliminated by the author's frequent use of quotation marks to suggest non-literal usages. "…does this imply that history, philosophy, and natural science are uncreative and unimaginative?" is an example of a rhetorical question that eliminates (D). Eagleton does occasionally quote other sources, but these quotations are not pithy maxims. **Thus (E) is the best answer.**

3. The "organized violence" to which Eagleton refers is later explained as the figurative, literary, and rhetorical devices employed by writers of "the literary." Thus, (B) is eliminated. (C) is the study of those devices, arguably the origin of the "disproportion."(D) is not strictly wrong, but is too general to be the best answer. (E) is one of the qualities of the disproportion, not its explanation. As clarified in the rest of the paragraph, the disproportion between signifier and signified is an "excess" of device. **Thus, (A) is the best answer.**

4. (A) and (D) are ways of describing the effects to language that identify literature. (C) is a formal or linguistic name for literary text. (E) is too broad a term that can include any use of any language. (B) describes the "whole stock of formal literary elements" that make a literary text literary. **Thus, (B) is the best answer.**

5. (A) is probably the least tempting choice for a careful reader, as Eagleton's discussion of archaic usages that sound poetic to contemporary ears precedes his distinction between the "deviatory" and the "poetic." (B) is eliminated by the fact that Eagleton mentions slang as an example of language that is *not* poetic. (D) expresses the reverse of the issue, slang being "deviatory." Similarly, (E) expresses the opposite of Eagleton's intent, since slang is not "ordinary." (C), however, is expressed when Eagleton writes, "not all linguistic deviations are poetic. Slang, for example." **Thus, (C) is the correct answer.**

Sample free-response item:

Carefully read Professor Terry Eagleton's essay, "What is Literature," in which he argues the case that "literature" is a social construct that ultimately cannot be explained in a single definition. After you read the passage, write an essay in which you evaluate the extent to which Eagleton's use of literary and rhetorical devices helps him communicate his hypothesis to his reader.

Sample Student Essay

In arriving at an answer to the ultimately unanswerable question, "What is Literature," Professor Terry Eagleton writes, "some literature is verbally self-regarding, while some highly wrought rhetoric is not literature." This statement tempts a reader to ask whether Eagleton considers his own introduction to literary theory to be literature. While Eagleton obviously strives to deliver a thorough discussion of an esoteric topic—and he hopes to keep his readers awake in the bargain—there are periods in his essay in which he seems too aware of himself and his topic, too "verbally self-regarding," and his style almost gets in the way of his point. Similes that are too obviously shocking and "unusual" or "ultra-specific" uses of words (set off in "quotation marks") are puzzling at best and, at worst, downright distracting.

Professor Eagleton is clearly writing on the near-impossible topic of arriving at a coherent and cohesive definition of "literature" or "the literary." He is writing to an admittedly difficult audience, undergraduates taking an introductory course in literary theory, quite possibly to fulfill a "humanities requirement." One can, therefore, fully appreciate any trick the professor has up his sleeve to enliven the subject and make it both comprehensible and palatable to his intended audience. Throughout the essay, he strives to keep the tone light, his attitude flip. The assertion of his introductory hypothesis is something of a rhetorical challenge to his reader to disagree: "If there is..., then it would seem obvious that there is..." Not merely "if...then" or "if...it follows," but "...it would seem obvious..." Only the blind would miss it.

In these opening paragraphs, Eagleton uses both first person plural ("We can begin") and second person ("You can define it") to draw the reader in, to make this essay, not a dissertation, but a conversation. Throughout the essay, Eagleton maintains this conversational tone, establishing a rapport with his presumably reluctant reader. Rhetorical questions invite both English majors and non- to sympathize with one another: Could "[defining literature as creative or imaginative writing] imply that history, philosophy, and natural science are uncreative and unimaginative?")

Eagleton is also careful to provide background information—the paragraphs on Formalism and the Russian Formalists for example—so that both non-English majors and introductory-level students of literature can follow the main thrust of the argument without puzzling over facts and details.

So there is much that Eagleton does, structurally and rhetorically, to connect with his reader and bring a potentially impenetrable topic into the realm of the comprehensible. There is also much, however, that he does, linguistically and rhetorically, that distracts the reader and almost undoes the effects of his less-unsettling techniques.

To highlight with quotation marks a word or phrase that is being used in an unconventional or non-literal sense is not unheard of. The "air quote" has come into popular use for just this purpose. One may want to suggest sarcastically that the argument he had with his significant other was a "discussion." One may emphasize her obsession by calling it an "interest." It is a legitimate technique and can be effective if not overdone.

Through the course of this essay, however, Eagleton uses this technique approximately 145 times. That means for an essay of around 6,500 words, around every forty-fifth word is in quotation marks. Not all of these quotation-mark uses are truly unorthodox; nor are they all the first appearance of a word that needs to be emphasized. When he sets off words like "devices" and "functions" with quotation marks, Eagleton is suggesting that he means something other than their literal meanings; but in the sentence, "'Devices' included sound, imagery, rhythm, syntax, metre, rhyme, narrative techniques, in fact the whole stock of formal literary elements," the word "devices" is used quite literally. Devices do include sound, imagery...

Even such innocuous and uncontroversial terms as "fact," "fiction," and "historical" find themselves set in quotation marks, not once, and not only with the word's first use, but with subsequent uses as well. If one were to jerk one's head and assume a different tone of voice every time he encountered a word in quotations marks that was not a part of a direct quotation, parts of this essay would give him a stiff neck and sound as if they were being read by split-personalities. Emphasis is emphasis, but when a writer emphasizes everything, then nothing gets emphasized.

And the reader's hearing too many voices in his head, especially when these voices are not contributing any real emphasis or difference in meaning, distracts from the overall point of the essay.

The overuse of quotation marks, however, is not the only effect that probably hurts more than it helps. Eagleton is trying to build and maintain rapport with an audience he may feel is disinterested at best. That is the probable reason for his striving to find the unexpected, the shocking, in an otherwise mundane topic. He does, however, try too hard at times. Literature, whether it can be defined or not, is generally considered to be art, a thing beautiful. One expects any simile that attempts to explain literature to somehow communicate that beauty. It is purely for the surprise effect, therefore, that Eagleton finds himself, not once but twice, comparing literary study to entomology, and literature to insects. The reader can understand the point and can appreciate the value of the surprising comparison, but it is also worth asking if the surprise isn't perhaps too much of a stretch, too contrived, and if Eagleton isn't trying too hard.

Professor Eagleton, then, has taken on a difficult task. The overall essay can *be judged only as immensely successful. Eagleton's glib tone, his frequent examples, many of which are surprising and humorous, and his obvious wit help establish an unlikely rapport with his introductory-level students. There are times, however, when like the literature he is struggling to define, he seems to be too aware of his own effect. These are the times when the essay suffers, and the reader has more the urge to retreat than continue onward.* ❦

Exercise Three:

Questions 11-15. Carefully read the address and then select the best answers to the multiple-choice questions that follow.

The following passage is a summary/paraphrase of Professor Terry Eagleton's essay, "What is Literature?" Read both the original essay and the summary, paying close attention, not only to the ideas expressed, but to the language, including any literary, linguistic, or rhetorical devices both authors use.

What is Literature?
A paraphrase, summary, and adaptation of the opening chapter of Terry Eagleton's *Introduction to Literary Theory*

By Dr. Barry Laga

The Problem

1   Have you ever felt ashamed or secretive about books you like because they are not on approved reading lists? Have you ever had a teacher, friend, or parent tell you that what you are reading isn't "literature," that it may have words printed on a page, but it is somehow inferior in quality to other books? That is, it might be "literature" in the broad sense of the term (words on a page) but it's not "literary"?

2   Well, the problem with such judgments is that if you press someone about her definition of "literature" or "literariness," she will have a hard time finding a criteria that works for everything we have ever called literature. Although many have tried to define what "literature" is or what makes something "literary," no one has successfully defined literature in such a way that it accounts for the complexities of language and the wide variety of written texts. Consider the following proposals:

Literature Is Imaginative Writing

3   Some define literature as writing which is "imaginative" or fictive, as opposed to factual, true, or historical. This seems reasonable until we realize that…

4   (1) what counts as "fact" varies with cultures and time periods. Is the book of Genesis (and the entire Bible for that matter) fact or fiction? Are the legends and myths of Greek, Scandinavia, and Native Americans fact or fiction? Is Darwin's *Origin of Species* fact or fiction? Are news reports fact or fiction?

5   (2) What is clearly imaginative writing is often not considered literature. For example, comic books, computer game stories, and Harlequin Romances are usually excluded from the category of "literature" even though they are certainly imaginative.

6   (3) A lot of what we do consider literature is more like history (i.e. Boswell's *Biography of Samuel Johnson*, Claredon's *History of the Rebellion*) or philosophy (i.e. the works of Mill, Ruskin, Newman). In sum, fact vs. fiction is not a helpful way to distinguish between what is literary and what is not. There are also a lot of "facts" in novels, and many novels are based on real historical events.

Literature is Extraordinary Language

7 *Victor Shklovsky (early 20th century Russian formalist)*

> *Habitualization devours objects, clothes, furniture, one's wife, and the fear of war. If all the complex lives of many people go on unconsciously, then such lives are as if they had never been. Art exists to help us recover the sensation of life; it exists to make us feel things, to make the stone stony. The end of art is to give a sensation of the object as seen, not as recognized. The technique of art is to make objects 'unfamiliar,' to make forms difficult, to increase the difficulty and length of perception is an aesthetic end in itself and must be prolonged. Art is a way of experiencing the artfulness of an object; the object is not important.*

8   Perhaps it is the way we use language. As some argue, literature transforms and intensifies ordinary language. If I say, "Thou still unravished bride of quietness," then you know it's literature or you know that I'm using "literary" language. The language is different from everyday speech in texture, rhythm and resonance. The sentence, "This is awfully squiggly handwriting!" doesn't sound literary, does it? However, there are also some problems.

9   (1) "Unordinary" speech depends upon a norm from which to deviate. But the specialized vocabulary used in sports, dance, music, small town diners, Glaswegian dockworkers, etc., or even everyday slang varies widely from the norm, but we don't classify that language as "literary." For example, most if not all of our swear words employ metaphorical/poetic language. Isn't the sentence 'You're an asshole!" literary because of its use of metaphor? The language "defamiliarizes" or "estranges" the ordinary.

10   (2) There isn't a universal norm. One person's norm may be another's deviation. "Sh**kicker" for "cowboy boot" may be poetic to someone from New York, but it's everyday speech in Laramie.

11   Many Americans think British words for everyday items seem poetic. For example, I smiled at a sign posted in a shopping mall in Salisbury: "Watch Out for Slow Moving Plants." Apparently "plants" are forms of heavy equipment or machinery. For Brits, this sign is rather literal, but I enjoyed the figurative language. I won't think of machinery or flowers in quite the same way.

12   (3) Finally, the sentence above "This is awfully squiggly handwriting!" doesn't sound literary, but it comes from Knut Hamsun's novel *Hunger*. Therefore, what is literary depends upon the context. Anything read in an English class could count as literature simply because it is read for English.

Literature Is Pragmatic Speech

13 Perhaps literature is "non-useful" writing, writing that doesn't help us do something pragmatic. There are still several problems.

14 (1) One could read anything as "non-useful." That is, I could easily read a shopping list and point out the interesting metaphors, beautiful sounds, imagery, etc. or...

15 (2) I could read *Moby Dick* to find out how to kill whales. In fact, I have used a novel about sled dogs to train my own dogs. Is that book no longer "literature" once I turn it into a "how-to" book?

Literature Is "Good" Writing

16 Perhaps something is literary because the text is the kind of writing we like to read; it's a highly valued kind of writing. In this case, anything can be literature, and anything can stop being literature. The important implication is that we don't get to decide what is literature because our parents, teachers, exams, textbooks, etc., define that for us. We are trained to value the kind of writing that they value. This doesn't mean that we are empty vessels with no ability to think for ourselves. However, our "personal" values and criteria are not personal, but social. These social institutions provide us with a range of possibilities, and social values are notoriously difficult to change.

Conclusions

17 "Literature" and the "literary" then are highly subjective categories. We can't decide whether or not something is "literature" or "literary" simply by looking at its form or language. Shakespeare's works have not always been valued as literature, and his works may not be valued in the future.

18 *For example, Plato wanted to ban poetry from his ideal republic, save for "hymns to the gods and praises of famous men."*

Disappointed?

19 You may feel dissatisfied because we will never come up with a concrete definition, but that is the point. As Terry Eagleton points out, "we can drop once and for all the illusion that the category "literature" is objective in the sense of being eternally given and immutable." He goes on to say that our opinions and value-judgments are not neutral either, that "the ways in which what we say and believe connects with the power structure and power-relations of the society we live in." In other words, your opinions about literature and literariness are not just your opinions. They are related to how and where you were raised and educated. Importantly, our environment encourages us to accept some values but not others, support the activities of some groups but not others, or exclude some choices as unacceptable. Therefore, how we define literature reveals what we have been taught to value and what we have been taught to reject. This is important for you because you are encouraged (perhaps even coerced) to learn what other people value and at the very minimum, what other people have made available for you to read.

20 This last insight is particularly important if you plan on teaching, for you will help shape the perceptions of your students. Again, have you ever had a teacher tell you that

the novel you are reading is "not literature," "escapist," or just "fun reading"? Can you see the potential problem here, especially when it comes to passing tests, getting into college, and pleasing others, including yourself? Do you recognize that the source of your values may not even be you?

21   Another way to frame this insight is to say that I tried to encourage you to ask different questions, questions that I have found far more useful. Asking "Is it literature?" or "Is it good literature?" is not as productive or interesting as asking...

- What does one's definition of "literature" reveal about one's attitudes, beliefs, values, training, or socialization (in short, one's ideological affiliation)?
- How do definitions and categories of "literature" and especially definitions of "good literature" coincide with specific political issues like "Who should govern?" "Who should have what role or function in society?" "What kinds of behaviors and belief should be excluded or included?"

22   Put yet another way, I would encourage you to look at definitions, reading lists, evaluations, etc., as a way to learn about your own set of values, your own particular school system, and your culture at large. As you will discover, a quick glance at the race, gender, class, sexuality, nationality, and time period of authors you have had to read in school will reveal something about whose ideology (system of values, beliefs, and history) is valorized, privileged, and passed on to other generations. Therefore, what and how you read is a political issue because it has to do with relations and structures of power. Lists of "masterpieces," "essential reading," or tables of contents in anthologies are not benign and innocent. Instead, they display cultural values. We need to take them seriously, for they tell us in their own way a lot about ourselves and our society. ❧

Multiple-choice questions:

11. The primary reason for the direct address in the section titled "The Problem" is to
    A. establish rapport with the reader.
    B. suggest the didactic purpose of the essay.
    C. introduce the essay's central hypothesis.
    D. reflect the opening paragraphs of the original.
    E. illustrate the universal appeal of literature.

12. According to the essay, literature is all of the following EXCEPT
    A. sensible.
    B. surprising.
    C. skillful.
    D. inspiring.
    E. fanciful.

13. The author of the summary/paraphrase invites his readers to think about the issue and draw their own conclusions by his frequent use of
   A. enumeratio.
   B. direct address.
   C. connotative understandings.
   D. apostrophe.
   E. rhetorical questions.

14. Compared to the original, the summary/paraphrase can best be described as
   A. better detailed.
   B. more intimate.
   C. less pedantic.
   D. more pragmatic.
   E. less subjective.

15. The closing paragraph of the summary hints at what type of relationship between "benign and innocent" and "cultural values"?
   A. complementary.
   B. antithetical.
   C. supplemental.
   D. coincidental.
   E. revelatory.

Free Response Item:

Carefully read Dr. Barry Laga's summary/paraphrase of Terry Eagleton's essay, "What is Literature?" paying close attention, not only to the ideas expressed but also to the techniques Laga employs to express them. Then, write a thoughtful and well-supported essay in which you analyze the voice and tone of the summary and evaluate the extent to which they contribute to the overall effectiveness of the summary.

Analyzing Tone, Mood, and Effect

CHAPTER 3

TONE IS USUALLY DEFINED as the attitude of the writer, whether he or she is angry, fervent, bored, whimsical, etc.

Mood is more general; it is the overall feeling of the work. It is largely inferred by the reader based on the author's tone, as well as his or her use of other elements like imagery, metaphor and simile, symbolism, etc.

Effect, then, is the reader's emotional, psychological, and practical response to the tone and mood of the text. It is closely related to the author's purpose. An author, for example, may choose to inform by being entertaining, humorous, glib. Another might decide that inciting his or her reader to anger might be the best way of persuading the reader.

Writers whose works you read know how to use the tools of tone and mood to create their desired effect on their readers. When you laugh at a humorous anecdote or pause in reflective sorrow at the end of a memorial, chances are that that is exactly the response or the effect that the writer wanted the piece to have. To know your response and to acknowledge it is often sufficient; after all, much of the reading we do is purely for our own purposes, and there is no need to over think our reactions.

Still, the writer, the editor, the critic, and the student must, at times, probe deeper and examine *how* the author achieves the desired effect; how his or her word choice, sentence structure, use of figurative and rhetorical devices, etc., help to create the tone; what other elements contribute to the mood of the text; and exactly how the writer achieves the desired effect on the reader.

Formal/Academic/Authoritative

Much of the nonfiction you will read throughout your education will be instructional or informative, written by experts in their field. For the most part, these experts will not want their voices to interfere with their subject matter. By the same token, however, the experts want to make certain they convey their expertise to their readers.

Academic lecturers and speakers, too, strive for a fragile balance between their personal presence and their subject matter. While, certainly, readers and listeners of these scholars do want to hear what *these experts* have to say about their subjects, it is equally true that they want to hear what the experts have to say *about their subjects*.

Read the following memorial, an essay highlighting the life, character, and achievements of Irving Kristol. It has been annotated to point out to you the techniques: word choice, sentence structure, use of figurative devices, that Epstein uses to create and maintain a formal yet sympathetic tone.

After you examine the passage and the accompanying notes, look at how a student taking the AP Language exam might respond to multiple-choice questions and a free-response item dealing with how Joseph Epstein communicates with his reader and creates reader sympathy for the subject of his memorial.

A Genius of Temperament
Joseph Epstein remembers Irving Kristol

JOSEPH EPSTEIN

1   As the last of the New York intellectuals depart the planet, it becomes apparent that Irving Kristol, who published less than most of them, had a wider and deeper influence on his time than all of them.[1]

2   Just how and why is not all that clear, but it is so. Nor is it clear how best to describe Irving. He wasn't a writer exactly, or at least not primarily; neither was he chiefly an editor, though he in fact edited some of the best intellectual magazines of his day. He wrote political journalism, but to call him a political journalist is severely to limit him. That baggy-pants term public intellectual doesn't do the job, either. He was over his lifetime associated with various institutions—magazines, universities, think tanks—but he always seemed somehow slightly outside of, somehow larger than, all of them.[2]

3   Irving[3] was the ultimate free-lance. If my father were alive,[4] he would say of Irving Kristol that he worked out of his car, with the irony added that Irving, who grew up in New York to immigrant parents, never learned to drive. *Sui generis* was what Irving

---

Sample Student Commentary

[1] Epstein begins with something of an antithesis: Kristol wrote less, but influenced more. That creates an immediate sense of suspense, as the reader wonders what kind of influence Kristol had and how he managed to have such a deep one.

[2] This paragraph is a wonderful example of definition by negation. We do not know what Kristol was, but we know what he was not.

[3] Because this is a memorial, and Epstein wants to establish a sympathy between his reader and his subject, he uses the man's first name, rather than referring to him as "Kristol" or "Mr. Kristol."

[4] Note the correct use of the subjunctive: if contrary to fact. "If my father were alive," Epstein doesn't write, "If my father was alive."

was—an amazing figure, whose like we shall probably not see again for the simple reason that no one quite like him existed before.[5]

4   He wrote with clarity and force, subtlety and persuasiveness, but, unlike a true writer, didn't feel the need to do it all the time. He was a splendid speaker, non-oratorical, casual, off-the-cuff division: witty, smart, commonsensical, always with a point to make, one that one[6] hadn't considered before. I recall once hearing Irving introduced by Christopher DeMuth in a room that had a large movie screen behind the speaker's desk. "I see," said Christopher, "that Irving has brought his usual full panoply of audio-visual aids." "Yes," replied Irving, "a cigarette," which he took out of his pocket and tapped on the desk before beginning to speak.[7]

5   Irving's reigning intellectual note was that of skepticism. As an intellectual, he lived by ideas, but at the same time he greatly distrusted them. All ideas for him, like saints for George Orwell, were guilty until proven innocent.[8] "Create a concept and reality leaves the room," Ortega y Gasset wrote, and my guess is that Irving would have seconded the motion.[9]

6   In the realm of ideas, he preferred those that existed in the world as it is as against those that had to be imposed by elaborate argument or government fiat.

7   At the same time, he liked to play with ideas. I remember a Chinese dinner with him at which he tried out the idea that Modernism in the arts was the devil's work. He meant the actual capital-D Devil. Was he serious? I'm not certain even now, but the discussion, in which Irving argued that Modernist art undermined tradition and as such human confidence in institutions, was provocative in the best sense, causing a true believer (that would be me) to defend Modernism by arguing that the best of it was based precisely on tradition.[10]

8   Irving himself did not provoke. I never saw him angry. Polemical though he could be in his political journalism, I never heard him put down political or intellectual enemies in conversation.[11] If I could have any of his gifts, it would be his extraordinary ability not to take things personally. Accusations, insults, obloquy, all seemed to bounce off him. He had a genius of temperament.[12]

Sample Student Commentary

[5] Another juxtaposition of antithetical ideas—not seen again because never seen before—heightens the sense of Kristol's uniqueness that Epstein is trying to establish.

[6] While some readers consider this use of "one" too formal, Epstein does not want to use an inappropriate second person. To say, "…one that you hadn't considered…" is stylistically immature.

[7] This anecdote provides a brief illustration of the assertion that Kristol was one who spoke "off the cuff."

[8] Epstein is alluding to George Orwell's 1950 essay, "Reflections on Gandhi," which begins, "Saints should always be judged guilty until they are proven innocent."

[9] José Ortega y Gasset was a Spanish philosopher and essayist. His most influential work was done during the early twentieth century while the Spanish government was in a constant state of turmoil, oscillating between monarchy, republicanism, and dictatorship. His works develop the idea that one cannot separate one's sense of self from his/her circumstances, and there are a multitude of perspectives from which a "truth" can be viewed and understood.

[10] Epstein provides another illustrative anecdote. Notice that both illustrations so far are personal to Epstein. He is establishing his intimacy with Kristol.

[11] A polemic is an argumentative piece that tries to establish the superiority of its thesis over all others.

[12] Hence the title of this memorial.

9　　He also seemed to be without vanity. I never heard him claim credit for any of the things that obituarists are now claiming for him:[13] helping to elect Ronald Reagan, launching neoconservatism, discovering youthful talent, and the rest of it. I never heard him quote himself, or remind other people of things he had written, or make any claims about himself whatsoever. I once told him that I thought Encounter, which he edited with Stephen Spender in London, and on which, I am certain, he did the lion's share of the work, was the best intellectual journal of my lifetime, but my praise appeared only to embarrass him. He didn't seem to wish to talk much about it.[14]

10　　Irving's specialty was the insertion of common sense into places where one wasn't accustomed to find it. He advised the young not to bring along a novel when being interviewed for a job, because, however mistakenly, it creates the impression of dreaminess. When Michael Joyce became the head of the Olin Foundation, with responsibility for doling out large sums of money, Irving, while congratulating him, told him that in his new job he could promise him two things: First, he would never eat another bad lunch; and, second, no one would ever speak truthfully to him again.[15] I once gave a lecture on friendship in which I made the argument that we mustn't expect our friends to share our opinions, but look instead for something beyond mere opinion to that more important entity, point of view. Irving, who was in the audience, told me afterwards that I had a good point, and he agreed with it, "except of course for Israel and Palestine."

11　　The older one gets as a writer the fewer people are around whose approval means much. Irving was one of those remaining people for me. When I heard that he took pleasure in my short stories, I was genuinely delighted. He once introduced me at a talk I gave at the American Enterprise Institute, saying that I was in the tradition of the cosmopolitan wits. I was so pleased by this that before beginning my talk I couldn't refrain from saying that being introduced in this way by Irving I felt as if I were Andy Williams introduced by Frank Sinatra saying this guy can really sing, or Rodney Dangerfield introduced by Charlie Chaplin saying this guy has some wonderful moves.[16]

12　　Irving was an extraordinarily selfless husband—a feminist in action if decidedly not in ideology. By this I mean that in Irving's biography, in the early 1940s, there is a lacuna, during which he took time away from his own then youthful career so that his wife Bea (who is of course Gertrude Himmelfarb, the historian of Victorian intellectual culture) could do her graduate studies at the University of Chicago and later research for her doctorate in London. How many men, of whatever political views, would have done that 60 years ago?[17]

13　　Irving and Bea were the Nick and Nora Charles of American intellectual life.[18] They

---

Sample Student Commentary

[13] Notice how indirectly Epstein makes these claims. He is not claiming these things; Kristol did not claim them; obituarists are currently claiming them.

[14] Epstein's third personal illustration.

[15] Epstein's pronoun use does become unclear, but the sentence seems to read that it was Joyce who would never eat another bad lunch or be spoken to truthfully again.

[16] Another personal reflection.

[17] This is, of course, a rhetorical question. Epstein expects that the answer will be "none."

[18] Another allusion, this one to the popular culture husband-and-wife detective team. The purpose of this allusion is to illustrate the equity in Kristol's marriage.

were always on the case together. They had a marriage in which the question of equality seemed simply never to have arisen. Congruent in their opinions, perfectly joined in what they valued, they were as united as any couple I have ever known.

14 One of my fondest memories[19] is of a panel at Harvard on which sat Irving, Michael Walzer, Martin Peretz, and Norman Podhoretz.[20] I don't recall the subject, but only that Irving, without being the least pushy about it, dominated, lighting up the room with his easy wit and charming good sense. I looked over at Bea, who was sitting a few rows in front of me and to my left, and could see how utterly enthralled she was by her husband's brilliance. After more than 50 years of life together, she still had a crush on him. I didn't have the least difficulty understanding why. ℮

Joseph Epstein is a contributing editor to *The Weekly Standard*. His third collection of short stories, *The Love Song of A. Jerome Minkoff*, was published in 2010.

Sample Student Commentary

[19] Since he opens his final paragraph with his "fondest" memory, perhaps Epstein has been following order of magnitude as the organizational pattern for his illustrations.

[20] All three are public intellectuals and theorists. Peretz had been an associate professor at Harvard.

Sample multiple-choice questions:

1. The nature of most of Epstein's allusions suggests that he expects his reader to be

    A. upper-middle-class professional.

    B. educated and well-read.

    C. politically conservative.

    D. philosophically inclined.

    E. intellectually elite.

2. In the second paragraph, the expression "worked out of his car" most likely means that Kristol

    A. never learned how to drive.

    B. traveled extensively.

    C. worked periodically.

    D. filled myriad positions.

    E. wielded great influence.

3. The examples provided in the third paragraph suggest that a great part of Kristol's appeal lay in the

    A. style of his public addresses.

    B. ability to make his listeners think.

    C. clarity and persuasiveness of his writing.

    D. extreme volume of his output.

    E. casual manner with which he worked.

4. All of the following contribute to the intimate and admiring tone of this essay EXCEPT

    A. *allusions to other writers and thinkers.*

    B. personal reminiscences and anecdotes.

    C. general and anonymous attributions.

    D. speculation.

    E. negation.

5. Based on its context in the fourth paragraph, the word *skepticism* most nearly means

    A. doubt.

    B. distrust.

    C. *uncertainty.*

    D. cynicism.

    E. disbelief.

Answers and Explanations:

1. The majority of the names Epstein mentions in this memorial—George Orwell, Christopher DeMuth, José Ortega y Gasset, Irving, Michael Walzer, Martin Peretz, Norman Podhoretz, et al—are intellectuals, thinkers, and writers. Recognizing their names and knowing what they do would not necessarily suggest a reader's socio-economic status or profession (A). And, although the majority of the people alluded to are conservative or neoconservative (C), one would not have to be a conservative to recognize their names and understand the allusion. (D) is tempting, but not the best answer as there are also political implications in the allusions. While some might consider the persons alluded to be "intellectually elite" (E), there is nothing to suggest that the reader would have to be elitist to understand the allusions. **(B) is the best answer. Whatever one's economic status or political persuasion, any educated or well-read individual could be familiar with the names to which Epstein alludes.**

2. Epstein writes that the fact that Kristol never learned how to drive renders the observation that he "worked out of his car" ironic, so (A) is clearly eliminated. (B) is too literal a reading of the expression and is also negated by (A). (C) is tempting, but not the best answer as it connotes periods of inactivity or unemployment. (E) is eliminated by the fact there is no necessary relationship between the expression and Kristol's influence. **The expression, however, is preceded and followed by brief mentions of the various positions Kristol filled and work he did. Thus, (D) is the best answer.**

3. While the most detailed illustration involves Kristol's casual manner of speaking (A), this is offered as an illustration of a larger point. (B) is likewise mentioned, but it is another aspect of Kristol's speaking manner. (C), too, is mentioned but cannot be considered the point of the paragraph. (D) is contradicted by (C) as well as Epstein's opening comment

about Kristol's having more influence even though he actually wrote less. **(E), then, is the best answer. Epstein writes that Kristol wrote "unlike a true writer," and he spoke "non-oratorical[ly]." In other words, he did what he did in a casual, non-self-conscious manner.**

4. (B) is, of course, Epstein's primary means of suggesting the closeness he shared with Kristol. There is not a single illustrative anecdote about Kristol that does not also involve Epstein. (C) allows Epstein to mention certain accomplishments—"helping to elect Ronald Reagan, launching neoconservatism, discovering youthful talent"—claims that apparently originate with "obituarists," and not with him. (D) is evident when Epstein writes, "I am certain, he did the lion's share of the work." From the beginning of the essay, Epstein employs negation (E) to admit the difficulty of identifying this man he admired into a particular group or class. Epstein's allusions (A), however, help to give the reader an understanding of Kristol, but they do not contribute to our understanding of Epstein's admiration of his subject. **Thus, (A) is the best answer.**

5. Certainly, all of the choices are synonyms of *skepticism*, so the key to this question is which shade of meaning is meant in the context of this passage. Epstein writes, "Irving's reigning intellectual note was that of skepticism. As an intellectual, he lived by ideas, but at the same time he greatly distrusted them. All ideas for him, like saints for George Orwell, were guilty until proven innocent." (A) is, therefore, somewhat less desirable as "doubt" does not necessarily connote the possibility of accepting the idea. (B) might tempt some who see the word in the text, but again, Epstein suggests the possibility of Kristol's accepting an idea, and "distrust" alone does not connote this possibility. (D) and (E) are even stronger levels of doubt, and can be excluded. (C) suggests both the current hesitance to accept an idea (all saints are presumed guilty) while acknowledging that the idea might be proven acceptable in the future (until proven innocent). **Thus, (C) is the best answer.**

Sample free-response item:

Carefully read the memorial. "A Genius of Temperament: Joseph Epstein remembers Irving Kristol." In the essay, Epstein recounts the accomplishments and his personal memories of the late writer and thinker, Irving Kristol. After reading the passage, write an essay in which you analyze the techniques Epstein uses to introduce his reader to Irving Kristol and to convey to the reader his sense of personal loss. Do not merely summarize the essay.

Sample Student Essay

In his article, "A Genius of Temperament," Joseph Epstein uses anecdotes as his primary vehicle to explain to the reader who his subject, Irving Kristol, was and why his death was such a loss for Epstein. Within his anecdotes, Epstein relates stories in which he and Kristol interacted; these anecdotes show Kristol to have been someone Epstein admired greatly. More importantly, they serve to connect the reader to the way Epstein feels about Kristol by presenting Kristol as he lived rather than as the aggregate of his ideas.

Epstein uses anecdotes throughout the memorial for two purposes. The first of these is to humanize Kristol. Instead of writing primarily about Kristol's thoughts and ideas, which are abstractions, Epstein portrays Kristol in social situations, especially those in which Epstein was present. By showing Kristol in interactions with others, Epstein tells the reader that Kristol was a person and a friend first and foremost, and a purveyor of ideas second. Through this technique, Epstein is also able to show Kristol's good qualities in a way that simply enumerating them could not, making Kristol seem more real to the reader. This humanizes Kristol and disposes the reader toward a sympathetic reaction. After all, it is much easier to care about someone if one can understand that someone as an actual person rather than simply the collection of ideas the person embodies.

The second purpose—to convey to the reader an acute sense of personal loss—follows directly from the first. Epstein always refers to his subject by his first name, Irving, signaling that this will not be an emotionally detached piece of writing. Using Kristol's first name establishes a sort of intimacy between Epstein and Kristol and reinforces to the reader that the two were close. Through humanizing Kristol and showing that he was a much-admired friend, Epstein makes readers aware of how they would feel if they had lost someone close to them. The anecdotes are essential to this rhetorical strategy; while an obituary would simply relate facts about Kristol's life, Epstein's memorial connects the two men in a way that historical facts alone cannot. For Epstein, the experience of Kristol—the way he presented ideas—is more important than the ideas themselves. Great thoughts outlive those who present them, but few are able to present great thoughts in gracious style. To Epstein, Kristol was one of those select few. Losing someone who could present that experience is clearly damaging to Epstein.

At the same time that Epstein is explaining why Kristol is important to him, he is also showing the reader who Kristol was. The introduction defines Kristol by negation; Epstein tells us all the things that Kristol was not as a way to explain his unique nature. The anecdotes serve to reinforce the qualities Epstein describes. Rather than simply write that Kristol has an off-the-cuff speaking style, Epstein gives the reader an anecdote in which this style is displayed; when Epstein writes that Kristol was "without vanity," he includes an anecdote in which Kristol is embarrassed by praise. Kristol displayed these qualities in real events, and Epstein's descriptions of these events have a more powerful effect on the reader than if Epstein were simply to list several good qualities Kristol possessed.

The effect of Epstein's anecdotes should not be understated. The anecdote is a powerful rhetorical device precisely because it is born of a human experience and, therefore, is easy for a human to identify with. By aligning his memorial with very human experiences, Epstein portrays his subject as a well-rounded person, rather than someone who is simply the sum of his accomplishments. ❧

Exercise One:

Questions 1-5. Read the following passage carefully before you choose your answers.

Bruce Catton (1899-1978) was a Civil War specialist whose early career included reporting for various newspapers. In 1954 he received both the Pulitzer Prize for historical work and the National Book Award. Catton served as Director of Information for the United States Department of Commerce and wrote many books, including Mr. Lincoln's Army *(1951),* Glory Road *(1952),* A Stillness at Appomattox *(1953),* The Hallowed Ground *(1956),* America Goes to War *(1958),* The Coming Fury *(1961),* Terrible Swift Sword *(1963),* Never Call Retreat *(1965),* Waiting for the Morning Train: An American Boyhood *(1972), and* Gettysburg: The Final Fury *(1974). For five years, Catton edited* American Heritage.

In this passage, Catton examines two contrasting historical figures and how they come to symbolize the causes for which they fought.

GRANT AND LEE: A STUDY IN CONTRASTS

BRUCE CATTON

1   WHEN ULYSSES S. GRANT and Robert E. Lee met in the parlor of a modest house at Appomattox Court House, Virginia, on April 9, 1865, to work out the terms for the surrender of Lee's Army of Northern Virginia, a great chapter on American life came to a close, and a great new chapter began.

2   These men were bringing the Civil War to its virtual finish. To be sure, other armies had yet to surrender, and for a few days the fugitive Confederate government would struggle desperately and vainly, trying to find some way to go on living now that its chief support was gone. But in effect it was all over when Grant and Lee signed the papers. And the little room where they wrote out the terms was the scene of one of the poignant, dramatic contrasts in American History.

3   They were two strong men these oddly different generals, and they represented the strengths of two conflicting currents that through them, had come into final collision.

4   Back of Robert E Lee was the notion that the old aristocratic concept might somehow survive and be dominant in American life. Lee was tidewater Virginia, and in his background were family, culture, and tradition...the age of chivalry transplanted to a New World which was making its own legends and its own myths. He embodied a way of life that had come down through the age of knighthood and the English country squire. America was a land that was beginning all over again, dedicated to nothing much more complicated than the rather hazy belief that all men had equal rights and should have an equal chance in the world. In such a land Lee stood for the feeling that it was somehow of advantage to human society to have a pronounced inequality in the social structure. There should be a leisure class, backed by ownership of land; in turn, society itself should be tied to the land as the chief source of wealth and influence. It would bring forth (according to this ideal) a class of men with a strong sense of obligation to the community; men who lived not to gain advantage for themselves, but to meet the solemn obligations which had been laid on them by the very fact that they were privileged. From

them the country would get its leadership. To them it could look for higher values—of thought, of conduct, or personal deportment—to give it strength and virtue.

5   Lee embodied the noblest elements of this aristocratic ideal. Through him, the landed nobility justified itself. For four years, the Southern states had fought a desperate war to uphold the ideals for which Lee stood. In the end, it almost seemed as of the Confederacy fought for Lee; as if he himself was the Confederacy…the best thing that the way of life for which the Confederacy stood could ever have to offer. He had passed into legend before Appomattox. Thousands of tired, underfed, poorly clothed Confederate soldiers, long since past the simple enthusiasm of the early days of the struggle, somehow considered Lee the symbol of everything for which they had been willing to die. But they could not quite put this feeling into words. If the Lost Cause, sanctified by so much heroism and so many deaths, had a living justification, its justification was General Lee.

6   Grant, the son of a tanner on the Western frontier, was everything Lee was not. He had come up the hard way and embodied nothing in particular except the eternal toughness and sinewy fiber of the men who grew up beyond the mountains. He was one of a body of men who owed reverence and obeisance to no one, who were self-reliant to a fault, who cared hardly anything for the past but who had a sharp eye for the future.

7   These frontier men were the precise opposites of the tidewater aristocrats. Back of them, in the great surge that had taken people over the Alleghenies and into the opening Western country, there was a deep, implicit dissatisfaction with a past that had settled into grooves. They stood for democracy, not from any reasoned conclusion about the proper ordering of human society, but simply because they had grown up in the middle of democracy and knew how it worked. Their society might have privileges, but they would be privileges each man had won for himself. Forms and patterns meant nothing. No man was born to anything, except perhaps to a chance to show how far he could rise. Life was competition.

8   Yet along with this feeling had come a deep sense of belonging to a national community. The Westerner who developed a farm, opened a shop, or set up in business as a trader could hope to prosper only as his own community prospered—and his community ran from the Atlantic to the Pacific and from Canada down to Mexico. If the land was settled, with towns and highways and accessible markets, he could better himself. He saw his fate in terms of the nation's own destiny. As its horizons expanded, so did his. He had, in other words, an acute dollars-and-cents stake in the continued growth and development of his country.

9   And that, perhaps, is where the contrast between Grant and Lee becomes most striking. The Virginia aristocrat, inevitably, saw himself in relation to his own region. He lived in a static society which could endure almost anything except change. Instinctively, his first loyalty would go to the locality in which that society existed. He would fight to the limit of endurance to defend it, because in defending it he was defending everything that gave his own life its deepest meaning.

10   The Westerner, on the other hand, would fight with an equal tenacity for the broader concept of society. He fought so because everything he lived by was tied to growth, expansion, and a constantly widening horizon. What he lived by would survive or fall with the nation itself. He could not possibly stand by unmoved in the face of an attempt

to destroy the Union. He would combat it with everything he had, because he could only see it as an effort to cut the ground out from under his feet.

11   So Grant and Lee were in complete contrast, representing two diametrically opposed elements in American life. Grant was the modern man emerging; beyond him, ready to come on the stage was the great age of steel and machinery, of crowded cities and a restless burgeoning vitality. Lee might have ridden down from the old age of chivalry, lance in hand, silken banner fluttering over his head. Each man was the perfect champion for his cause, drawing both his strengths and his weaknesses from the people he led.

12   Yet it was not all contrast, after all. Different as they were—in background, in personality, in underlying aspiration—these two great soldiers had much in common. Under everything else, they were marvelous fighters. Furthermore, their fighting qualities were really very much alike. Each man had, to begin with, the great virtue of utter tenacity and fidelity. Grant fought his way down the Mississippi Valley in spite of acute personal discouragement and profound military handicaps. Lee hung on in the trench at Petersburg after hope born of a fighter's refusal to give up a long as he can still remain on his feet and lift his two fists.

13   Daring and resourcefulness they had, too: the ability to think faster and move faster than the enemy. These were the qualities which gave Lee the dazzling campaigns of Second Manassas and Chancellorsville and won Vicksburg for Grant.

14   Lastly, and perhaps greatest of all, there was the ability, at the end, to turn quickly from the war to peace once the fighting was over. Out of the way these two men behaved at Appomattox came the possibility of peace of reconciliation. It was a possibility not wholly realized, in the year to come, but which did, in the end, help the two sections to become one nation again…after a war whose bitterness might have seemed to make such a reunion wholly impossible. No part of either man's life became him more than the part he played in their brief meeting in the McLean house at Appomattox. Their behavior there put all succeeding generations of Americans in their debt. Two great Americans, Grant and Lee—very different, yet under everything very much alike. Their encounter at Appomattox was one of the great moments of American history. ❧

"Grant and Lee: A Study in Contrast" was written as a chapter of The American Story, *1990,*
Bruce Catton. *"Grant and Lee: A Study in Contrasts." Excerpted from* The American Story *edited by Earl Schenck Miers. Copyright © Earl Schenck Miers. Reprinted with permission from the United States Capitol Historical Society.*

Multiple-choice questions:

1. As it is used in the second paragraph, the word *virtual* most nearly means
   A. actual.
   B. official.
   C. practical.
   D. effective.
   E. absolute.

2. Through the course of this passage, Catton elevates Grant and Lee to the status of

A. historical personages.

B. mythical archetypes.

C. cultural icons.

D. political symbols.

E. social satires.

3. The most prevalent literary and rhetorical device used in this passage is

A. antithesis.

B. hyperbole.

C. paradox.

D. amplification.

E. metaphor.

4. Catton's tone throughout can best be described as

A. poignant.

B. optimistic.

C. neutral.

D. condemning.

E. laudatory.

5. Catton most likely intends the sentence, *"Thousands of tired, underfed, poorly clothed Confederate soldiers...considered Lee the symbol of everything for which they had been willing to die,"* (paragraph 5) to be read as a(n)

A. analogy.

B. literal statement.

C. hypothesis.

D. broad generalization.

E. allusion.

Free Response Item:

Carefully read Bruce Catton's "Grant and Lee: A Study in Contrasts." Then, write a well-supported essay in which you analyze Catton's diction, sentence structure, and other language choices and how they help him achieve his desired tone and effect.

✖ Conversationally Formal

Many writers, lecturers, and speakers have a great desire to be a presence to their audience. Their voices are as important—possibly even more important—than the subject matter itself. Readers of motivational writers, political writers, even humorists and commentators are often as interested in the writer as they are in the subject matter. These writers know that, in order to appeal to their readers, they must adopt a tone, create a mood, that will appeal to the reader without distracting from the subject matter.

Consider the following passage, the speech delivered by author and activist Elie Wiesel on the occasion of his receiving the Nobel Peace Prize on December 10, 1986. A survivor of the Holocaust and author of numerous works including the novels *Night* and *Dawn*, Wiesel was awarded the Nobel Prize in large part to honor his ceaseless efforts to decry human rights violations like Apartheid and to keep the world always aware of historical and current incidents of genocide.

Wiesel's speech has been annotated to point out to you the various strategies: word choice, sentence structure, uses of literary and rhetorical devices that point to how Wiesel constructs his address to engage his audience. After you examine the passage and the accompanying notes, look at how a student taking the AP Language exam might respond to multiple-choice questions and a free-response item dealing with how Wiesel achieves and maintains a formal, yet sympathetic tone.

Elie Wiesel
The Nobel Peace Prize
Acceptance Speech 1986

1   IT IS WITH A PROFOUND sense of humility[1] that I accept the honor you have chosen to bestow upon me.[2] I know: your choice transcends me.[3] This both frightens and pleases me.[4]

2   It frightens me because I wonder: do I have the right to represent the multitudes who have perished?[5] Do I have the right to accept this great honor on their behalf?...I do not.[6] That would be presumptuous. No one may speak for the dead, no one may interpret their mutilated dreams and visions.

Sample Student Commentary

[1] The oxymoron of "profound" and "humility" ironically draws attention to the speaker while ostensibly deflecting it.

[2] Interesting construction. Of course Wiesel is accepting an award conferred, but what effect is added by his acknowledgment "you have chosen to bestow…"?

[3] This sentence is ambiguous. Does the choice transport Wiesel beyond himself, or does the choice include a class of people of which Wiesel is merely a member?

[4] Not quite an oxymoron, but another juxtaposition of almost antithetical ideas.

[5] This clarifies part of the ambiguity of the previous paragraph.

[6] To raise a question and then provide an answer is a device called hypophora.

3   It pleases me because I may say that this honor belongs to all the survivors and their children, and through us, to the Jewish people with whose destiny I have always identified.[7]

4   I remember: it happened yesterday or eternities ago.[8] A young Jewish boy discovered the kingdom of night. I remember his bewilderment, I remember his anguish. It all happened so fast. The ghetto. The deportation. The sealed cattle car. The fiery altar upon which the history of our people and the future of mankind were meant to be sacrificed.[9]

5   I remember:[10] he asked his father: "Can this be true?" This is the twentieth century, not the Middle Ages. Who would allow such crimes to be committed? How could the world remain silent?"[11]

6   And now the boy is turning to me: "Tell me," he asks. "What have you done with my future? What have you done with your life?"[12]

7   And I tell him that I have tried. That I have tried to keep memory alive, that I have tried to fight those who would forget. Because if we forget, we are guilty, we are accomplices.[13]

8   And then I explained to him how naive we were, that the world did know and remain silent. And that is why I swore never to be silent whenever and wherever human beings endure suffering and humiliation. We must always take sides. Neutrality helps the oppressor, never the victim. Silence encourages the tormentor, never the tormented.[14] Sometimes we must interfere. When human lives are endangered, when human dignity is in jeopardy, national borders and sensitivities become irrelevant. Wherever men or women are persecuted because of their race, religion, or political views, that place must—at that moment—become the center of the universe.

9   Of course, since I am a Jew profoundly rooted in my peoples' memory and tradition, my first response is to Jewish fears, Jewish needs, Jewish crises. For I belong to a traumatized generation, one that experienced the abandonment and solitude of our people. It would be unnatural for me not to make Jewish priorities my own: Israel, Soviet Jewry, Jews in Arab lands…But there are others as important to me. Apartheid is, in my view, as abhorrent as anti-Semitism. To me, Andrei Sakharov's isolation is as much of a disgrace as Josef Biegun's imprisonment. As is the denial of Solidarity and its leader Lech Walesa's

---

Sample Student Commentary

[7] This further clarifies the ambiguity of the first paragraph.

[8] Another interesting juxtaposition. Perhaps Wiesel's uncertainty contributes to his humble, common man persona.

[9] This paragraph contains a series of stylistic sentence fragments.

[10] The repetition of "I remember" at the beginning of two successive paragraphs is an example of anaphora. It contributes both emphasis to the material and a rhythm to the spoken delivery of that material.

[11] Spoken aloud, as they would be in a speech, these rhetorical questions invite Wiesel's listeners to pause and ponder their own answers to these unanswerable questions.

[12] Wiesel's use of dialogue, both here and in the rhetorical questions in the previous paragraph, help create the tone of a storyteller.

[13] Up until now, Wiesel's use of first person has been singular, referring only to himself. Now, his use of the plural involves his listeners and readers as well.

[14] The use of the absolutes "always" and "never" emphasizes the passion with which Wiesel intends these sentences to be read. The parallel structure further intensifies this passion.

right to dissent. And Nelson Mandela's interminable imprisonment.[15]

10   There is so much injustice and suffering crying out for our attention: victims of hunger, of racism, and political persecution, writers and poets, prisoners in so many lands governed by the Left and by the Right. Human rights are being violated on every continent. More people are oppressed than free. And then, too, there are the Palestinians to whose plight I am sensitive but whose methods I deplore. Violence and terrorism are not the answer. Something must be done about their suffering, and soon. I trust Israel, for I have faith in the Jewish people. Let Israel be given a chance, let hatred and danger be removed from her horizons, and there will be peace in and around the Holy Land.

11   Yes, I have faith. Faith in God and even in His creation. Without it no action would be possible. And action is the only remedy to indifference: the most insidious danger of all. Isn't this the meaning of Alfred Nobel's legacy? Wasn't his fear of war a shield against war?

12   There is much to be done, there is much that can be done. One person—a Raoul Wallenberg, an Albert Schweitzer, one person of integrity, can make a difference, a difference of life and death. As long as one dissident is in prison, our freedom will not be true. As long as one child is hungry, our lives will be filled with anguish and shame. What all these victims need above all is to know that they are not alone; that we are not forgetting them, that when their voices are stifled we shall lend them ours, that while their freedom depends on ours, the quality of our freedom depends on theirs.

13   This is what I say to the young Jewish boy wondering what I have done with his years. It is in his name that I speak to you and that I express to you my deepest gratitude. No one is as capable of gratitude as one who has emerged from the kingdom of night. We know that every moment is a moment of grace, every hour an offering; not to share them would mean to betray them. Our lives no longer belong to us alone; they belong to all those who need us desperately.

14   Thank you, Chairman Aarvik. Thank you, members of the Nobel Committee. Thank you, people of Norway, for declaring on this singular occasion that our survival has meaning for mankind. 🐚

From Les Prix Nobel. The Nobel Prizes 1986, *Editor Wilhelm Odelberg, [Nobel Foundation],* Stockholm, 1987 *Copyright © The Nobel Foundation 1986*

Sample Student Commentary
[15] Specific examples and parallel sentence fragments continue to communicate Wiesel's passion.

Sample multiple-choice questions:

1. **The most likely purpose of the oxymoron in the opening sentence of this address is to**
   A. surprise and delight the reader.
   B. clarify the thesis.
   C. *create reader sympathy.*
   D. create authorial distance.
   E. point out an apparent contradiction.

2. **"The boy" referred to in paragraph 4 most likely refers to**
   A. a young Holocaust survivor.
   B. a young Holocaust victim.
   C. an archetype of Holocaust victims.
   D. Wiesel's father.
   E. *Wiesel himself.*

3. **Which of the following best signals Wiesel's shift in focus from personal to universal?**
   A. *"…if we forget, we are guilty, we are accomplices…" (paragraph 7)*
   B. "…the world did know and remain silent." (paragraph 8)
   C. "I remember." (paragraph 4, 5)
   D. "…the history of our people and the future of mankind…" (paragraph 4)
   E. "But there are others as important to me." (paragraph 9)

4. **The overall tone of this speech transitions from**
   A. passionate to imploring.
   B. *reluctant to challenging.*
   C. entreating to impassioned.
   D. bewildered to concerned.
   E. reminiscent to convicted.

5. **Through the course of his address, Wiesel does all of the following EXCEPT**
   A. thank the Nobel prize committee.
   B. accept the award in the name the oppressed.
   C. declare himself to be a Jew.
   D. challenge his listeners to activism.
   E. *condemn those who violate human rights.*

Answers and Explanations:

1. Certainly "surprise and delight" (A) is a common goal of writers and speakers; the phrase "profound sense of humility" is almost a cliché in the context of acceptance speeches. Whether this speech is likely to advance an argument has not yet been determined, and even if there is a thesis, it has not yet been introduced. Thus, (B) is eliminated. This being a speech, Wiesel would not want to create a distance between himself and his audience (D). If anything, he would want to establish intimacy. (E) might tempt a few, but the oxymoron *is* an apparent contradiction, it does not point to another one. **(C) is the best choice as Wiesel wants to establish his humility and gratitude and not alienate himself from his audience by boasting of the award he is accepting.**

2. From the paragraph that begins, "I remember: it happened yesterday or eternities ago," it is clear that Wiesel is sharing a personal memory and that he is the boy discovering the evil in the world and bewildered by it. Thus, it is clear that, when the boy asks the man how the man has spent his life, it is the memory of young Wiesel challenging the mature Wiesel. (A), therefore, is true, and (B) is tempting, but these are not the best answers in the context of the speech. (C) is likewise true, but also too general given the context. (D) is eliminated by the fact it is clear from elsewhere in the speech that Wiesel himself was a Holocaust survivor, and his father would not have been a boy during that period. **Given the full rhetorical context, however, and the conceit of Wiesel remembering his own childhood in the third person, (E) is the best answer.**

3. (B) might tempt but occurs after the shift, as Wiesel is developing the details of his new focus. (C) occurs before the shift. Clearly the anaphora establishes that the focus here is still on Wiesel and his own memories. (D) is a summative statement, leading to the conclusion, and it occurs well after the shift. (E) might be tempting, but it signals Wiesel's shift from Jew to "others." He has already broadened his focus from himself alone. **(A) is the first occurrence of first person plural, in which Wiesel leaves his personal remembrance and gratitude and begins to include his audience in his entreaty. Thus, (A) is the best answer.**

4. The speech begins with Wiesel's wondering, "do I have the right to represent the multitudes who have perished?" This suggests his reluctance to fulfill the role demanded by his accepting the award. Wiesel transitions to his conclusion by saying, "There is much to be done, there is much that can be done." **Thus, (B) is the best answer.** (A) might tempt, as there is, indeed, passion through the speech, but Wiesel's tone can never be said to be imploring. Likewise, he challenges, but there are no words or phrases that suggest "entreating," (C). The boy Wiesel admits to having been bewildered (D), but this is not the overall tone of his address at this point. Likewise, while there is memory in the first part of the speech, it is bitter memory and cannot be called "reminiscence" (E). Nor is it the overall tone of this portion.

5. The first and final paragraphs eliminate (A). (B) is eliminated by his early admission, "your choice transcends me." (C) is eliminated by his declaration, "…I am a Jew profoundly rooted in my peoples' memory and tradition." Wiesel's several calls to action include, "We must always take sides. Neutrality helps the oppressor, never the victim. Silence encourages the tormentor, never the tormented. Sometimes we must interfere," and culminate in, "action is the only remedy to indifference: the most insidious danger of all." Thus, (D) is eliminated. **While he names several instances of oppression, never does he curse or condemn the oppressor. Thus, (E) is the best answer.**

Sample free-response item:

Carefully read Elie Wiesel's Nobel Peace Prize Acceptance Speech. Then, write an essay in which you analyze Wiesel's use of diction and rhetorical devices in order to establish and maintain a tone that will both engage and challenge his audience.

Sample Student Essay

In his 1986 Nobel Peace Prize Acceptance speech, writer and activist Elie Wiesel adopts an appropriately humble tone in order to express his gratitude for the honor, as well as to challenge his audience to rouse themselves from their apathy and indifference and take action against oppression and the violation of human rights. He achieves his engaging and challenging tone through the effective use of antithetical juxtapositions like oxymoron, repetition of key words and phrases, and rhetorical questions that invite his hearers to examine their own hearts and consciences. The result is a call to action that is at once humble and inspiring, gracious yet motivating.

Wiesel begins his address with the near-cliché that he accepts the award with "profound...humility." Having been chosen to receive the award "both frightens and pleases" him. These antithetical juxtapositions—not quite oxymorons, but close—draw the audience's attention to the speaker, even as he appears to draw attention away from himself. He is carefully affecting an air of humility, not wanting to alienate his audience at this personal and professional pinnacle.

This humble tone is further maintained through the use of a hypophora that clearly suggests self-doubt: "Do I have the right...? I do not."

The next significant portion of the speech comprises Wiesel's memory of the Holocaust, his bewilderment at the depths of human brutality and indifference. Of course, this is the acknowledgement of one of the reasons for Weisel's being given the award, but it is also another opportunity for the speaker to engage the audience, to personalize the issue that will soon be broached. Wiesel employs anaphora, a refrain-like repetition of significant words or phrases, to evoke this sympathy from his listener. "I remember," Wiesel writes, "A young Jewish boy..." "I remember his anguish," he continues. "*I remember,*" he concludes, "*he asks his father...*" The anaphora lends a cadence to the recitation of facts; it hints at Weisel's involvement in the episode he is remembering. It makes him human, vulnerable in the eyes of the audience. He is no longer only Elie Wiesel, Nobel Peace Prize Laureate, but he is a young Jewish Holocaust victim.

Once he has established his humble, vulnerable tone; once he has achieved an emotional connection with his audience, Weisel can confidently cite instance after instance of oppression and human rights violations—Andrei Sakharov's isolation, Josef Biegun's imprisonment, apartheid and Nelson Mandela's [then ongoing] imprisonment—without sounding as if he were lecturing or preaching. He has already established his humanity, humility, and vulnerability. In the event, however, that his recitation has indeed compromised his desired effect, Weisel closes this section of his speech and begins the transition to his conclusion with two rhetorical questions: "*Isn't this the meaning of Alfred Nobel's legacy? Wasn't his fear of war a shield against war?*"

These questions require no answer; Wiesel is simply inviting his audience to examine their own consciences.

Elie Wiesel's 1986 Nobel Peace Prize acceptance speech, then, is a highly effective address, planned and delivered with the intent to engage his audience, motivate them to shake off their indifference, and establish his own humanity and humility. The voice of the writer and speaker is, in this speech, as powerful as is the subject matter the speaker is addressing. ॐ

Exercise Two:

Questions 6-10. Read the following passage carefully before you choose your answers.

One of the key components of the Nobel Prize ceremony each December is the delivery of the Nobel Lecture. The following passage is the lecture delivered by Nobel Peace Prize laureate Elie Wiesel in 1986. In his lecture, Wiesel, a survivor of the Holocaust, writer, and human rights activist, contemplates the paradox of human existence: the need to remember versus the desire to forget.

Elie Wiesel
The Nobel Peace Prize
Nobel Lecture
NOVEMBER 11, 1986

Hope, Despair and Memory

1   A HASIDIC LEGEND TELLS us that the great Rabbi Baal-Shem-Tov, Master of the Good Name, also known as the Besht, undertook an urgent and perilous mission: to hasten the coming of the Messiah. The Jewish people, all humanity were suffering too

much, beset by too many evils. They had to be saved, and swiftly. For having tried to meddle with history, the Besht was punished; banished along with his faithful servant to a distant island. In despair, the servant implored his master to exercise his mysterious powers in order to bring them both home.

2 "Impossible", the Besht replied. "My powers have been taken from me."

3 "Then, please, say a prayer, recite a litany, work a miracle."

4 "Impossible", the Master replied, "I have forgotten everything." They both fell to weeping.

5 Suddenly the Master turned to his servant and asked: "Remind me of a prayer—any prayer ."

6 "If only I could," said the servant. "I too have forgotten everything."

7 "Everything—absolutely everything?"

8 "Yes, except—"

9 "Except what?"

10 "Except the alphabet."

11 At that the Besht cried out joyfully: "Then what are you waiting for? Begin reciting the alphabet and I shall repeat after you…" And together the two exiled men began to recite, at first in whispers, then more loudly: "*Aleph, beth, gimel, daleth…*" And over again, each time more vigorously, more fervently; until, ultimately, the Besht regained his powers, having regained his memory.

12 I love this story, for it illustrates the messianic expectation—which remains my own. And the importance of friendship to man's ability to transcend his condition. I love it most of all because it emphasizes the mystical power of memory. Without memory, our existence would be barren and opaque, like a prison cell into which no light penetrates; like a tomb which rejects the living. Memory saved the Besht, and if anything can, it is memory that will save humanity. For me, hope without memory is like memory without hope.

13 Just as man cannot live without dreams, he cannot live without hope. If dreams reflect the past, hope summons the future. Does this mean that our future can be built on a rejection of the past? Surely such a choice is not necessary. The two are not incompatible. The opposite of the past is not the future but the absence of future; the opposite of the future is not the past but the absence of past. The loss of one is equivalent to the sacrifice of the other.

14 A recollection. The time: After the war. The place: Paris. A young man struggles to readjust to life. His mother, his father, his small sister are gone. He is alone. On the verge of despair. And yet he does not give up. On the contrary, he strives to find a place among the living. He acquires a new language. He makes a few friends who, like himself, believe that the memory of evil will serve as a shield against evil; that the memory of death will serve as a shield against death.

15 This he must believe in order to go on. For he has just returned from a universe where God, betrayed by His creatures, covered His face in order not to see. Mankind, jewel of his creation, had succeeded in building an inverted Tower of Babel, reaching not toward heaven but toward an anti-heaven, there to create a parallel society, a new "creation" with its own princes and gods, laws and principles, jailers and prisoners. A world where the past no longer counted—no longer meant anything.

16   Stripped of possessions, all human ties severed, the prisoners found themselves in a social and cultural void. "Forget," they were told, "Forget where you came from; forget who you were. Only the present matters." But the present was only a blink of the Lord's eye. The Almighty himself was a slaughterer: it was He who decided who would live and who would die; who would be tortured, and who would be rewarded. Night after night, seemingly endless processions vanished into the flames, lighting up the sky. Fear dominated the universe. Indeed this was another universe; the very laws of nature had been transformed. Children looked like old men, old men whimpered like children. Men and women from every corner of Europe were suddenly reduced to nameless and faceless creatures desperate for the same ration of bread or soup, dreading the same end. Even their silence was the same for it resounded with the memory of those who were gone. Life in this accursed universe was so distorted, so unnatural that a new species had evolved. Waking among the dead, one wondered if one was still alive.

17   And yet real despair only seized us later. Afterwards. As we emerged from the nightmare and began to search for meaning. All those doctors of law or medicine or theology, all those lovers of art and poetry, of Bach and Goethe, who coldly, deliberately ordered the massacres and participated in them. What did their metamorphosis signify? Could anything explain their loss of ethical, cultural and religious memory? How could we ever understand the passivity of the onlookers and—yes—the silence of the Allies? And question of questions: Where was God in all this? It seemed as impossible to conceive of Auschwitz with God as to conceive of Auschwitz without God. Therefore, everything had to be reassessed because everything had changed. With one stroke, mankind's achievements seemed to have been erased. Was Auschwitz a consequence or an aberration of "civilization"? All we know is that Auschwitz called that civilization into question as it called into question everything that had preceded Auschwitz. Scientific abstraction, social and economic contention, nationalism, xenophobia, religious fanaticism, racism, mass hysteria. All found their ultimate expression in Auschwitz.

18   The next question had to be, why go on? If memory continually brought us back to this, why build a home? Why bring children into a world in which God and man betrayed their trust in one another?

19   Of course we could try to forget the past. Why not? Is it not natural for a human being to repress what causes him pain, what causes him shame? Like the body, memory protects its wounds. When day breaks after a sleepless night, one's ghosts must withdraw; the dead are ordered back to their graves. But for the first time in history, we could not bury our dead. We bear their graves within ourselves.

20   For us, forgetting was never an option.

21   Remembering is a noble and necessary act. The call of memory, the call to memory, reaches us from the very dawn of history. No commandment figures so frequently, so insistently, in the Bible. It is incumbent upon us to remember the good we have received, and the evil we have suffered. New Year's Day, *Rosh Hashana*, is also called *Yom Hazikaron*, the day of memory. On that day, the day of universal judgment, man appeals to God to remember: our salvation depends on it. If God wishes to remember our suffering, all will be well; if He refuses, all will be lost. Thus, the rejection of memory becomes a divine

curse, one that would doom us to repeat past disasters, past wars.

22   Nothing provokes so much horror and opposition within the Jewish tradition as war. Our abhorrence of war is reflected in the paucity of our literature of warfare. After all, God created the Torah to do away with iniquity, to do away with war*. Warriors fare poorly in the Talmud: Judas Maccabeus is not even mentioned; Bar-Kochba is cited, but negatively†. David, a great warrior and conqueror, is not permitted to build the Temple; it is his son Solomon, a man of peace, who constructs God's dwelling place. Of course some wars may have been necessary or inevitable, but none was ever regarded as holy. For us, a holy war is a contradiction in terms. War dehumanizes, war diminishes, war debases all those who wage it. The Talmud says, "*Talmidei hukhamim shemarbin shalom baolam*" (It is the wise men who will bring about peace). Perhaps, because wise men remember best.

23   And yet it is surely human to forget, even to want to forget. The Ancients saw it as a divine gift. Indeed if memory helps us to survive, forgetting allows us to go on living. How could we go on with our daily lives, if we remained constantly aware of the dangers and ghosts surrounding us? The Talmud tells us that without the ability to forget, man would soon cease to learn. Without the ability to forget, man would live in a permanent, paralyzing fear of death. Only God and God alone can and must remember everything.

24   How are we to reconcile our supreme duty towards memory with the need to forget that is essential to life? No generation has had to confront this paradox with such urgency. The survivors wanted to communicate everything to the living: the victim's solitude and sorrow, the tears of mothers driven to madness, the prayers of the doomed beneath a fiery sky.

25   They needed to tell the child who, in hiding with his mother, asked softly, very softly: "Can I cry now?" They needed to tell of the sick beggar who, in a sealed cattle-car, began to sing as an offering to his companions. And of the little girl who, hugging her grandmother, whispered: "Don't be afraid, don't be sorry to die...I'm not." She was seven, that little girl who went to her death without fear, without regret.

26   Each one of us felt compelled to record every story, every encounter. Each one of us felt compelled to bear witness. Such were the wishes of the dying, the testament of the dead. Since the so-called civilized world had no use for their lives, then let it be inhabited by their deaths.

27   The great historian Shimon Dubnov served as our guide and inspiration. Until the moment of his death he said over and over again to his companions in the Riga ghetto: "*Yidden, shreibt un fershreibt*" (Jews, write it all down). His words were heeded. Overnight, countless victims become chroniclers and historians in the ghettos, even in the death camps. Even members of the *Sonderkommandos*, those inmates forced to burn their fellow inmates' corpses before being burned in turn, left behind extraordinary documents. To testify became an obsession. They left us poems and letters, diaries and fragments of novels, some known throughout the world, others still unpublished.

---

* The Torah comprises the first five books of Scriptures, the Law as given to Moses during the Hebrews' forty-year Exodus. The Talmud is the record of the Oral Law, which includes rabbinical interpretation, commentary, and elaboration on Torah.

† Judah Maccabeus led the struggle against Antiochus IV of Syria. His defeat of the Syrians and reconsecration of the Temple is commemorated in the Jewish holiday Hanukkah. Simon Bar-Kochba was the leader of a Hebrew revolt against the Romans, 132-135 A.D.

28 After the war we reassured ourselves that it would be enough to relate a single night in Treblinka, to tell of the cruelty, the senselessness of murder, and the outrage born of indifference: it would be enough to find the right word and the propitious moment to say it, to shake humanity out of its indifference and keep the torturer from torturing ever again. We thought it would be enough to read the world a poem written by a child in the Theresienstadt ghetto to ensure that no child anywhere would ever again have to endure hunger or fear. It would be enough to describe a death-camp "Selection," to prevent the human right to dignity from ever being violated again.

29 We thought it would be enough to tell of the tidal wave of hatred which broke over the Jewish people for men everywhere to decide once and for all to put an end to hatred of anyone who is "different"—whether black or white, Jew or Arab, Christian or Moslem—anyone whose orientation differs politically, philosophically, sexually. A naive undertaking? Of course. But not without a certain logic.

30 We tried. It was not easy. At first, because of the language; language failed us. We would have to invent a new vocabulary, for our own words were inadequate, anemic.

31 And then too, the people around us refused to listen; and even those who listened refused to believe; and even those who believed could not comprehend. Of course they could not. Nobody could. The experience of the camps defies comprehension.

32 Have we failed? I often think we have.

33 If someone had told us in 1945 that in our lifetime religious wars would rage on virtually every continent, that thousands of children would once again be dying of starvation, we would not have believed it. Or that racism and fanaticism would flourish once again, we would not have believed it. Nor would we have believed that there would be governments that would deprive a man like Lech Walesa of his freedom to travel merely because he dares to dissent. And he is not alone. Governments of the Right and of the Left go much further, subjecting those who dissent, writers, scientists, intellectuals, to torture and persecution. How to explain this defeat of memory?

34 How to explain any of it: the outrage of Apartheid which continues unabated. Racism itself is dreadful, but when it pretends to be legal, and therefore just, when a man like Nelson Mandela is imprisoned, it becomes even more repugnant. Without comparing Apartheid to Nazism and to its "final solution"—for that defies all comparison—one cannot help but assign the two systems, in their supposed legality, to the same camp. And the outrage of terrorism: of the hostages in Iran, the coldblooded massacre in the synagogue in Istanbul, the senseless deaths in the streets of Paris. Terrorism must be outlawed by all civilized nations—not explained or rationalized, but fought and eradicated. Nothing can, nothing will justify the murder of innocent people and helpless children. And the outrage of preventing men and women like Andrei Sakharov, Vladimir and Masha Slepak, Ida Nudel, Josef Biegun, Victor Brailowski, Zakhar Zonshein, and all the others known and unknown from leaving their country. And then there is Israel, which after two thousand years of exile and thirty-eight years of sovereignty still does not have peace. I would like to see this people, which is my own, able to establish the foundation for a constructive relationship with all its Arab neighbors, as it has done with Egypt. We must exert pressure on all those in power to come to terms.

35 And here we come back to memory. We must remember the suffering of my people, as

we must remember that of the Ethiopians, the Cambodians, the boat people, Palestinians, the Mesquite Indians, the Argentinean "*desaparecidos*"—the list seems endless.

36   Let us remember Job who, having lost everything—his children, his friends, his possessions, and even his argument with God—still found the strength to begin again, to rebuild his life. Job was determined not to repudiate the creation, however imperfect, that God had entrusted to him.

37   Job, our ancestor. Job, our contemporary. His ordeal concerns all humanity. Did he ever lose his faith? If so, he rediscovered it within his rebellion. He demonstrated that faith is essential to rebellion, and that hope is possible beyond despair. The source of his hope was memory, as it must be ours. Because I remember, I despair. Because I remember, I have the duty to reject despair. I remember the killers, I remember the victims, even as I struggle to invent a thousand and one reasons to hope.

38   There may be times when we are powerless to prevent injustice, but there must never be a time when we fail to protest. The Talmud tells us that by saving a single human being, man can save the world. We may be powerless to open all the jails and free all the prisoners, but by declaring our solidarity with one prisoner, we indict all jailers. None of us is in a position to eliminate war, but it is our obligation to denounce it and expose it in all its hideousness. War leaves no victors, only victims. I began with the story of the Besht. And, like the Besht, mankind needs to remember more than ever. Mankind needs peace more than ever, for our entire planet, threatened by nuclear war, is in danger of total destruction. A destruction only man can provoke, only man can prevent. Mankind must remember that peace is not God's gift to his creatures, it is our gift to each other.

From Nobel Lectures, Peace 1981-1990, Editor-in-Charge Tore Frängsmyr, Editor Irwin Abrams, World Scientific Publishing Co., Singapore, 1997 Copyright © The Nobel Foundation 1986

Multiple-choice questions:

6. The opening of this lecture can best be described as a

   A. fable.

   B. parable.

   C. legend.

   D. anecdote.

   E. illustration.

7. Through the course of his lecture, Wiesel employs all of the following antitheses EXCEPT

   A. remembering and forgetting.

   B. war and peace.

   C. past and future.

   D. living and dead.

   E. wisdom and memory.

8. The "metamorphosis" to which Wiesel refers in paragraph 17 denotes a change from

    A. cultured to barbaric.

    B. educated to foolish.

    C. artistic to pragmatic.

    D. creative to destructive.

    E. aesthetic to ascetic.

9. As it is used in paragraph 22, the word *paucity* most likely means

    A. superiority.

    B. elimination.

    C. scarcity.

    D. preponderance.

    E. abhorrence.

10. The organizational and structural pattern of this lecture can best be described as

    A. linear.

    B. episodic.

    C. antithetical.

    D. cyclic.

    E. circular.

Free Response Item:

Carefully read Elie Wiesel's 1986 Nobel Peace Prize acceptance speech. Then, write a well-supported essay in which you analyze the techniques Wiesel uses to establish and maintain his rapport with his audience.

Humorous/Sarcastic

Remember that tone reflects the attitude of the writer toward his or her subject and toward his or her audience. If the writer considers the subject matter trivial or ridiculous—perhaps even a waste of time—this opinion might be reflected in the writer's tone. Similarly, if the writer considers his or her audience to be silly, irrational, or illogical, this, too, might be reflected in the tone.

Indeed, much of the most entertaining and memorable writing, fiction and nonfiction, achieves its value through a satiric, ironic, humorous, or sarcastic tone. Many popular columnists mock themselves and their lives in their writing, while many political and social commentators mock what they perceive to be the shortcomings in our political leaders or social trends.

The issue for the Advanced Placement scholar, of course, is not only to identify and name the tone, but also to analyze how the writer creates the tone and what effect the tone evokes in the reader.

Consider the following passage, a famous gubernatorial veto of a bill. In 1949, the General Assembly of the State of Illinois sent "An Act to Provide Protection to Insectivorous Birds by Restraining Cats" to Illinois governor Adlai Stevenson for his signature. Instead, he vetoed the bill and returned it to the legislature with the statement that follows. The passage has been annotated to point out to you the techniques—word choice, sentence structure, rhetorical and literary devices—that Stevenson used to convey, not only the fact of and reasons for the veto, but also his attitude toward the infamous "Cat Bill" and the legislature that sent the bill to him.

After you examine the passage and notes, look at how a student taking the AP Language exam might respond to multiple-choice questions and a free-response item dealing with the tone of this veto and its intended effect on its audience.

Famous "Cat Bill Veto," April 23, 1949

To the Honorable, the Members of the Senate of the Sixth-sixth General Assembly:

1 I herewith return, without my approval, Senate Bill No. 93, entitled, "An Act to Provide Protection to Insectivorous Birds by Restraining Cats."[1] This is the so-called "Cat Bill." I veto and withhold my approval from this Bill for the following reasons:[2]

2 It would impose fines on owners or keepers who permitted their cats to run at large off their premises. It would permit any person to capture, or call upon the police to pick up and imprison, cats at large. It would permit the use of traps. The bill would have statewide application—on farms, in villages, and in metropolitan centers.[3]

3 This legislation has been introduced in the past several sessions of the Legislature, and it has, over the years, been the source of much comment—not all of which has been in a serious vein.[4] It may be that the General Assembly has now seen fit to refer it to one who can view it with a fresh outlook. Whatever the reasons for passage at this session, I cannot believe there is a widespread public demand for this law or that it could, as a practical matter, be enforced.

Sample Student Commentary

[1] The title of the bill suggests that the purpose of the bill is actually to protect insect-eating birds.

[2] Much of the overly formal word choice is merely conventional. Legal and governmental documents still use highly formal, largely archaic, wording and phrasing.

[3] Although the members of the General Assembly know the terms of the bill, Stevenson's larger audience—the people of the State of Illinois—probably need this brief orientation.

[4] This is probably an understatement. Previous attempts at passing this bill have probably met with mockery.

4   Furthermore, I cannot agree that it should be the declared public policy of Illinois that a cat visiting a neighbor's yard or crossing the highway is a public nuisance.[5] It is in the nature of cats to do a certain amount of unescorted roaming. Many live with their owners in apartments or other restricted premises, and I doubt if we want to make their every brief foray an opportunity for a small game hunt by zealous citizens[6]—with traps or otherwise. I am afraid this Bill could only create discord, recrimination and enmity. Also consider the owner's dilemma: To escort a cat abroad on a leash is against the nature of the cat, and to permit it to venture forth for exercise[7] unattended into a night of new dangers is against the nature of the owner. Moreover, cats perform useful service, particularly in rural areas, in combating rodents— work they necessarily perform alone and without regard for property lines.

5   We are all interested in protecting certain varieties of birds. That cats destroy some birds, I well know, but I believe this legislation would further but little the worthy cause to which its proponents give such unselfish effort.[8] The problem of cat versus bird is as old as time. If we attempt to resolve it by legislation, who knows but what we may be called upon to take sides as well in the age old problems of dog versus cat, bird versus bird, or even bird versus worm.[9] In my opinion, the State of Illinois and its local governing bodies already have enough to do without trying to control feline delinquency.[10]

6   For these reasons, and not because I love birds the less or cats the more,[11] I veto and withhold my approval from Senate Bill No. 93.

Respectfully, ADLAI E. STEVENSON, Governor

Veto Messages of Adlai E. Stevenson, Governor of Illinois, on Senate and House Bills Passed by the 66th General Assembly of Illinois. Springfield: State of Illinois, 1949. 🍎

Sample Student Commentary

[5] Compare Stevenson's summary of this bill with the actual intent as suggested by the bill's title. "Public nuisance," in this context, is almost hyperbole.

[6] More hyperbole. The exaggeration highlights what Stevenson sees as the silliness of the provisions of the bill.

[7] Stevenson is not being openly mocking, but his use of formal, euphemistic words and phrases (escort a cat abroad, etc.) suggests his attitude. This out-of-place formality renders the topic laughable.

[8] Again, note the out-of-place formality of the language. Also note the apparent compliment to proponents of the bill.

[9] This predicting of growing problems in the future is a logical fallacy known as the slippery slope. In this context, however, Stevenson is probably being intentionally ridiculous.

[10] "Feline delinquency" is a play on words. In 1949, "juvenile delinquency" was still a relatively new concept, and state legislatures were still debating how to dispense justice to underage offenders.

[11] *In My Bondage and My Freedom*, Frederick Douglass wrote, "It is not that I love Maryland less, but freedom more." Stevenson is playing on this famous antithesis.

Sample multiple-choice questions:

1. **Which of the following understatements most clearly suggests Stevenson's attitude toward the "Cat Bill"?**

   A. "It would impose fines on owners or keepers who permitted their cats to run at large…"

   B. "…it has, over the years, been the source of much comment…"

   C. *"…not all of which has been in a serious vein."*

   D. "…I cannot believe there is a widespread public demand for this law…"

   E. "I doubt we want to make their every foray an opportunity for a small game hunt by zealous citizens"

2. **To convey his disdain for this bill, Stevenson employs all of the following EXCEPT**

   A. hyperbole.

   B. understatement.

   C. euphemism.

   D. word play.

   E. *double entendre.*

3. **Which of the following lines can most accurately be considered the climax of this passage?**

   A. "…dog versus cat, bird versus bird, or even bird versus worm."

   B. "…not because I love birds the less or cats the more…"

   C. "I am afraid this Bill could only create discord, recrimination and enmity."

   D. *"I cannot believe there is a widespread public demand for this law…"*

   E. "The bill would have statewide application…"

4. **Given the overall tone of this passage, Stevenson's dual purpose in writing is most likely to**

   A. amend and chastise.

   B. inform and reconcile.

   C. entertain and encourage.

   D. *reject and reprove.*

   E. cajole and condemn.

5. **Stevenson uses phrases like "herewith return," "veto and withhold my approval," "It would impose," "It would permit," etc., in order to maintain a tone of**

   A. *official legality.*

   B. extreme invective.

   C. sincere disapproval.

   D. lighthearted mockery.

   E. arbitrary authority.

Answers and Explanations:

1. (A) is a statement of fact, not an understatement. (B) is possibly an understatement, but it does not necessarily connote mockery or chastisement. (D) is merely a statement of opinion. (E) is both an opinion and a hyperbole, not an understatement. (C), however, suggests possible mockery while understating the extent or nature of the comments that have not all been in "a serious vein." **Thus, (C) is the best answer.**

2. (A) is eliminated by the line, "I doubt if we want to make their every brief foray an opportunity for *a small game hunt by zealous citizens—with traps* or otherwise." (B) is eliminated by "This legislation has…been the source of much comment—not all of which has been in a serious vein," and (C) by "To *escort a cat* abroad on a leash is against the nature of the cat, and to permit it to *venture forth for exercise…*" The pun "feline delinquents" eliminates (D). The language is, however, rather straightforward. There are no truly ambiguous words or expressions that could mean two things at the same time. **Thus (E) is the best answer.**

3. The climax being the highest point, the strongest reason for vetoing the bill, and the strongest rebuke of the bill and the legislature, (B) is eliminated because it is a humorous mock-allusion, but it is a part of the conclusion, after the climax has already been achieved. (C) and (D) are both statements of opinion, but neither is rich in either tone or content. (E) is a statement of fact and constitutes a part of the introduction to the passage. The slippery-slope in the fifth paragraph points out the ridiculous character of the bill by exaggerating the potential consequences. **Thus (A) is the best answer.**

4. (A) might tempt some, but Stevenson is vetoing the bill, not sending it back to the General Assembly for amendment. There is an element of information (B) in the passage, but it is a veto, not a plea for reconciliation between the legislative and executive branches. (C) is fairly easily eliminated because, while the passage might indeed be entertaining, it is, first and foremost, a legal document. (E) can also be easily eliminated when the reader realizes that Stevenson is not merely toying with the legislature, but *condemn* is too strong a word for his disapproval. As the passage is a veto, it is clearly Stevenson's purpose to reject the bill, and the hyperbole and understatement that lend sarcasm to the veto indicate an intent to mildly reprove the legislature that passed such a silly bill. **Thus, (D) is the best answer.**

5. Much of the success of this passage is that Stevenson manages to point out and criticize the silliness of the "Cat Bill" without stooping to insult and outright mockery (B). Even those who would read this passage as sincere (C), with no hint of irony, should realize that the quoted lines in this question neither denote nor connote disapproval. The overall tone of the piece is certainly lighthearted mockery (D), but again, the specific phrases quoted are neither lighthearted nor mocking. While the passage is authoritative—it

is a veto—Stevenson's exercise of this authority is certainly not without reason, or arbitrary. The passage is, however, an official veto from the governor. Certain language conventions must be observed in the drafting of such an official document. **Thus (A) is the best answer.**

Sample free-response item:

Carefully read Governor Adlai Stevenson's 1949 "Cat Bill Veto." Stevenson (1900-1965) was the governor of the State of Illinois from 1948 to 1952. In 1952 and four years later, he was the Democratic Party's candidate for President of the United States. He then served as the United States Ambassador to the United Nations. In this gubernatorial veto, Stevenson expresses clear and specific reasons for rejecting the bill and mildly chastises the Illinois General Assembly for sending such a trivial matter to him for his signature.

After you read Governor Stevenson's veto, write an essay in which you analyze the techniques Stevenson uses to maintain a delicate balance in tone between what is expected of an official legal document and the underlying derision he expresses for those who passed the bill.

Do not merely summarize the passage.

Sample Student Essay

Adlai Stevenson's famous 1949 "Cat Bill Veto," while ostensibly a simple veto message to the General Assembly of Illinois, is also a vehicle by which Governor Stevenson expresses disdain for the Legislature, who have passed what he sees as an unnecessary bill. While writing in a style appropriate for a legal document and avoiding outright insult, Mr. Stevenson nevertheless manages to convey his disdain through the use of several rhetorical techniques. Skillfully utilizing hyperbole, understatement, and overly formal language, Stevenson makes clear to the reader that he will not abide what he sees as a frivolous use of time by the Legislature.

The stated purpose of the bill is to protect birds by ensuring that cats are not allowed to wander unrestricted. A great divide exists between the opinions of Mr. Stevenson and those of the Legislature concerning the urgency of this problem. In the fourth paragraph, Stevenson uses hyperbole to exaggerate what will happen as a result of the bill. He claims that the bill's passing will cause the free roaming of cats to be labeled a "public nuisance" and will result in "small game hunt[s]," creating "discord, recrimination, and enmity" among the citizens of Illinois. By exaggerating what will happen as a result of the bill's passing, Stevenson is effectively chastising the Legislature by showing them that their solution is disproportionate to the problem.

Governor Stevenson also believes that the problem the bill purports to solve is not much of a problem at all. He uses understatement in the third paragraph to chide the Legislature for sending a frivolous bill to his desk. The key to this paragraph is the first sentence, which reads, "This legislation has been introduced in the past several sessions of the Legislature, and it has, over the years, been the source of much comment—not all of which has been in a serious vein." The understatement lies in the second half of the sentence. Were Stevenson to have written that the bill has been openly joked about in Legislative sessions, the tone of the veto message would have turned to one of clear disdain instead of gentle chastising. Because this section comes so early in the veto message, he would have had to maintain that tone throughout the rest of the document in order to achieve stylistic consistency, as sudden shifts of tone can be jarring for the reader. Because this is a veto message, Stevenson does not believe the bill merits passing. If this is the case, and the Legislature has discussed this bill in its past several sessions, then it is clear to the reader that Mr. Stevenson believes the Legislature has used a substantial portion of its time on a project without merit.

The Legislature believes that the problem of cats attacking birds is so important that a bill must be passed to solve it. Stevenson clearly disagrees, and he uses excessively formal language in an ironic manner to rebuke the Legislature while avoiding insulting them outright. Governor Stevenson writes at a level of formality more appropriate for a rousing speech than for a simple message to the Legislature. The disparity between the level of formality required and that which is delivered highlights the absurdity of the bill. Surely, only landmark pieces of legislation would be written about in the flowery language Stevenson employs, but the reader has been aware since the second paragraph that he believes the bill is ill-conceived, not desired by the public, and impossible to enforce. By delivering his veto message in language better suited to important purposes, the Governor subtly informs the Legislature that they should be spending time on important matters, not pointless ones such as the "Cat Bill."

In using these rhetorical devices, Stevenson presents the "Cat Bill" as a complete waste of time while managing not to insult the Legislature directly. Though it is possible that members of the Legislature may have been offended by the arch manner in which he couches his dissent, the message itself meets the standards for a gubernatorial veto. Governor Stevenson's veto message is playful but serious, putting an end to the "Cat Bill" without shaming the Legislature. ❦

Exercise Three:

Questions 11-15. Read the following passage carefully before you choose your answers.

This passage contains three accounts of a speech delivered by former slave, abolitionist, and feminist Sojourner Truth.

1   THE NEARLY EPIC CHARACTER, Sojourner Truth, was born a slave in New York State in 1797. As a slave, she was given the name Isabella Baumfree. She escaped slavery in 1827 and took the name Sojourner Truth in 1843 when she embarked on her speaking endeavor, becoming a well-known opponent of slavery and supporter of women's rights. She delivered her best-known speech—which eventually came to be known as "Ain't I a Woman?"—at the Women's Convention in Akron, Ohio, on May 29, 1851.

2   The speeches that follow are the three printed versions of Ms. Truth's address that have been widely circulated. The first was published a month after the convention by Marius Robinson, an abolitionist and newspaper editor who had attended the convention.

3 **Sojourner Truth's address as it appeared in the *Anti-Slavery Bugle* of Salem, Ohio, June 1851:**

I want to say a few words about this matter. I am a woman's rights. I have as much muscle as any man, and can do as much work as any man. I have plowed and reaped and husked and chopped and mowed, and can any man do more than that? I have heard much about the sexes being equal. I can carry as much as any man, and can eat as much too, if I can get it. I am as strong as any man that is now. As for intellect, all I can say is, if a woman have a pint, and a man a quart—why can't she have her little pint full? You need not be afraid to give us our rights for fear we will take too much,—for we can't take more than our pint'll hold. The poor men seems to be all in confusion, and don't know what to do. Why children, if you have woman's rights, give it to her and you will feel better. You will have your own rights, and they won't be so much trouble. I can't read, but I can hear. I have heard the bible and have learned that Eve caused man to sin. Well, if woman upset the world, do give her a chance to set it right side up again. The Lady has spoken about Jesus, how he never spurned woman from him, and she was right. When Lazarus died, Mary and Martha came to him with faith and love and besought him to raise their brother. And Jesus wept and Lazarus came forth. And how came Jesus into the world? Through God who created him and the woman who bore him. Man, where was your part? But the women are coming up blessed be God and a few of the men are coming up with them. But man is in a tight place, the poor slave is on him, woman is coming on him, he is surely between a hawk and a buzzard.

4   Twelve years later, in May 1863, Frances Dana Gage, a feminist and abolitionist activist and writer, who had presided over the 1851 Akron convention, published a very different version—different in both content and tone. Gage's version was published again in 1875, 1881, and 1889 and became the most familiar account. The problems presented in accepting this account as authoritative include Gage's inclusion of the oft-repeated phrase, "Ain't I a Woman?"; this has come to be used as the speech's title, and the fact that Gage attributes a southern dialect to Ms. Truth, when in fact, Truth had been a slave in New York. By her own accounts, Sojourner Truth gave birth to five children, one of whom was sold into slavery—not the thirteen claimed by Gage.

5 It was in her 1863 recollection of the Convention and Truth's speech that Gage created the legend that the former slave braved a mob of angry white men in order to make her address, which won the mob's sympathy. In 1851, however, Gage herself had reported that the city of Akron had welcomed the women's convention, and the crowd to which Truth spoke was friendly and supportive.

6 **Sojourner Truth's address as republished by Frances Gage in 1863 including Gage's recreation of the dialect in which Ms. Truth allegedly delivered her address and both the speaker's and the crowd's reactions:**

Wall, chilern, whar dar is so much racket dar must be somethin' out o' kilter. I tink dat 'twixt de niggers of de Souf and de womin at de Norf, all talkin' 'bout rights, de white men will be in a fix pretty soon. But what's all dis here talkin"bout?

Dat man ober dar say dat womin needs to be helped into carriages, and lifted ober ditches, and to hab de best place everywhar. Nobody eber helps me into carriages, or ober mud-puddles, or gibs me any best place!" [And raising herself to her full height, and her voice to a pitch like rolling thunders, she asked] "And a'n't I a woman? Look at me! Look at me! Look at my arm! [and she bared her right arm to the shoulder, showing her tremendous muscular power]. I have ploughed, and planted, and gathered into barns, and no man could head me! And a'n't I a woman? I could work as much and eat as much as a man—when I could get it—and bear de lash as well! And a'n't I a woman? I have borne thirteen chilern, and seen 'em mos' all sold off to slavery, and when I cried out with my mother's grief, none but Jesus heard me! And a'n't I a woman?

7 Den dey talks 'bout dis ting in de head; what dis dey call it? ["Intellect," whispered some one near.] "Dat's it, honey. What's dat got to do wid womin's rights or nigger's rights? If my cup won't hold but a pint, and yourn holds a quart, wouldn't ye be mean not to let me have my little half-measure full?" [And she pointed her significant finger, and sent a keen glance at the minister who had made the argument. The cheering was long and loud.]

8 Den dat little man in black dar, he say women can't have as much rights as men, 'cause Christ wan't a woman! Whar did your Christ come from?" [Rolling thunder couldn't have stilled that crowd, as did those deep, wonderful tones, as she stood there with outstretched arms and eyes of fire. Raising her voice still louder, she repeated,] "Whar did your Christ come from? From God and a woman! Man had nothin' to do wid Him." [Oh, what a rebuke that was to that little man.]

9 [Turning again to another objector, she took up the defense of Mother Eve. I can not follow her through it all. It was pointed, and witty, and solemn; eliciting at almost every sentence deafening applause; and she ended by asserting:] "If de fust woman God ever made was strong enough to turn de world upside down all alone, dese women togedder [and she glanced her eye over the platform] ought to be able to turn it back, and get it right side up again! And now dey is asking to do it, de men better let 'em." [Long-continued cheering greeted this.] "Bleeged to ye for hearin' on me, and now old Sojourner han't got nothin' more to say."

10 **Later, Frances Gage's version of the speech began to appear in standard, modern English:**
Well, children, where there is so much racket there must be something out of kilter. I think that 'twixt the negroes of the South and the women at the North, all talking about rights, the white men will be in a fix pretty soon. But what's all this here talking about?

11   That man over there says that women need to be helped into carriages, and lifted over ditches, and to have the best place everywhere. Nobody ever helps me into carriages, or over mud-puddles, or gives me any best place! And ain't I a woman? Look at me! Look at my arm! I have ploughed and planted, and gathered into barns, and no man could head me! And ain't I a woman? I could work as much and eat as much as a man—when I could get it—and bear the lash as well! And ain't I a woman? I have borne thirteen children, and seen most all sold off to slavery, and when I cried out with my mother's grief, none but Jesus heard me! And ain't I a woman?

12   Then they talk about this thing in the head; what's this they call it? [member of audience whispers, "intellect"] That's it, honey. What's that got to do with women's rights or negroes' rights? If my cup won't hold but a pint, and yours holds a quart, wouldn't you be mean not to let me have my little half measure full?

13   Then that little man in black there, he says women can't have as much rights as men, 'cause Christ wasn't a woman! Where did your Christ come from? Where did your Christ come from? From God and a woman! Man had nothing to do with Him.

14   If the first woman God ever made was strong enough to turn the world upside down all alone, these women together ought to be able to turn it back, and get it right side up again! And now they is asking to do it, the men better let them.

15   Obliged to you for hearing me, and now old Sojourner ain't got nothing more to say. ॐ

Multiple-choice questions:

11. The evolution of the speech from the first to the third accounts can best be described as from
    A. reasoned to impassioned.
    B. intellectual to uneducated.
    C. formal to colloquial.
    D. ambivalent to purposeful.
    E. respectful to provocative.

12. The repeated phrase, "Ain't I a woman," can best be described as a(n)

A. anaphora.

B. epistrophe.

C. prologue.

D. epigram.

E. refrain.

13. Truth's addressing the members of her audience as "children" is most likely intended to convey her

A. affection.

B. confusion.

C. disdain.

D. rancor.

E. uncertainty.

14. Editor Frances Gage's use of bracketed text is most likely intended to help her

A. clarify Truth's language.

B. recreate the audience's experience.

C. intensify the speech's passion.

D. disparage Sojourner Truth.

E. glamorize the character of the speaker.

15. What purpose or intent is suggested by the evolution of the speech, from the earliest account to the most recent?

A. to heighten reader sympathy

B. to broaden audience appeal

C. to intensify reader reaction

D. to seek public approval

E. to influence public opinion

Free Response Item:

Carefully read the various accounts of Sojourner Truth's famous address. Then, write an essay in which you analyze the changes—in both language and content—made by the editors of each speech, noting how the changes both alter and preserve what has come to be regarded as Truth's distinctive voice. Do not merely review or summarize the various alterations.

12. The repeated phrase "Ain't I a woman," can best be described as a(n)

15. What purpose or intent is suggested by the evolution of the speech, from the earliest accounts to the most recent?
   E. to influence public opinion

Analyzing structure and organizational patterns

CHAPTER 4

JUST AS TONE AND MOOD are easily confused or taken to be synonymous, *structure* and *organization* are often mistaken to mean the same thing. The truth is, however, that the careful reader and writer know that the two, while related, are different aspects of the written piece and serve fairly specific purposes.

Structure suggests the presentation and development of information across the overall piece. The five paragraph essay has a formal, though basic, structure. The formal introduction, body, and conclusion describes a structure. To outline the progression of ideas from the first word of the passage to the concluding sentence, to note how one idea transitions to the next and how the reader's attention is drawn to the final point is a method examining the structure of the piece.

The *organization* or *organizational pattern* has to do with how the information is presented within the piece. The writer may develop a thesis by mentioning minor points first and lead up to the climactic, big idea. A writer might focus first on physical actions and reactions and then move into thoughts and feelings. An organizational pattern like thesis-antithesis might repeat itself several times in the same article, each paragraph revealing the opposing sides of an argument.

Both structure and organization reveal something about the author's purpose, the intended audience, and the relationship of author to reader to subject.

As with the other elements of writing, the critic and student must sometimes examine a passage, not only with the intent of identifying whether the piece is tightly, formally, or casually structured and how the information within the passage is organized, but also to discern how the structure and organization helps the writer achieve his or her purpose.

Unlike literary and rhetorical devices, logical fallacies, and the like, various structures and organizational patterns do not have names by which they can be identified and defined. Certainly, one can talk about "narrative structure," but even within that formal sounding scheme is an infinite array of variations. At best, a reader, scholar, or critic can describe the structure or organizational pattern of a passage.

As a student, you are probably familiar with terms like *thesis-proof, comparison-contrast*, and so on. These describe the organizational patterns within a passage, how the information is presented within each paragraph and from one paragraph to another. Terms like *linear, circular*, and *cyclic* can be used to describe the progression of material throughout the overall passage—how the passage is structured.

Linear passages proceed from point A to B, then to point C, eventually arriving at their final point. It is a common structure for informative and persuasive essays. *Circular* passages may appear linear, proceeding from point to point until the reader finds that the writer has brought the passage back to point A—though, certainly, the reader understands point A with more depth or clarity than he or she did at the beginning of the passage. *Cyclic* passages lead from point A to a concluding point, but their progression is not a straight line. Rather, the writer of such a passage will occasionally diverge from the main thread of ideas to provide the reader with additional information or to expand upon personal feelings about the topic. Always, however, the writer eventually returns to the point at which he or she began and then proceeds to the next point. It takes skillful writers to construct such passages and not lose themselves or the reader along the way.

All writing is structured, and the structure of a professional piece is always intentional. Even an apparent lack of structure is a structure. Because the writer may be writing for purely personal reasons, and because he or she may not want to be overly obvious in trying to attain his or her purpose, the writer may choose a casual form for the passage. Many modern writers of nonfiction prefer casual or informal structures in order to establish and maintain a conversational tone and an intimacy with the reader that might be lost if the passage were more formally structured.

The issue for the Advanced Placement scholar, of course, is not only to identify and name a passage's structure and organizational pattern, but to analyze how the writer has crafted the passage so that it meets his or her purpose, conveying the information, expressing the view, and affecting the reader in the desired ways.

Read the following speech, presented by a newly elected Prime Minister of Great Britain, Winston Churchill on the eve of Britain's official involvement in World War II. It has been annotated to point out to you the techniques: word choice, sentence structure, use of rhetorical devices that Churchill uses to both inform and encourage the House of Commons to take the appropriate action.

After you examine the passage and the accompanying notes, look at how a student taking the AP Language exam might respond to multiple-choice questions and a free-response item dealing with how Churchill has structured his speech to achieve the greatest impact in a relatively small amount of time.

On his first entrance into the House of Commons as Britain's new Prime Minister on 13 May 1940, Winston Churchill received only a lukewarm reception from the assembly. Outgoing Prime Minister Neville Chamberlain was heartily cheered. The new and less-popular Prime Minister then made the following statement. It was the beginning of World War II. The armies of Adolf Hitler were swarming across Europe. They seemed unstoppable as they conquered country after country. Eventually, even the survival of Britain itself seemed doubtful. Churchill's speech has come to be regarded as one of the greatest national calls-to-arms ever proclaimed.

Blood, Sweat and Tears
by Sir Winston Churchill

MAY 13TH 1940

1 ON FRIDAY EVENING LAST, I received from His Majesty the mission to form a new administration. It was the evident will of' Parliament and the nation that this should be conceived on the broadest possible basis and that it should include all parties.[1]

2 I have already completed the most important part of this task.

3 A war cabinet has been formed of five members, representing, with the Labour, Opposition, and Liberals, the unity of the nation. It was necessary that this should be done in one single day on account of the extreme urgency and rigor of events.[2] Other key positions were filled yesterday. I am submitting a further list to the king tonight. I hope to complete the appointment of principal ministers during tomorrow.[3]

4 The appointment of other ministers usually takes a little longer. I trust when Parliament meets again this part of my task will be completed and that the administration will be complete in all respects. I considered it in the public interest to suggest to the Speaker that the House should be summoned today. At the end of today's proceedings, the adjournment of the House will be proposed until May 21 with provision for earlier meeting if need be. Business for that will be notified to MPs at the earliest opportunity.

5 I now invite the House by a resolution to record its approval of the steps taken and declare its confidence in the new government.[4]

6 The resolution:

7 "That this House welcomes the formation of a government representing the united and inflexible resolve of the nation to prosecute the war with Germany to a victorious conclusion."

8 To form an administration of this scale and complexity is a serious undertaking in

---

Sample Student Commentary

[1] Churchill begins with a fairly typical introduction. Starting by specifying when he was instructed to create the new administration suggests the information here may be organized in chronological order.

[2] This informative sentence looks both to the past—the formation of the war cabinet—and the future—the source of the urgency.

[3] The rest of the paragraph continues the chronological order.

[4] This short paragraph constitutes a clear and formal transition.

itself. But we are in the preliminary phase of one of the greatest battles in history. We are in action at many other points—in Norway and in Holland—and we have to be prepared in the Mediterranean. The air battle is continuing, and many preparations have to be made here at home.

9   In this crisis I think I may be pardoned if I do not address the House at any length today, and I hope that any of my friends and colleagues or former colleagues who are affected by the political reconstruction will make all allowances for any lack of ceremony with which it has been necessary to act.

10   I say to the House as I said to ministers who have joined this government, I have nothing to offer but blood, toil, tears, and sweat. We have before us an ordeal of the most grievous kind. We have before us many, many months of struggle and suffering.

11   You ask, what is our policy? I say it is to wage war by land, sea, and air. War with all our might and with all the strength God has given us, and to wage war against a monstrous tyranny never surpassed in the dark and lamentable catalogue of human crime. That is our policy.

12   You ask, what is our aim?[5] I can answer in one word. It is victory. Victory at all costs—Victory in spite of all terrors—Victory, however long and hard the road may be, for without victory there is no survival.

13   Let that be realized. No survival for the British Empire, no survival for all that the British Empire has stood for, no survival[6] for the urge, the impulse of the ages, that mankind shall move forward toward his goal.

14   I take up my task in buoyancy and hope.[7] I feel sure that our cause will not be suffered to fail among men. I feel entitled at this juncture, at this time, to claim the aid of all and to say, "Come then, let us go forward together with our united strength." ❧

Sample Student Commentary

[5] As this is a speech being delivered directly to Churchill's intended audience, the use of hypophora as a transition is particularly effective.

[6] The anaphora in both this and the preceding paragraphs contributes not only to emphasis, but also to the organization of ideas.

[7] Note the circular nature of the speech. Churchill returns to where he began—the task of forming a new administration to face the mounting crisis.

Sample multiple-choice questions:

1. The primary purpose of this speech is most likely to

A. inspire the nation.

B. defend Churchill's position.

C. *inform the Parliament.*

D. solicit guidance.

E. rectify misapprehensions.

2. The information presented in the paragraph following the resolution strongly suggests that war with Germany

    A. is imminent.

    B. has already begun.

    C. cannot be avoided.

    D. cannot be won.

    E. will be long and difficult.

3. The "evident will" of Parliament in the first paragraph, and Churchill's final entreaty suggest that one of Churchill's goals is to

    A. defeat the Nazis.

    B. lead an effective government.

    C. unify a fractious nation.

    D. encourage a nervous Parliament.

    E. oversee an efficient war effort.

4. What important structural function does the anaphora in the tenth and eleventh paragraphs serve?

    A. connect the ideas of victory and survival

    B. transition between the topics of these two paragraphs

    C. contrast the expectation of victory with the fear of failure

    D. reconcile the need for victory with the desire to survive

    E. prepare the reader for the final entreaty

5. The two-fold function of the hypophoras in the two paragraphs that begin, "You ask..." is transition and

    A. contrast.

    B. emphasis.

    C. elaboration.

    D. encouragement.

    E. rapport.

Answers and Explanations:

1. (A) might tempt those students who actually read the introductory note, but the inspirational aspect of the speech is a relatively small portion, rhetorically positioned to end the speech on a powerful note. This speech was also delivered before the House of Commons, not to the nation as a whole. (B) might also be mildly tempting, but there is no evidence that Churchill's call to war or his request for the resolution is being challenged; nor is there evidence that the members do not understand the situation with which they are faced (E). (D) is fairly easily eliminated by the fact that Churchill is informing the House, not asking what has been done and remains to do. **(C), then, is the best answer.**

The speech begins with Churchill's informing the House of his mandate from the king and continues with a description of what he has already done and what he still needs to do—with a proposed timeline for when he intends to accomplish the rest.

2. While paragraph 8, "we are in the preliminary phase of one of the greatest battles in history," might suggest (A), the next two sentences: "We are in action at many other points...The air battle is continuing..." **clearly establishes (B) as the correct answer.** (C) is true but not the most compelling choice. (E) is likewise true, but not mentioned in the paragraph in question. (D) is refuted by the sentiment expressed in the rest of the speech.

3. The "evident will" is that Churchill's administration "should include all parties." His final entreaty is for "us [the nation] to go forward together with our united strength." (A) is clearly one of Churchill's goals, but it is not suggested in the final sentence of the speech. (B) is logical, but it is an inference rather than anything Churchill himself admits. There is nothing in the speech to suggest that Parliament is nervous (D). (E) is also a logical inference, given Churchill's desire to move swiftly with the formation of his government, but it is not a focus of the sentence in question. Churchill's stated endeavor to establish his government "on the broadest possible basis" and his entreaty to face the crisis with "united strength" **clearly establish (C) as the best answer.**

4. The anaphora in the tenth paragraph involves the word *victory*, and the anaphora in the eleventh paragraph involves the phrase *no survival*. Since the first occurrence of the second anaphora appears in the tenth paragraph in the context that the one is necessary for the other, (B) is not an attractive choice. Churchill does not admit to a fear of failure (C); he merely asserts that there can be no survival without victory. As victory and survival are not contradictory, they do not need to be reconciled (D). (E) has some truth, but it is not the most compelling choice. The concatenation of the *victory* anaphora with the *no survival* anaphora, however, connects (A) the two ideas and provides unity. **Thus, (A) is the best answer.**

5. There is no contrast between waging war and winning, so (A) is not an attractive choice. As the second paragraph does transition to a new, though related topic (victory) and not a further discussion of the previous one (waging war), (B) and (C) are also not attractive. (D) might be mildly tempting, but Churchill expresses more fervor and the need to prevail than confidence that they will prevail. By directly addressing his audience ("You ask...") and involving them in a conversation of sorts, it is clear that Churchill is building rapport with a group that does not necessarily love him. **Thus, (E) is the best answer.**

Sample free-response item:

Carefully read Winston Churchill's famous *Blood, Sweat, and Tears* speech, delivered before the British House of Commons on 13 May 1940. Churchill, newly elected to the office of Prime Minister, updates the House of Commons on his progress in the establishment of his administration and war cabinet and on the British preparedness to wage a successful war against Nazi Germany.

After reading the passage, write an essay in which you describe how Churchill's use of structural and organizational elements and linguistic and rhetorical devices contributes to the clarity and power of this brief address. Avoid summary.

Sample Student Essay

In his "Blood, Sweat, and Tears" speech, Winston Churchill delivers a brief and rousing speech to the British House of Commons in which he outlines the direction Britain will take while he is in office. Through careful organization, Churchill presents this information in a way that is designed to make a powerful impact upon the listener. The contrast between the two halves of the speech—the first half being strictly informational and formal, the second being declaratory and rousing through the use of several rhetorical techniques—imbues Churchill's words with urgency and clarity and leaves no room for argument.

The speech can be considered to have two halves. The first half comprises Churchill's explanation to the British House of Commons of both what he has already done and what he intends to do. This information is delivered with brief formality; as an address to the House of Commons, the message must be formal, and this portion of the speech is deliberately brief in order to match the sense of urgency with which Churchill and the British government must act. The language fits Churchill's purpose: there are no flashy turns of phrase or rhetorical tricks to be found in this section, as none would be necessary for such a simple address. Churchill is economical with his language here, making the transition to the second half that much more effective.

What begins as a simple address concerning governmental duties becomes something more in the second half of the speech, as the tone changes from one of simply delivering information to one of rousing people to action. After a short transition in which he explains the crisis facing Britain, Churchill employs several rhetorical devices— in stirring contrast to the first half of the speech. Churchill makes his position known to the House through the use of hypophora. In two short paragraphs, Churchill lays out both the policy and the goal of the British government, leaving little room for argument. As Churchill is the incoming Prime Minister, this communicates to the House that he is prepared for the office and more than likely makes the members more positively disposed toward him. By posing these questions and answering them himself, Churchill also maintains the theme of urgent action that pervades this speech; as there is no time for petty argument, Churchill does not give the House the opportunity to argue. Their objectives have been clearly stated, and that is what they shall strive for.

In naming the purpose and goal of the new government, Churchill also uses anaphora for emphasis. When he mentions that their policy is to wage war "by land, sea, and air", he repeats the word "war" two more times in quick succession. When he names their purpose as "victory", he repeats this as well. There is a clear and logical procession through these ideas and into the next paragraph, in which he again uses anaphora to emphasize that without victory there is "no survival." Through their policy of waging war "with all the strength God has given" them, they will achieve victory. By achieving victory, they also achieve survival. The logical structure of the speech leads directly to these ideas being inextricably associated with one another.

With a popular Prime Minister leaving office, Churchill's ascension could have been a time of great turmoil within the British government. By laying out his policies and goals in a clear and powerful manner, Churchill signals to the House of Commons that he has already prepared for the task at hand. The brevity of the message suggests urgency, and Churchill's no-nonsense attitude ensures that the House will see the onset of World War II in the same manner. The time for infighting and indecision is past, and strong, firm leadership is required in difficult times. Through this speech, Churchill effectively sets the agenda, while also building support in a time of transition. ❧

Exercise One:

Questions 1-5. Read the following passage carefully before you choose your answers.

John Fitzgerald Kennedy (1917-1963) was the thirty-fifth President of the United States, defeating Richard Nixon in one of the closest presidential elections in American history. At his inauguration, Kennedy became the second-youngest President, the first President born in the twentieth century, and the first Boy Scout to become President. He won the 1957 Pulitzer Prize for biography for his bestselling Profiles in Courage, the only President to have won this award. His brief term in office was marked by such historical events as the Bay of Pigs Invasion, the Cuban Missile Crisis, the building of the Berlin Wall and the resultant Berlin Airlift, the beginning of the Space Race with the Soviet Union, the advancement of the Civil Rights Movement, and the beginning of the Vietnam conflict. He was assassinated on November 22, 1963, at the age of 46 and became one of only two Presidents to be buried in Arlington National Cemetery.

His inaugural address, delivered on Friday, January 20, 1961, is well remembered as both a look backward at the recent trials experienced by the United States and a look forward to triumphs yet to come. Recognizing the rancor of the election that he has recently won, Kennedy calls for reconciliation and unification, even as he challenges all Americans to take up the task that lies before them.

John F. Kennedy *Inaugural Address*

FRIDAY, JANUARY 20, 1961

1 VICE PRESIDENT JOHNSON, Mr. Speaker, Mr. Chief Justice, President Eisenhower, Vice President Nixon, President Truman, reverend clergy, fellow citizens, we observe today not a victory of party, but a celebration of freedom—symbolizing an end, as well as a beginning—signifying renewal, as well as change. For I have sworn before you and Almighty God the same solemn oath our forebears prescribed nearly a century and three quarters ago.

2 The world is very different now. For man holds in his mortal hands the power to abolish all forms of human poverty and all forms of human life. And yet the same revolutionary beliefs for which our forebears fought are still at issue around the globe—the belief that the rights of man come not from the generosity of the state, but from the hand of God.

3 We dare not forget today that we are the heirs of that first revolution. Let the word go forth from this time and place, to friend and foe alike, that the torch has been passed to a new generation of Americans—born in this century, tempered by war, disciplined by a hard and bitter peace, proud of our ancient heritage—and unwilling to witness or permit the slow undoing of those human rights to which this Nation has always been committed, and to which we are committed today at home and around the world.

4 Let every nation know, whether it wishes us well or ill, that we shall pay any price, bear any burden, meet any hardship, support any friend, oppose any foe, in order to assure the survival and the success of liberty.

5 This much we pledge—and more.

6 To those old allies whose cultural and spiritual origins we share, we pledge the loyalty of faithful friends. United, there is little we cannot do in a host of cooperative ventures. Divided, there is little we can do—for we dare not meet a powerful challenge at odds and split asunder.

7 To those new States whom we welcome to the ranks of the free, we pledge our word that one form of colonial control shall not have passed away merely to be replaced by a far more iron tyranny. We shall not always expect to find them supporting our view. But we shall always hope to find them strongly supporting their own freedom—and to remember that, in the past, those who foolishly sought power by riding the back of the tiger ended up inside.

8 To those peoples in the huts and villages across the globe struggling to break the bonds of mass misery, we pledge our best efforts to help them help themselves, for whatever period is required—not because the Communists may be doing it, not because we seek their votes, but because it is right. If a free society cannot help the many who are poor, it cannot save the few who are rich.

9 To our sister republics south of our border, we offer a special pledge—to convert our good words into good deeds—in a new alliance for progress—to assist free men and free governments in casting off the chains of poverty. But this peaceful revolution of hope cannot become the prey of hostile powers. Let all our neighbors know that we shall join with them to oppose aggression or subversion anywhere in the Americas. And let every other power know that this Hemisphere intends to remain the master of its own house.

10   To that world assembly of sovereign states, the United Nations, our last best hope in an age where the instruments of war have far outpaced the instruments of peace, we renew our pledge of support—to prevent it from becoming merely a forum for invective—to strengthen its shield of the new and the weak—and to enlarge the area in which its writ may run.

11   Finally, to those nations who would make themselves our adversary, we offer not a pledge but a request: that both sides begin anew the quest for peace, before the dark powers of destruction unleashed by science engulf all humanity in planned or accidental self-destruction.

12   We dare not tempt them with weakness. For only when our arms are sufficient beyond doubt can we be certain beyond doubt that they will never be employed.

13   But neither can two great and powerful groups of nations take comfort from our present course—both sides overburdened by the cost of modern weapons, both rightly alarmed by the steady spread of the deadly atom, yet both racing to alter that uncertain balance of terror that stays the hand of mankind's final war.

14   So let us begin anew—remembering on both sides that civility is not a sign of weakness, and sincerity is always subject to proof. Let us never negotiate out of fear. But let us never fear to negotiate.

15   Let both sides explore what problems unite us instead of belaboring those problems which divide us.

16   Let both sides, for the first time, formulate serious and precise proposals for the inspection and control of arms—and bring the absolute power to destroy other nations under the absolute control of all nations.

17   Let both sides seek to invoke the wonders of science instead of its terrors. Together let us explore the stars, conquer the deserts, eradicate disease, tap the ocean depths, and encourage the arts and commerce.

18   Let both sides unite to heed in all corners of the earth the command of Isaiah—to "undo the heavy burdens...and to let the oppressed go free."

19   And if a beachhead of cooperation may push back the jungle of suspicion, let both sides join in creating a new endeavor, not a new balance of power, but a new world of law, where the strong are just and the weak secure and the peace preserved.

20   All this will not be finished in the first 100 days. Nor will it be finished in the first 1,000 days, nor in the life of this Administration, nor even perhaps in our lifetime on this planet. But let us begin.

21   In your hands, my fellow citizens, more than in mine, will rest the final success or failure of our course. Since this country was founded, each generation of Americans has been summoned to give testimony to its national loyalty. The graves of young Americans who answered the call to service surround the globe.

22   Now, the trumpet summons us again—not as a call to bear arms, though arms we need; not as a call to battle, though embattled we are—but a call to bear the burden of a long twilight struggle, year in and year out, "rejoicing in hope, patient in tribulation"—a struggle against the common enemies of man: tyranny, poverty, disease, and war itself.

23   Can we forge against these enemies a grand and global alliance, North and South, East and West, that can assure a more fruitful life for all mankind? Will you join in that historic effort?

24   In the long history of the world, only a few generations have been granted the role of defending freedom in its hour of maximum danger. I do not shrink from this responsibility—I welcome it. I do not believe that any of us would exchange places with any other people or any other generation. The energy, the faith, the devotion which we bring to this endeavor will light our country and all who serve it—and the glow from that fire can truly light the world.

25   And so, my fellow Americans: ask not what your country can do for you—ask what you can do for your country.

26   My fellow citizens of the world: ask not what America will do for you, but what together we can do for the freedom of man.

27   Finally, whether you are citizens of America or citizens of the world, ask of us the same high standards of strength and sacrifice which we ask of you. With a good conscience our only sure reward, with history the final judge of our deeds, let us go forth to lead the land we love, asking His blessing and His help, but knowing that here on earth God's work must truly be our own. ❧

Multiple-choice questions:

1. All of the following are identifiable segments of Kennedy's speech EXCEPT the

  A. introduction.

  B. address to the world.

  C. challenge to America's enemies.

  D. conciliation.

  E. challenge to the American people.

2. The oxymoron in the second paragraph elaborates upon which of the following statements?

  A. The world is very different now. (paragraph 2)

  B. ...the same revolutionary beliefs...are still at issue around the globe... (paragraph 2)

  C. ...we observe today not a victory of party, but a celebration of freedom... (paragraph 1)

  D. We dare not forget today we are the heirs of that first revolution. (paragraph 3)

  E. The torch has been passed to a new generation. (paragraph 3)

3. The brief paragraph, "This much we pledge—and more," (paragraph 5) functions primarily as a(n)

  A. introduction.

  B. conclusion.

  C. thesis.

  D. premise.

  E. transition.

4. One of the chief rhetorical devices Kennedy uses to provide a sense of formal structure to his speech is
   A. epistrophe.
   B. apostrophe.
   C. anaphora.
   D. parallelism.
   E. chiasmus.

5. Which of the following best describes the overall organizational pattern of the speech?
   A. general to specific
   B. order of magnitude
   C. local to global
   D. thesis to antithesis
   E. past to future

Free Response Item:

Carefully read President John F. Kennedy's *Inaugural Address*. Then, write a well-reasoned and well-supported essay in which you analyze how Kennedy uses rhetorical devices to maintain a conversational tone, yet a clear and compelling structure.

Now, consider the following passage. Published in the *Birmingham News* on April 12, 1963, "A Call for Unity" is a statement made by eight white Alabama clergymen. In it, these clergymen agree that social injustice exists, but they argue that the battle against racial segregation is best fought in the courts, not in the streets. Dr. Martin Luther King, Jr., had been invited to Birmingham to organize a series of non-violent protests. On April 6, twenty-nine protestors were arrested as they marched from the Gaston Motel to the Birmingham Federal Building. King himself was arrested during a similar protest on April 12. It was while in jail that Dr. King read this statement.

The clergymen's statement has been annotated to point out to you the various techniques and conventions used by writers to convey their views in a manner that will be clear and powerful to their readers. After you examine the passage and the accompanying notes, look at how a student taking the AP Language exam might respond to multiple-choice questions and a free-response item dealing with how the clergymen achieve their purpose.

A Call for Unity

1 WE THE UNDERSIGNED CLERGYMEN[1] are among those who, in January, issued[2] "an appeal for law and order and common sense," in dealing with racial problems in Alabama. We expressed understanding that honest convictions in racial matters could properly be pursued in the courts, but urged that decisions of those courts should in the meantime be peacefully obeyed.[3]

2 Since that time there had been some evidence of increased forbearance and a willingness to face facts. Responsible citizens have undertaken to work on various problems which cause racial friction and unrest. In Birmingham, recent public events have given indication that we all have opportunity for a new constructive and realistic approach to racial problems.[4]

3 However,[5] we are now confronted by a series of demonstrations by some of our Negro citizens, directed and led in part by outsiders. We recognize the natural impatience of people who feel that their hopes are slow in being realized. But we are convinced that these demonstrations are unwise and untimely.[6]

4 We agree rather[7] with certain local Negro leadership which has called for honest and open negotiation of racial issues in our area. And we believe this kind of facing of issues can best be accomplished by citizens of our own metropolitan area, white and Negro, meeting with their knowledge and experience of the local situation. All of us need to face that responsibility and find proper channels for its accomplishment.

5 Just as we formerly pointed out that "hatred and violence have no sanction in our religious and political traditions," we also point out that such actions as incite to hatred and violence, however technically peaceful[8] those actions may be, have not contributed to the resolution of our local problems. We do not believe that these days of new hope are days when extreme measures are justified in Birmingham.

6 We commend the community as a whole, and the local news media and law enforcement officials in particular, on the calm manner in which these demonstrations have been

---

Sample Student Commentary

[1] Notice that the writers identify themselves as "clergymen," not merely "citizens." They are possibly suggesting that their positions should afford them enhanced influence or credibility.

[2] Notice the word choice; they issued, not submitted. What might the distinctions between those two words suggest?

[3] The opening paragraph immediately recalls the past, thus suggesting the organization of the letter will follow chronological order.

[4] The second paragraph follows the chronological order by addressing the period between the past in the first paragraph and the present.

[5] The first two paragraphs have presented important background information, not unlike the exposition in a formally structured narrative plot. This paragraph introduces the conflict, event, or situation that motivates the writing of this letter.

[6] Thesis-antithesis: "We recognize...But we are convinced..."

[7] The structural and organizational patterns mirror one another: thesis-antithesis, point and counter-point, local resident versus outsider.

[8] Do not miss the powerful implication of this sentence. The writers are essentially condemning the recent demonstrations as violence posing as non-violence.

handled. We urge the public[9] to continue to show restraint should the demonstrations continue, and the law enforcement officials to remain calm and continue to protect our city from violence.

7   We further strongly urge[10] our own Negro community[11] to withdraw support from these demonstrations, and to unite locally in working peacefully for a better Birmingham. When rights are consistently denied, a cause should be pressed in the courts and in negotiations among local leaders, and not in the streets. We appeal to both our white and Negro citizenry to observe the principles of law and order and common sense.[12] 🌑

Bishop C.C.J. Carpenter, D.D., LL.D., Episcopalian Bishop of Alabama

Bishop Joseph A. Durick, D.D., Auxiliary Bishop, Roman Catholic Diocese of Mobile, Birmingham

Rabbi Milton L. Grafman, Temple Emanu-El, Birmingham, Alabama

Bishop Paul Hardin, Methodist Bishop of the Alabama-West Florida Conference

Bishop Nolan B. Harmon, Bishop of the North Alabama Conference of the Methodist Church

Rev. George M. Murray, D.D., LL.D, Bishop Coadjutor, Episcopal Diocese of Alabama

Rev. Edward V. Ramage, Moderator, Synod of the Alabama Presbyterian Church in the United States

Rev. Earl Stallings, Pastor, First Baptist Church, Birmingham, Alabama

---

Sample Student Commentary

[9] Note the progression from "we commend" to "we urge."

[10] From "urge" in the previous paragraph to "strongly urge."

[11] There has also been something of a progression from "the community as a whole," to "the public," to "our own Negro community."

[12] Ultimately, the passage turns out to be circular in structure, beginning with an appeal for "common sense," and ending with an identical appeal.

Sample multiple-choice questions:

1. All of the following are juxtaposed, antithetical points in the organizational plans EXCEPT

A. local versus national.

B. Negro versus white.

C. *clergy versus lay.*

D. violent versus peaceful.

E. gradual versus immediate.

2. Given the narrative structure established in the first and second paragraphs, which of the following best identifies the climax of the letter?

A. *"...we also point out that such actions as incite to hatred and violence, however technically peaceful those actions may be, have not contributed to the resolution of our local problems." (paragraph 5)*

B. "However, we are now confronted by a series of demonstrations by some of our Negro citizens..." (paragraph 3)

C. "...we are convinced that these demonstrations are unwise and untimely." (paragraph 3)

D. "...we believe this kind of facing of issues can best be accomplished by citizens of our own metropolitan area, white and Negro, meeting with their knowledge and experience of the local situation..." (paragraph 4)

E. "We urge the public to continue to show restraint should the demonstrations continue..." (paragraph 6)

3. Which of the following, from the third paragraph, best establishes the primary conflict of this letter?

A. Negro citizens

B. demonstrations

C. natural impatience

D. hopes

E. *outsiders*

4. Paragraph six signals a shift in purpose from

A. persuasive to reflective.

B. reflective to persuasive.

C. persuasive to informative.

D. *informative to persuasive.*

E. reflective to informative.

5. Which of the following best describes the relationship of this letter to the January letter mentioned in the first paragraph?

A. rebuttal

B. retraction

C. *continuation*

D. prelude

E. reiteration

Answers and Explanations:

1. (A) is eliminated by the writers' pointing out that the recent demonstrations have been organized, in part, by "outsiders" and their call for "citizens of our own metropolitan area" to negotiate racial harmony. (B) is easily eliminated by the overall subject matter of the letter and its historical and social context. (D) is eliminated by the writers' urging the "law enforcement officials to remain calm and continue to protect our city from violence," and their call to "unite locally in working peacefully for a better Birmingham." (E) is eliminated by the writers' insistence that the findings of the courts "should *in the meantime* be peacefully obeyed," and in their claim, "We recognize the natural impatience of people who feel that their hopes are slow in being realized. *But…*" The letter, however, though written by clergymen who possibly hope to use their status to bolster their influence and credibility, never draws a distinction between clergy and laypersons. **Thus, (C) is the best answer.**

2. (B) is clearly a transition, certainly increasing the magnitude of the information, but not yet the climax. (C) might be tempting, as it is a strong statement, but it is not the strongest choice available or the strongest statement issued by the writers of the letter. (D) is more a bit of exposition than a mounting or climactic argument. (E) is a relatively mild statement that begins to lead to the conclusion. (A), however, is a strong statement of condemnation, the highest point of the writers' plea for non-violence, and the highest point in their criticism of the outside agitators who have organized the demonstrations. **Thus, (A) is the best answer.**

3. While the writers admit that "some of [their] Negro citizens" have participated in the demonstrations, they have also admitted that others in the Negro community have cooperated with their efforts at negotiation and judicial action. Thus, (A) is eliminated. (B) does name the key issue, but the fact of demonstrations alone is not at the heart of the writers' concern. (C) and (D) are, in fact, in conflict, but this is the admitted conflict of the Negro community, not the concern of the writers of this letter. Their issue is not only the fact of the demonstrations but the fact that these demonstrations have been "directed and led in part by outsiders," even though "responsible citizens have undertaken to work on various problems which cause racial friction and unrest." **Thus, (E) is the best answer.**

4. Paragraphs one and two are essentially informative in nature, identifying the writers and providing a summary of past events leading to the present crisis. The use of "urge" and "strongly urge" in paragraphs six and seven clearly signals a shift from this informative purpose to a persuasive one. **Thus, (D) is the only reasonable answer.**

5. Clearly, the writers neither rebut (A) nor retract (B) anything from their earlier letter. If anything, they reiterate the opinions expressed in the January letter and elaborate upon

them, adding their thoughts on the recent demonstrations. (D) is eliminated by the knowledge that a later publication cannot be a prelude to an earlier one. (E) is tempting, as the writers do reiterate many of their sentiments from the earlier letter. However, in addition to reiterating those sentiments, they add their thoughts on the recent demonstrations and attempt to persuade the public to end them. **Thus, (C) is the best answer.**

Sample free-response item:

Carefully read the Alabama clergymen's "A Call for Unity." Then, write a thoughtful and well-organized essay in which you examine the structure and organizational patters on the letter and how they help the writers achieve their intended purpose. Do not merely summarize the passage.

Sample Student Essay

In "A Call for Unity," eight Alabama clergymen exhort the local population, specifically, the "Negro community," to stop peaceful protests in the streets and to instead trust their efforts to the established court systems. The document is organized so that it places examples the clergymen deem as good in direct opposition to those the clergymen deem as bad. The actual purpose and audience of the piece is concealed by the clergymen until almost the very end; they accomplish this through narrowing the focus of the piece gradually until the group they wish to reach is identified. The piece is carefully structured; the clergymen make their authority known early so that it percolates through the document.

The message follows several major organizational patterns. One of these is the juxtaposition of antithetical ideas. Because their intent is to inform the Negro community that its actions are not acceptable, the clergymen place concepts in opposition to one another from the third paragraph onward, signaling their preferences regarding the handling of the situation. In each case, the juxtaposition reveals what the clergymen deem the correct choice of action to be. The clergymen are careful to give the example of the "[r]esponsible citizens" before setting it against that of the demonstrators described in the following paragraph. Likewise, the bad example of these demonstrating "outsiders" is set against the good example of the "local Negro citizenship." Though no explanation is given as to why the actions of the demonstrators are wrong, the clergymen's point of view is evident. This pattern continues throughout the message.

Another important point of organization is the gradual narrowing of focus, from all citizens to the "Negro community," which reveals the intended audience and purpose of the piece. The message begins by describing the work of "[r]esponsible citizens," but narrows its focus to "some of our Negro citizens" when introducing the problem which the message purports to solve. Likewise, commendations go to the "community as a whole" and "the public," but members of the "Negro community" who support the demonstrations are implicitly criticized. By narrowing the focus to a select group when describing the problem, the clergymen inform that group—in this case, the "Negro community"—that they are in the wrong.

The structure of the piece also lends to its effectiveness and purpose. The clergymen begin the message by appealing to their authority as clergymen. Their authority should give the message an air of moral righteousness—whether their advice is morally correct or not. This interpretation is strengthened by the fact that the clergymen had previously "issued" a similar tract. The fact that they "issued" this document connotes that the document was to be obeyed as a command. In another antithetical juxtaposition, they later set their authority against that of the "outsiders" fomenting civil discord. Because there is little evidence of actual logical argument, the clergymen use their authority to make their point, trusting that their audience will be predisposed to accept their ideas.

"A Call for Unity" is intended to be a persuasive piece, but there seems to be a strange disconnect between the beliefs of the clergymen and reality. The clergymen write that "rights are consistently denied," but they insist that the fight for those rights should happen in a courtroom or in negotiation with local leaders—the same people who consistently chose to deny those rights. Though the piece is effective in making known the position of the clergymen, it may not have been as effective in convincing those who did not already share the clergymen's opinions. 🥭

Exercise Two:

Questions 6-10. Read the following passage carefully before you choose your answers.

On April 16, 1963, while incarcerated in the Birmingham, Alabama, jail for his role in organizing and executing the demonstrations condemned in the Alabama clergymen's "A Call for Unity," Dr. Martin Luther King, Jr., wrote his famous reply: "Letter from Birmingham Jail." It was first published in the June 12, 1963, edition of The Christian Century, *and in the June 24, 1963, issue of* The New Leader. *It was reprinted shortly thereafter in* The Atlantic Monthly. *King included the full text in his 1964 book* Why We Can't Wait.

Letter from Birmingham Jail
—DR. MARTIN LUTHER KING, JR.

16 April 1963

My Dear Fellow Clergymen:

1   While confined here in the Birmingham city jail, I came across your recent statement calling my present activities "unwise and untimely." Seldom do I pause to answer criticism of my work and ideas. If I sought to answer all the criticisms that cross my

desk, my secretaries would have little time for anything other than such correspondence in the course of the day, and I would have no time for constructive work. But since I feel that you are men of genuine good will and that your criticisms are sincerely set forth, I want to try to answer your statement in what I hope will be patient and reasonable terms.

2 I think I should indicate why I am here in Birmingham, since you have been influenced by the view which argues against "outsiders coming in." I have the honor of serving as president of the Southern Christian Leadership Conference, an organization operating in every southern state, with headquarters in Atlanta, Georgia. We have some eighty five affiliated organizations across the South, and one of them is the Alabama Christian Movement for Human Rights. Frequently we share staff, educational and financial resources with our affiliates. Several months ago the affiliate here in Birmingham asked us to be on call to engage in a nonviolent direct action program if such were deemed necessary. We readily consented, and when the hour came we lived up to our promise. So I, along with several members of my staff, am here because I was invited here. I am here because I have organizational ties here.

3 But more basically, I am in Birmingham because injustice is here. Just as the prophets of the eighth century B.C. left their villages and carried their "thus saith the Lord" far beyond the boundaries of their home towns, and just as the Apostle Paul left his village of Tarsus and carried the gospel of Jesus Christ to the far corners of the Greco Roman world, so am I compelled to carry the gospel of freedom beyond my own home town. Like Paul, I must constantly respond to the Macedonian call for aid.

4 Moreover, I am cognizant of the interrelatedness of all communities and states. I cannot sit idly by in Atlanta and not be concerned about what happens in Birmingham. Injustice anywhere is a threat to justice everywhere. We are caught in an inescapable network of mutuality, tied in a single garment of destiny. Whatever affects one directly, affects all indirectly. Never again can we afford to live with the narrow, provincial "outside agitator" idea. Anyone who lives inside the United States can never be considered an outsider anywhere within its bounds.

5 You deplore the demonstrations taking place in Birmingham. But your statement, I am sorry to say, fails to express a similar concern for the conditions that brought about the demonstrations. I am sure that none of you would want to rest content with the superficial kind of social analysis that deals merely with effects and does not grapple with underlying causes. It is unfortunate that demonstrations are taking place in Birmingham, but it is even more unfortunate that the city's white power structure left the Negro community with no alternative.

6 In any nonviolent campaign there are four basic steps: collection of the facts to determine whether injustices exist; negotiation; self purification; and direct action. We have gone through all these steps in Birmingham. There can be no gainsaying the fact that racial injustice engulfs this community. Birmingham is probably the most thoroughly segregated city in the United States. Its ugly record of brutality is widely known. Negroes have experienced grossly unjust treatment in the courts. There have been more unsolved bombings of Negro homes and churches in Birmingham than in any other city in the nation. These are the hard, brutal facts of the case. On the basis of these conditions, Negro leaders sought to negotiate with the city fathers. But the latter consistently refused to engage in good faith negotiation.

7   Then, last September, came the opportunity to talk with leaders of Birmingham's economic community. In the course of the negotiations, certain promises were made by the merchants—for example, to remove the stores' humiliating racial signs. On the basis of these promises, the Reverend Fred Shuttlesworth and the leaders of the Alabama Christian Movement for Human Rights agreed to a moratorium on all demonstrations. As the weeks and months went by, we realized that we were the victims of a broken promise. A few signs, briefly removed, returned; the others remained. As in so many past experiences, our hopes had been blasted, and the shadow of deep disappointment settled upon us. We had no alternative except to prepare for direct action, whereby we would present our very bodies as a means of laying our case before the conscience of the local and the national community. Mindful of the difficulties involved, we decided to undertake a process of self purification. We began a series of workshops on nonviolence, and we repeatedly asked ourselves: "Are you able to accept blows without retaliating?" "Are you able to endure the ordeal of jail?" We decided to schedule our direct action program for the Easter season, realizing that except for Christmas, this is the main shopping period of the year. Knowing that a strong economic-withdrawal program would be the by product of direct action, we felt that this would be the best time to bring pressure to bear on the merchants for the needed change.

8   Then it occurred to us that Birmingham's mayoral election was coming up in March, and we speedily decided to postpone action until after election day. When we discovered that the Commissioner of Public Safety, Eugene "Bull" Connor, had piled up enough votes to be in the run off, we decided again to postpone action until the day after the run off so that the demonstrations could not be used to cloud the issues. Like many others, we waited to see Mr. Connor defeated, and to this end we endured postponement after postponement. Having aided in this community need, we felt that our direct action program could be delayed no longer.

9   You may well ask: "Why direct action? Why sit ins, marches and so forth? Isn't negotiation a better path?" You are quite right in calling for negotiation. Indeed, this is the very purpose of direct action. Nonviolent direct action seeks to create such a crisis and foster such a tension that a community which has constantly refused to negotiate is forced to confront the issue. It seeks so to dramatize the issue that it can no longer be ignored. My citing the creation of tension as part of the work of the nonviolent resister may sound rather shocking. But I must confess that I am not afraid of the word "tension." I have earnestly opposed violent tension, but there is a type of constructive, nonviolent tension which is necessary for growth. Just as Socrates felt that it was necessary to create a tension in the mind so that individuals could rise from the bondage of myths and half truths to the unfettered realm of creative analysis and objective appraisal, so must we see the need for nonviolent gadflies to create the kind of tension in society that will help men rise from the dark depths of prejudice and racism to the majestic heights of understanding and brotherhood. The purpose of our direct action program is to create a situation so crisis packed that it will inevitably open the door to negotiation. I therefore concur with you in your call for negotiation. Too long has our beloved Southland been bogged down in a tragic effort to live in monologue rather than dialogue.

10   One of the basic points in your statement is that the action that I and my associates have taken in Birmingham is untimely. Some have asked: "Why didn't you give the new city administration time to act?" The only answer that I can give to this query is that the new Birmingham administration must be prodded about as much as the outgoing one, before it will act. We are sadly mistaken if we feel that the election of Albert Boutwell as mayor will bring the millennium to Birmingham. While Mr. Boutwell is a much more gentle person than Mr. Connor, they are both segregationists, dedicated to maintenance of the status quo. I have hope that Mr. Boutwell will be reasonable enough to see the futility of massive resistance to desegregation. But he will not see this without pressure from devotees of civil rights. My friends, I must say to you that we have not made a single gain in civil rights without determined legal and nonviolent pressure. Lamentably, it is an historical fact that privileged groups seldom give up their privileges voluntarily. Individuals may see the moral light and voluntarily give up their unjust posture; but, as Reinhold Niebuhr has reminded us, groups tend to be more immoral than individuals.

11   We know through painful experience that freedom is never voluntarily given by the oppressor; it must be demanded by the oppressed. Frankly, I have yet to engage in a direct action campaign that was "well timed" in the view of those who have not suffered unduly from the disease of segregation. For years now I have heard the word "Wait!" It rings in the ear of every Negro with piercing familiarity. This "Wait" has almost always meant "Never." We must come to see, with one of our distinguished jurists, that "justice too long delayed is justice denied."

12   We have waited for more than 340 years for our constitutional and God given rights. The nations of Asia and Africa are moving with jetlike speed toward gaining political independence, but we still creep at horse and buggy pace toward gaining a cup of coffee at a lunch counter. Perhaps it is easy for those who have never felt the stinging darts of segregation to say, "Wait." But when you have seen vicious mobs lynch your mothers and fathers at will and drown your sisters and brothers at whim; when you have seen hate filled policemen curse, kick and even kill your black brothers and sisters; when you see the vast majority of your twenty million Negro brothers smothering in an airtight cage of poverty in the midst of an affluent society; when you suddenly find your tongue twisted and your speech stammering as you seek to explain to your six year old daughter why she can't go to the public amusement park that has just been advertised on television, and see tears welling up in her eyes when she is told that Funtown is closed to colored children, and see ominous clouds of inferiority beginning to form in her little mental sky, and see her beginning to distort her personality by developing an unconscious bitterness toward white people; when you have to concoct an answer for a five year old son who is asking: "Daddy, why do white people treat colored people so mean?"; when you take a cross county drive and find it necessary to sleep night after night in the uncomfortable corners of your automobile because no motel will accept you; when you are humiliated day in and day out by nagging signs reading "white" and "colored"; when your first name becomes "nigger," your middle name becomes "boy" (however old you are) and your last name becomes "John," and your wife and mother are never given the respected title "Mrs."; when you are harried by day and haunted by night by the fact that you are a Negro, living constantly at tiptoe stance, never quite knowing what to expect next,

and are plagued with inner fears and outer resentments; when you are forever fighting a degenerating sense of "nobodiness"—then you will understand why we find it difficult to wait. There comes a time when the cup of endurance runs over, and men are no longer willing to be plunged into the abyss of despair. I hope, sirs, you can understand our legitimate and unavoidable impatience. You express a great deal of anxiety over our willingness to break laws. This is certainly a legitimate concern. Since we so diligently urge people to obey the Supreme Court's decision of 1954 outlawing segregation in the public schools, at first glance it may seem rather paradoxical for us consciously to break laws. One may well ask: "How can you advocate breaking some laws and obeying others?" The answer lies in the fact that there are two types of laws: just and unjust. I would be the first to advocate obeying just laws. One has not only a legal but a moral responsibility to obey just laws. Conversely, one has a moral responsibility to disobey unjust laws. I would agree with St. Augustine that "an unjust law is no law at all."

13   Now, what is the difference between the two? How does one determine whether a law is just or unjust? A just law is a man made code that squares with the moral law or the law of God. An unjust law is a code that is out of harmony with the moral law. To put it in the terms of St. Thomas Aquinas: An unjust law is a human law that is not rooted in eternal law and natural law. Any law that uplifts human personality is just. Any law that degrades human personality is unjust. All segregation statutes are unjust because segregation distorts the soul and damages the personality. It gives the segregator a false sense of superiority and the segregated a false sense of inferiority. Segregation, to use the terminology of the Jewish philosopher Martin Buber, substitutes an "I it" relationship for an "I thou" relationship and ends up relegating persons to the status of things. Hence segregation is not only politically, economically and sociologically unsound, it is morally wrong and sinful. Paul Tillich has said that sin is separation. Is not segregation an existential expression of man's tragic separation, his awful estrangement, his terrible sinfulness? Thus it is that I can urge men to obey the 1954 decision of the Supreme Court, for it is morally right; and I can urge them to disobey segregation ordinances, for they are morally wrong.

14   Let us consider a more concrete example of just and unjust laws. An unjust law is a code that a numerical or power majority group compels a minority group to obey but does not make binding on itself. This is difference made legal. By the same token, a just law is a code that a majority compels a minority to follow and that it is willing to follow itself. This is sameness made legal. Let me give another explanation. A law is unjust if it is inflicted on a minority that, as a result of being denied the right to vote, had no part in enacting or devising the law. Who can say that the legislature of Alabama which set up that state's segregation laws was democratically elected? Throughout Alabama all sorts of devious methods are used to prevent Negroes from becoming registered voters, and there are some counties in which, even though Negroes constitute a majority of the population, not a single Negro is registered. Can any law enacted under such circumstances be considered democratically structured?

15   Sometimes a law is just on its face and unjust in its application. For instance, I have been arrested on a charge of parading without a permit. Now, there is nothing wrong in having an ordinance which requires a permit for a parade. But such an ordinance becomes unjust when it is used to maintain segregation and to deny citizens the First-Amendment privilege of peaceful assembly and protest.

16   I hope you are able to see the distinction I am trying to point out. In no sense do I advocate evading or defying the law, as would the rabid segregationist. That would lead to anarchy. One who breaks an unjust law must do so openly, lovingly, and with a willingness to accept the penalty. I submit that an individual who breaks a law that conscience tells him is unjust, and who willingly accepts the penalty of imprisonment in order to arouse the conscience of the community over its injustice, is in reality expressing the highest respect for law.

17   Of course, there is nothing new about this kind of civil disobedience. It was evidenced sublimely in the refusal of Shadrach, Meshach and Abednego to obey the laws of Nebuchadnezzar, on the ground that a higher moral law was at stake. It was practiced superbly by the early Christians, who were willing to face hungry lions and the excruciating pain of chopping blocks rather than submit to certain unjust laws of the Roman Empire. To a degree, academic freedom is a reality today because Socrates practiced civil disobedience. In our own nation, the Boston Tea Party represented a massive act of civil disobedience.

18   We should never forget that everything Adolf Hitler did in Germany was "legal" and everything the Hungarian freedom fighters did in Hungary was "illegal." It was "illegal" to aid and comfort a Jew in Hitler's Germany. Even so, I am sure that, had I lived in Germany at the time, I would have aided and comforted my Jewish brothers. If today I lived in a Communist country where certain principles dear to the Christian faith are suppressed, I would openly advocate disobeying that country's antireligious laws.

19   I must make two honest confessions to you, my Christian and Jewish brothers. First, I must confess that over the past few years I have been gravely disappointed with the white moderate. I have almost reached the regrettable conclusion that the Negro's great stumbling block in his stride toward freedom is not the White Citizen's Counciler or the Ku Klux Klanner, but the white moderate, who is more devoted to "order" than to justice; who prefers a negative peace which is the absence of tension to a positive peace which is the presence of justice; who constantly says: "I agree with you in the goal you seek, but I cannot agree with your methods of direct action"; who paternalistically believes he can set the timetable for another man's freedom; who lives by a mythical concept of time and who constantly advises the Negro to wait for a "more convenient season." Shallow understanding from people of good will is more frustrating than absolute misunderstanding from people of ill will. Lukewarm acceptance is much more bewildering than outright rejection.

20   I had hoped that the white moderate would understand that law and order exist for the purpose of establishing justice and that when they fail in this purpose they become the dangerously structured dams that block the flow of social progress. I had hoped that the white moderate would understand that the present tension in the South is a necessary phase of the transition from an obnoxious negative peace, in which the Negro passively accepted his unjust plight, to a substantive and positive peace, in which all men will respect the dignity and worth of human personality. Actually, we who engage in nonviolent direct action are not the creators of tension. We merely bring to the surface

the hidden tension that is already alive. We bring it out in the open, where it can be seen and dealt with. Like a boil that can never be cured so long as it is covered up but must be opened with all its ugliness to the natural medicines of air and light, injustice must be exposed, with all the tension its exposure creates, to the light of human conscience and the air of national opinion before it can be cured.

21   In your statement you assert that our actions, even though peaceful, must be condemned because they precipitate violence. But is this a logical assertion? Isn't this like condemning a robbed man because his possession of money precipitated the evil act of robbery? Isn't this like condemning Socrates because his unswerving commitment to truth and his philosophical inquiries precipitated the act by the misguided populace in which they made him drink hemlock? Isn't this like condemning Jesus because his unique God consciousness and never ceasing devotion to God's will precipitated the evil act of crucifixion? We must come to see that, as the federal courts have consistently affirmed, it is wrong to urge an individual to cease his efforts to gain his basic constitutional rights because the quest may precipitate violence. Society must protect the robbed and punish the robber. I had also hoped that the white moderate would reject the myth concerning time in relation to the struggle for freedom. I have just received a letter from a white brother in Texas. He writes: "All Christians know that the colored people will receive equal rights eventually, but it is possible that you are in too great a religious hurry. It has taken Christianity almost two thousand years to accomplish what it has. The teachings of Christ take time to come to earth." Such an attitude stems from a tragic misconception of time, from the strangely irrational notion that there is something in the very flow of time that will inevitably cure all ills. Actually, time itself is neutral; it can be used either destructively or constructively. More and more I feel that the people of ill will have used time much more effectively than have the people of good will. We will have to repent in this generation not merely for the hateful words and actions of the bad people but for the appalling silence of the good people. Human progress never rolls in on wheels of inevitability; it comes through the tireless efforts of men willing to be co workers with God, and without this hard work, time itself becomes an ally of the forces of social stagnation. We must use time creatively, in the knowledge that the time is always ripe to do right. Now is the time to make real the promise of democracy and transform our pending national elegy into a creative psalm of brotherhood. Now is the time to lift our national policy from the quicksand of racial injustice to the solid rock of human dignity.

22   You speak of our activity in Birmingham as extreme. At first I was rather disappointed that fellow clergymen would see my nonviolent efforts as those of an extremist. I began thinking about the fact that I stand in the middle of two opposing forces in the Negro community. One is a force of complacency, made up in part of Negroes who, as a result of long years of oppression, are so drained of self respect and a sense of "somebodiness" that they have adjusted to segregation; and in part of a few middle-class Negroes who, because of a degree of academic and economic security and because in some ways they profit by segregation, have become insensitive to the problems of the masses. The other force is one of bitterness and hatred, and it comes perilously close to advocating violence. It is expressed in the various black nationalist groups that are springing

up across the nation, the largest and best known being Elijah Muhammad's Muslim movement. Nourished by the Negro's frustration over the continued existence of racial discrimination, this movement is made up of people who have lost faith in America, who have absolutely repudiated Christianity, and who have concluded that the white man is an incorrigible "devil."

23   I have tried to stand between these two forces, saying that we need emulate neither the "do nothingism" of the complacent nor the hatred and despair of the black nationalist. For there is the more excellent way of love and nonviolent protest. I am grateful to God that, through the influence of the Negro church, the way of nonviolence became an integral part of our struggle. If this philosophy had not emerged, by now many streets of the South would, I am convinced, be flowing with blood. And I am further convinced that if our white brothers dismiss as "rabble rousers" and "outside agitators" those of us who employ nonviolent direct action, and if they refuse to support our nonviolent efforts, millions of Negroes will, out of frustration and despair, seek solace and security in black nationalist ideologies—a development that would inevitably lead to a frightening racial nightmare.

24   Oppressed people cannot remain oppressed forever. The yearning for freedom eventually manifests itself, and that is what has happened to the American Negro. Something within has reminded him of his birthright of freedom, and something without has reminded him that it can be gained. Consciously or unconsciously, he has been caught up by the Zeitgeist, and with his black brothers of Africa and his brown and yellow brothers of Asia, South America and the Caribbean, the United States Negro is moving with a sense of great urgency toward the promised land of racial justice. If one recognizes this vital urge that has engulfed the Negro community, one should readily understand why public demonstrations are taking place. The Negro has many pent up resentments and latent frustrations, and he must release them. So let him march; let him make prayer pilgrimages to the city hall; let him go on freedom rides—and try to understand why he must do so. If his repressed emotions are not released in nonviolent ways, they will seek expression through violence; this is not a threat but a fact of history. So I have not said to my people: "Get rid of your discontent." Rather, I have tried to say that this normal and healthy discontent can be channeled into the creative outlet of nonviolent direct action. And now this approach is being termed extremist. But though I was initially disappointed at being categorized as an extremist, as I continued to think about the matter I gradually gained a measure of satisfaction from the label. Was not Jesus an extremist for love: "Love your enemies, bless them that curse you, do good to them that hate you, and pray for them which despitefully use you, and persecute you." Was not Amos an extremist for justice: "Let justice roll down like waters and righteousness like an ever flowing stream." Was not Paul an extremist for the Christian gospel: "I bear in my body the marks of the Lord Jesus." Was not Martin Luther an extremist: "Here I stand; I cannot do otherwise, so help me God." And John Bunyan: "I will stay in jail to the end of my days before I make a butchery of my conscience." And Abraham Lincoln: "This nation cannot survive half slave and half free." And Thomas Jefferson: "We hold these truths to be self evident, that all men are created equal . . ." So the question is not whether we will be extremists, but what kind of extremists we will be. Will we be extremists for hate or for love? Will we be extremists for the preservation of injustice or for the extension of justice? In that dramatic scene on Calvary's hill three men were crucified. We must never forget that all three were crucified for the same crime—the crime of extremism. Two were extremists for immorality, and thus fell below their environment. The other, Jesus Christ, was an extremist for love, truth and goodness, and thereby rose above his environment. Perhaps the South, the nation and the world are in dire need of creative extremists.

25   I had hoped that the white moderate would see this need. Perhaps I was too optimistic; perhaps I expected too much. I suppose I should have realized that few members of the oppressor race can understand the deep groans and passionate yearnings of the oppressed race, and still fewer have the vision to see that injustice must be rooted out by strong, persistent and determined action. I am thankful, however, that some of our white brothers in the South have grasped the meaning of this social revolution and committed themselves to it. They are still all too few in quantity, but they are big in quality. Some -such as Ralph McGill, Lillian Smith, Harry Golden, James McBride Dabbs, Ann Braden and Sarah Patton Boyle—have written about our struggle in eloquent and prophetic terms. Others have marched with us down nameless streets of the South. They have languished in filthy, roach infested jails, suffering the abuse and brutality of policemen who view them as "dirty nigger-lovers." Unlike so many of their moderate brothers and sisters, they have recognized the urgency of the moment and sensed the need for powerful "action" antidotes to combat the disease of segregation. Let me take note of my other major disappointment. I have been so greatly disappointed with the white church and its leadership. Of course, there are some notable exceptions. I am not unmindful of the fact that each of you has taken some significant stands on this issue. I commend you, Reverend Stallings, for your Christian stand on this past Sunday, in welcoming Negroes to your worship service on a nonsegregated basis. I commend the Catholic leaders of this state for integrating Spring Hill College several years ago.

26   But despite these notable exceptions, I must honestly reiterate that I have been disappointed with the church. I do not say this as one of those negative critics who can always find something wrong with the church. I say this as a minister of the gospel, who loves the church; who was nurtured in its bosom; who has been sustained by its spiritual blessings and who will remain true to it as long as the cord of life shall lengthen.

27   When I was suddenly catapulted into the leadership of the bus protest in Montgomery, Alabama, a few years ago, I felt we would be supported by the white church. I felt that the white ministers, priests and rabbis of the South would be among our strongest allies. Instead, some have been outright opponents, refusing to understand the freedom movement and misrepresenting its leaders; all too many others have been more cautious than courageous and have remained silent behind the anesthetizing security of stained glass windows.

28   In spite of my shattered dreams, I came to Birmingham with the hope that the white religious leadership of this community would see the justice of our cause and, with deep moral concern, would serve as the channel through which our just grievances could reach the power structure. I had hoped that each of you would understand. But again I have been disappointed.

29   I have heard numerous southern religious leaders admonish their worshipers to

comply with a desegregation decision because it is the law, but I have longed to hear white ministers declare: "Follow this decree because integration is morally right and because the Negro is your brother." In the midst of blatant injustices inflicted upon the Negro, I have watched white churchmen stand on the sideline and mouth pious irrelevancies and sanctimonious trivialities. In the midst of a mighty struggle to rid our nation of racial and economic injustice, I have heard many ministers say: "Those are social issues, with which the gospel has no real concern." And I have watched many churches commit themselves to a completely other worldly religion which makes a strange, un-Biblical distinction between body and soul, between the sacred and the secular.

30   I have traveled the length and breadth of Alabama, Mississippi and all the other southern states. On sweltering summer days and crisp autumn mornings I have looked at the South's beautiful churches with their lofty spires pointing heavenward. I have beheld the impressive outlines of her massive religious education buildings. Over and over I have found myself asking: "What kind of people worship here? Who is their God? Where were their voices when the lips of Governor Barnett dripped with words of interposition and nullification? Where were they when Governor Wallace gave a clarion call for defiance and hatred? Where were their voices of support when bruised and weary Negro men and women decided to rise from the dark dungeons of complacency to the bright hills of creative protest?"

31   Yes, these questions are still in my mind. In deep disappointment I have wept over the laxity of the church. But be assured that my tears have been tears of love. There can be no deep disappointment where there is not deep love. Yes, I love the church. How could I do otherwise? I am in the rather unique position of being the son, the grandson and the great grandson of preachers. Yes, I see the church as the body of Christ. But, oh! How we have blemished and scarred that body through social neglect and through fear of being nonconformists.

32   There was a time when the church was very powerful—in the time when the early Christians rejoiced at being deemed worthy to suffer for what they believed. In those days the church was not merely a thermometer that recorded the ideas and principles of popular opinion; it was a thermostat that transformed the mores of society. Whenever the early Christians entered a town, the people in power became disturbed and immediately sought to convict the Christians for being "disturbers of the peace" and "outside agitators."' But the Christians pressed on, in the conviction that they were "a colony of heaven," called to obey God rather than man. Small in number, they were big in commitment. They were too God-intoxicated to be "astronomically intimidated." By their effort and example they brought an end to such ancient evils as infanticide and gladiatorial contests. Things are different now. So often the contemporary church is a weak, ineffectual voice with an uncertain sound. So often it is an archdefender of the status quo. Far from being disturbed by the presence of the church, the power structure of the average community is consoled by the church's silent—and often even vocal—sanction of things as they are.

33   But the judgment of God is upon the church as never before. If today's church does not recapture the sacrificial spirit of the early church, it will lose its authenticity, forfeit the loyalty of millions, and be dismissed as an irrelevant social club with no meaning for

the twentieth century. Every day I meet young people whose disappointment with the church has turned into outright disgust.

34   Perhaps I have once again been too optimistic. Is organized religion too inextricably bound to the status quo to save our nation and the world? Perhaps I must turn my faith to the inner spiritual church, the church within the church, as the true ekklesia and the hope of the world. But again I am thankful to God that some noble souls from the ranks of organized religion have broken loose from the paralyzing chains of conformity and joined us as active partners in the struggle for freedom. They have left their secure congregations and walked the streets of Albany, Georgia, with us. They have gone down the highways of the South on tortuous rides for freedom. Yes, they have gone to jail with us. Some have been dismissed from their churches, have lost the support of their bishops and fellow ministers. But they have acted in the faith that right defeated is stronger than evil triumphant. Their witness has been the spiritual salt that has preserved the true meaning of the gospel in these troubled times. They have carved a tunnel of hope through the dark mountain of disappointment. I hope the church as a whole will meet the challenge of this decisive hour. But even if the church does not come to the aid of justice, I have no despair about the future. I have no fear about the outcome of our struggle in Birmingham, even if our motives are at present misunderstood. We will reach the goal of freedom in Birmingham and all over the nation, because the goal of America is freedom. Abused and scorned though we may be, our destiny is tied up with America's destiny. Before the pilgrims landed at Plymouth, we were here. Before the pen of Jefferson etched the majestic words of the Declaration of Independence across the pages of history, we were here. For more than two centuries our forebears labored in this country without wages; they made cotton king; they built the homes of their masters while suffering gross injustice and shameful humiliation -and yet out of a bottomless vitality they continued to thrive and develop. If the inexpressible cruelties of slavery could not stop us, the opposition we now face will surely fail. We will win our freedom because the sacred heritage of our nation and the eternal will of God are embodied in our echoing demands. Before closing I feel impelled to mention one other point in your statement that has troubled me profoundly. You warmly commended the Birmingham police force for keeping "order" and "preventing violence." I doubt that you would have so warmly commended the police force if you had seen its dogs sinking their teeth into unarmed, nonviolent Negroes. I doubt that you would so quickly commend the policemen if you were to observe their ugly and inhumane treatment of Negroes here in the city jail; if you were to watch them push and curse old Negro women and young Negro girls; if you were to see them slap and kick old Negro men and young boys; if you were to observe them, as they did on two occasions, refuse to give us food because we wanted to sing our grace together. I cannot join you in your praise of the Birmingham police department.

35   It is true that the police have exercised a degree of discipline in handling the demonstrators. In this sense they have conducted themselves rather "nonviolently" in public. But for what purpose? To preserve the evil system of segregation. Over the past few years I have consistently preached that nonviolence demands that the means we use must be as pure as the ends we seek. I have tried to make clear that it is wrong to use immoral means to attain moral ends. But now I must affirm that it is just as wrong,

or perhaps even more so, to use moral means to preserve immoral ends. Perhaps Mr. Connor and his policemen have been rather nonviolent in public, as was Chief Pritchett in Albany, Georgia, but they have used the moral means of nonviolence to maintain the immoral end of racial injustice. As T. S. Eliot has said: "The last temptation is the greatest treason: To do the right deed for the wrong reason."

36 I wish you had commended the Negro sit inners and demonstrators of Birmingham for their sublime courage, their willingness to suffer and their amazing discipline in the midst of great provocation. One day the South will recognize its real heroes. They will be the James Merediths, with the noble sense of purpose that enables them to face jeering and hostile mobs, and with the agonizing loneliness that characterizes the life of the pioneer. They will be old, oppressed, battered Negro women, symbolized in a seventy-two-year-old woman in Montgomery, Alabama, who rose up with a sense of dignity and with her people decided not to ride segregated buses, and who responded with ungrammatical profundity to one who inquired about her weariness: "My feets is tired, but my soul is at rest." They will be the young high school and college students, the young ministers of the gospel and a host of their elders, courageously and nonviolently sitting in at lunch counters and willingly going to jail for conscience' sake. One day the South will know that when these disinherited children of God sat down at lunch counters, they were in reality standing up for what is best in the American dream and for the most sacred values in our Judaeo Christian heritage, thereby bringing our nation back to those great wells of democracy which were dug deep by the founding fathers in their formulation of the Constitution and the Declaration of Independence.

37 Never before have I written so long a letter. I'm afraid it is much too long to take your precious time. I can assure you that it would have been much shorter if I had been writing from a comfortable desk, but what else can one do when he is alone in a narrow jail cell, other than write long letters, think long thoughts and pray long prayers?

38 If I have said anything in this letter that overstates the truth and indicates an unreasonable impatience, I beg you to forgive me. If I have said anything that understates the truth and indicates my having a patience that allows me to settle for anything less than brotherhood, I beg God to forgive me.

39 I hope this letter finds you strong in the faith. I also hope that circumstances will soon make it possible for me to meet each of you, not as an integrationist or a civil-rights leader but as a fellow clergyman and a Christian brother. Let us all hope that the dark clouds of racial prejudice will soon pass away and the deep fog of misunderstanding will be lifted from our fear drenched communities, and in some not too distant tomorrow the radiant stars of love and brotherhood will shine over our great nation with all their scintillating beauty.

40 Yours for the cause of Peace and Brotherhood, Martin Luther King, Jr. ☙

Multiple-choice questions:

6. Which of the following organizational patterns is predominant in King's letter?

A. thesis—proof

B. thesis—antithesis

C. comparison—contrast

D. order of magnitude

E. chronological order

7. The structure of King's letter was most likely determined by

A. the order in which his ideas occurred to him.

B. his readers' need for definition and explanation.

C. a logical progression of facts and examples.

D. the order of the Alabama clergymen's criticisms.

E. a need for clarity and persuasiveness.

8. To maintain unity throughout this long letter, King relies heavily on his

A. status as a Southern clergyman.

B. knowledge of history and theology.

C. position as an outsider in Birmingham.

D. desire for justice.

E. role as a civil-rights leader.

9. The structural plan of this letter can best be described as

A. linear.

B. tangential.

C. antithetical.

D. cyclic.

E. desultory.

10. The thirty-sixth paragraph (the fourth paragraph from the end) signals the beginning of King's conclusion by

A. disagreeing with the clergymen.

B. reiterating his thesis.

C. expressing a sentiment.

D. summing up his evidence.

E. predicting the future.

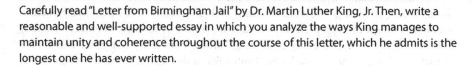

Free Response Item:

Carefully read "Letter from Birmingham Jail" by Dr. Martin Luther King, Jr. Then, write a reasonable and well-supported essay in which you analyze the ways King manages to maintain unity and coherence throughout the course of this letter, which he admits is the longest one he has ever written.

Now, consider the following passage, an opinion piece written in response to an earlier column. The passage has been annotated to point out to you the various means the writer has used to convey his personal disagreement with an earlier column and his view of what many in the United States consider the best schools, and to potentially influence the reader to acknowledge the validity of his view.

After you examine the passage and notes, look at how a student taking the AP Language exam might respond to multiple-choice questions and a free-response item dealing with the structure and organization of this column and its intended effect on the reader.

Obama's Good Students:
A dissent on the 'valedictocracy'.

BY JOSEPH EPSTEIN

DECEMBER 8, 2008, VOL. 14, NO. 12

1   LAST WEEK THE EXCELLENT David Brooks, in one of his columns in the *New York Times*, exulted over the high quality of people President-elect Barack Obama was enlisting in his new cabinet and onto his staff. The chief evidence for these people being so impressive, it turns out, is they all went to what the world—"that ignorant ninny," as Henry James called it—thinks superior schools. Harvard, Yale, Princeton, Stanford, the London School of Economics; like dead flies on flypaper,[1] the names of the schools Obama's new appointees attended dotted Brooks's column.

2   Here is the column's first paragraph:

3   Jan. 20, 2009, will be a historic day. Barack Obama (Columbia, Harvard Law) will take the oath of office as his wife, Michelle (Princeton, Harvard Law), looks on proudly. Nearby, his foreign policy advisers will stand beaming, including perhaps

---

Sample Student Commentary

[1] Clearly a negative association, suggesting Epstein's opinion of the persons and schools named.

[2] Epstein seems to assert a thesis by negation. His argument is implicit in his tone rather than explicit in his words.

Hillary Clinton (Wellesley, Yale Law), Jim Steinberg (Harvard, Yale Law) and Susan Rice (Stanford, Oxford D. Phil.).

4 This administration will be, as Brooks writes, "a valedictocracy." The assumption here is that having all these good students—many of them possibly "toll-frees," as high-school students who get 800s on their SATs used to be known in admissions offices—running the country is obviously a pretty good thing.[3] Brooks's one jokey line in the column has it that "if a foreign enemy attacks the United States during the Harvard-Yale game any time over the next four years, we're screwed." Since my appreciation of David Brooks is considerable, and since I agree with him on so many things, why don't I agree with him here?[4]

5 The reason is that, after teaching at a university for 30 years, I have come to distrust the type I think of as "the good student"[5] —that is, the student who sails through school and is easily admitted into the top colleges and professional schools. The good student is the kid who works hard in high school, piles up lots of activities, and scores high on his SATs, and for his efforts gets into one of the 20 or so schools in the country that ring the gong of success. While there he gets a preponderance of A's. This allows him to move on to the next good, or even slightly better, graduate, business, or professional school, where he will get more A's still, and move onward and ever upward. His perfect résumé in hand, he runs only one risk—that of catching cold from the draft created by all the doors opening for him wherever he goes, as he piles up scads of money, honors, and finally ends up being offered a job at a high level of government. He has, in a sense Spike Lee never intended, done the right thing.[6]

6 What's wrong with this? Am I describing anything worse than effort and virtue richly rewarded? I believe I am.[7] My sense of the good student is that, while in class, he really has only one pertinent question, which is, What does this guy, his professor at the moment, want? Whatever it is—a good dose of liberalism, libertarianism, feminism, conservatism—he gives it to him, in exchange for another A to slip into his backpack alongside all the others on his long trudge to the Harvard, Yale, Stanford law or business schools, and thence into the empyrean.

7 Murray Kempton once wrote that intellectual contentment in America consists in not giving a damn about Harvard.[8] Harvard—and Yale, Princeton, Stanford, and the others— has over the past three or four decades made this contentment easy to achieve. All these schools have done so by becoming, at least in their humanities and social sciences sides,

---

Sample Student Commentary

[3] The thesis, though clear, still remains more implicit than explicit. Rather than building his case, Epstein begins by dismissing the opposing view.

[4] The thesis is still not stated explicitly, but implied in a rhetorical question.

[5] Epstein is careful to make certain his reader knows the thesis is his opinion, what "[he] think[s] of as..."

[6] Epstein most likely knows this generalized summary will resonate with readers who already agree with him but will not convince those who do not. He probably does not intend this piece to be persuasive, but merely expressive of his view.

[7] These are not rhetorical questions. Since Epstein answers the questions he raises, he is advancing his argument by hypophora.

[8] Murray Kempton was a Pulitzer Prize-winning journalist. That he wrote this statement attributed to him is verifiable. Whether it is an accurate or true assessment is not.

more and more mired in the mediocre. The reason for this is the politicization of the subjects that these academics, who have only the blurriest notion of how academic freedom is supposed to work, have allowed to take over the universities.[9]

8   Harvard, I remember hearing some years ago,[10] is looking for a strong feminist. One should have thought it would be the other way round: feminism trying to establish a beachhead at Harvard. Not so. Like Gadarene swine,[11] the putatively best of American colleges have rushed to take on the worst of intellectual freight.[12] Behind the much-vaunted notion of diversity in contemporary universities is the attempt to make sure that no corpus of bad ideas isn't amply represented. In this attempt, the top universities have succeeded admirably.

9   The problem set for the good student, then, is to negotiate his way through this bramble of bad ideas.[13] My son, who went to Stanford, told me at the time that a not uncommon opening session in some of his classes was for a professor to announce that he was going to teach his course from the Marxist (or feminist or new historicist or Foucauldian) point of view, but he wanted the students to know that everyone in class was entirely free to disagree with him, and indeed he encouraged strong disagreement. My son was the boy who, from the back of the room, could be heard faintly muttering, "Yeah, sure, for a B-."[14]

10   I did my teaching at Northwestern University, where most of the students had what I came to regard as "the habits of achievement." They did the reading, most of them could write a respectable paper, many of them talked decently in response to my questions. They made it difficult for me to give them less than a B for the course. But the only students who genuinely interested me went beyond being good students to become passionate ones. Their minds, I could tell, were engaged upon more than merely getting another high grade. The number of such students was remarkably small; if I had to pin it down, I should say they comprised well under 3 percent, and not all of them received A's from me.

11   Meanwhile our good student, resembling no one so much as that Italian character in Catch-22 who claimed to have flourished under the fascists, then flourished under

---

Sample Student Commentary

[9] Notice that Epstein has shifted his focus from a criticism of President-elect Obama's proposed cabinet to a criticism of the schools themselves. Also notice that, in this purely expressive column, Epstein does not offer any specific examples or verifiable facts.

[10] For those readers still expecting a thesis-proof argument, note that Epstein continues to stay on the level of personal reflection, speculation, and opinion.

[11] In Matthew 8: 28-32, Jesus drives a legion of demons out of a possessed man. The demons enter a herd of swine, and the swine then run into the Sea of Galilee, where they drown. Clearly, the illusion suggests a mad and self-destructive mass action.

[12] Antithesis: the best versus the worst. Note, however, that these are evaluative terms—in the superlative, which is difficult at best to prove—and unelaborated by examples or illustrations.

[13] Between the last sentence of the previous paragraph and the first sentence of this paragraph, Epstein commits the logical fallacy of Begging The Question. Without establishing the accuracy of his assertion that the ideas taught in universities are "bad," he describes the "good student's" plight of having to "negotiate…this bramble of bad ideas."

[14] Epstein does here provide his reader with a specific, verifiable example. He does not, however, establish the truth or validity of his son's assertion.

the Communists, and was confident he would also flourish under the Americans, treks on his merry way.[15] From Yale to Harvard Law School, or Harvard to Yale Law School, or to one of the highly regarded (and content empty) business schools, he goes, as the Victorians had it, from strength to strength.

12 In recent years I have come to think that some of the worst people in the United States have gone to the Harvard or Yale Law Schools: Mr. and Mrs. Eliot Spitzer, Mr. and Mrs. William Clinton, and countless others.[16] And why not, since these institutions serve as the grandest receptacles in the land for our good students: those clever, sometimes brilliant, but rarely deep young men and women who, joining furious drive to burning if ultimately empty ambition, will do anything to get ahead.

13 Universities are of course the last bastion of snobbery in America. The problem is that the snobbery works. Nor is this snobbery likely to be seriously eroded in our lifetime. No parent whose child has the choice of going to Princeton or Arizona State is likely to advise the kid to become a Sun Devil. Go to one of the supposedly better schools and your chances for success in the great world increase, flat-out, no doubt about it. To have been accepted at one of the top schools means that a child has done what he was told, followed instructions, kept his eye on the prize, played the game, and won. But does it mean much more?

14 Harry S. Truman and Ronald Reagan were two of the greatest presidents of the twentieth century.[17] Truman didn't go to college at all, and Reagan, one strains to remember, went to Eureka College in Eureka, Illinois. Each was his own man, each, in his different way, without the least trace of conformity or hostage to received opinion or conventional wisdom. Schooling, even what passes for the best schooling, would, one feels,[18] have made either man less himself and thereby probably worse.

15 The presence and continued flourishing of Harvard, Yale, Princeton, Stanford, and the rest do perform a genuine service. They allow America to believe it has a meritocracy, even though there is no genuine known merit about it.[19] Perhaps one has to have taught at or otherwise had a closer look at these institutions to realize how thin they are. I myself feel their thinness so keenly that, on more than one occasion, I have, by way of informing one friend or acquaintance about another, said, "He went to Princeton and then to the Harvard Law School, but, really, he is much better than that."[20] ❦

Joseph Epstein, a contributing editor to *The Weekly Standard*, is the author most recently of *Fred Astaire*.

Sample Student Commentary

[15] Another allusion, this one from literature. Notice that it provides neither an example of the type of student Epstein is describing nor evidence that such students do, in fact, comprise the majority of university students.

[16] Again, Epstein has been very careful to inform his reader that his judgments are what he has come to think.

[17] Here Epstein begins to return his focus to his original topic: the value of President-elect Obama's "valedictocracy".

[18] Note the shift from Epstein's earlier first-person statements of opinion to this third-person suggestion that this assertion is a commonly held belief.

[19] After apparently beginning a transition back to his original topic—the President and cabinet—this final paragraph returns to a personal criticism of what he has called "the putatively best of American colleges."

[20] Epstein leaves his reader with a quotation, but not one that establishes others' agreement with his view. In this quotation, Epstein is quoting himself.

Sample multiple-choice questions:

1. The phrase in the first paragraph that most clearly asserts Mr. Epstein's argument is

    A. "the excellent David Brooks."

    B. "the high quality of people."

    C. "it turns out."

    D. "that ignorant ninny."

    E. "like dead flies on flypaper."

2. Structurally, the purpose of the second full paragraph is to

    A. illustrate Epstein's concern.

    B. provide important background.

    C. clarify the thesis.

    D. assuage the opposition.

    E. qualify the argument.

3. All of the following suggest the purpose of this column EXCEPT

    A. "I believe…" (paragraph 6).

    B. "I think of…" (paragraph 5).

    C. "many of them possibly…" (paragraph 4).

    D. "I have come to distrust…" (paragraph 5).

    E. "I remember hearing…" (paragraph 8).

4. The organizational pattern of this column can best be described as

    A. thesis-proof.

    B. thesis-antithesis.

    C. assertion-illustration.

    D. opinion-elaboration.

    E. enquiry-response.

5. The structure of this column can best be described as

    A. linear.

    B. cyclic.

    C. circular.

    D. desultory.

    E. tangential.

Answers and Explanations:

1. Because this column is a "dissent" and not a formal argument, Epstein is not obligated to state an explicit thesis. He can legitimately suggest his agreement or disagreement through attitude and tone. (A) is so early in the column that we do not even know the topic, let alone Epstein's position. As the phrase in itself does not convey irony or sarcasm, (B) suggests admiration. (C) is tempting, as the phrase begins to qualify the apparent admiration, but it is not the best answer. (D) might also be tempting, but it is a quotation, and it is still possible that Epstein will disagree with James. (E), however, is an unambiguously negative comparison qualifying the prestigious schools named in the column with which Epstein is disagreeing. It is the clearest impression thus far of how Epstein views the men and women named to the cabinet. **Thus, (E) is the best answer.**

2. As Epstein's entire column is founded upon another writer's work, it will be very difficult for anyone who has not read the column with which he disagrees to fully appreciate Epstein's dissent. (A) might tempt some students, but the paragraph is something stronger than merely an illustration. (C) is easily eliminated by the fact that Epstein has not specified a thesis, and the quoted paragraph certainly does nothing to explain Epstein's disagreement. Nowhere in the column does Epstein acknowledge or attempt to assuage his opposition (D). He is clearly writing this column for those who already essentially agree with him. And, as this column does not introduce or advance an argument *per se*, (E) is eliminated. **(B), however, is the best answer as it allows Epstein's reader to view firsthand the wording and tone of the piece with which he is disagreeing.**

3. The column is, by Epstein's admission, a "dissent." Clearly, the writer is expressing his view of the topic without expressly intending to persuade anyone to agree with him. Thus, any phrasing that emphasizes the basis of his statement in his personal view and experience, (A), (B), (D), and (E), suggests the column's non-persuasive purpose. (C), however, is different. This statement is not personal opinion but speculation—"possibly." **Thus, (C) is the best answer.**

4. Again, Epstein does not intend this piece to persuade those who do not already agree with him. His "thesis" is, at best, implied through tone and figurative language; and he offers no real, verifiable factual "proof" for any of his points. The few examples he does offer are more illustrative than informative or persuasive. Thus, (A) is clearly excluded. Epstein does not acknowledge an opposing view, so (B) is eliminated. (C) is tempting, but not all of Epstein's assertions are illustrated by allusion or example. Likewise, (E) might tempt some, but Epstein actually employs only one hypophora to support this choice. The entire column, however, is organized by Epstein's making an assertion—about the schools, the students who strive to attend them, and the persons who graduate from them—followed by an elaboration or expansion of that assertion. **Thus, (D) is the best answer.**

5. Remember that structure refers to the flow of information across the entire column. (A) is tempting, as the piece does begin by discussing the men and women nominated for President-elect Obama's cabinet, then shifts to a criticism of Ivy League schools and students who attend them; in addition, there are instances in which Epstein returns to a previously discussed topic, but (A) is not the best answer. The essay begins with Obama's proposed cabinet and ends with a general criticism of a person who attended Ivy League undergraduate and graduate school, never returning to Obama or the cabinet, so (C) is clearly eliminated. There are clear transitions from one point to the next, even as they cycle back to a previous point, so (D), though tempting to some, is eliminated. (E) is easily eliminated because not every point in the discussion is an immediate leap in a new direction from the previous point. Throughout the column, however, Epstein does return to the idea of the "good student" after he has seemed to move on. He does return to the impact of education on the quality of a presidential administration, and so on. **Thus, (B) is the best answer.**

Sample free-response item:

Carefully read Joseph Epstein's "Obama's Good Students: A dissent on the 'valedictocracy.'" Epstein is a former university professor and a regular columnist and author. In this column, he responds to an earlier column he read in which the author praised the credentials of the men and women then-President-elect Barack Obama had suggested for his cabinet.

After reading Epstein's dissent, write an essay in which you analyze how the structure and organizational pattern help Epstein to both achieve his stated purpose and possibly affect his reader's viewpoint.

Do not merely summarize the passage.

Sample Student Essay

In his article, "Obama's Good Students: A dissent on the 'valedictocracy,'" Joseph Epstein attacks the idea that a cabinet made up of "good students" from leading schools is good for the American government. Epstein organizes his ideas in a cyclical pattern; this allows him to return to previous ideas, bolstering them with new ideas from other topics he has developed in the interim. Though the article does not present any explicit arguments, Epstein criticizes the quality of the schools the nominees attended, thereby implicitly criticizing the quality of the nominees. Because he presents little factual information, he merely cycles from point to point; a logical argument would move directly from point to point, building steam as it progressed. Epstein's article, instead, interweaves its points, with the purpose of laying out his position and, possibly, changing the reader's view on elite universities.

Each paragraph of Epstein's article serves to develop one of two main ideas that

Epstein has previously introduced. Roughly, these ideas are as follows: first, leading universities (Harvard, Yale, etc.) are bad; second, the average, goal-driven student of these universities is bad. From these main points, the reader can extrapolate that Epstein believes the students of these universities have little merit and, therefore, the cabinet appointees are poor choices. To develop these main points, Epstein presents his ideas in a cyclical pattern. Where Epstein writes a paragraph attacking universities, he usually follows that paragraph with one attacking the "good student," and vice versa. The informal structure of the piece allows him to return to a point previously developed, as if remembering a particularly important bit of information while in conversation.

Epstein's article is more declaratory than argumentative. Instead of logical arguments, the reader is presented with assertions that Epstein backs up with anecdotes and opinions. This organizational pattern fits his purpose. Because this is not a persuasive piece, Epstein does not need to present arguments to convince the reader that he (Epstein) is correct. Epstein is free, then, to make assertions and expand upon them without the standard logical organizational pattern: present premises, present conclusion, show how conclusion logically follows from premises. One could assert that such a structure would have been inappropriate for this article, as it presents little in the way of factual information and is full of generalizations.

One could also make the argument that the goal of Epstein's piece is to slant the reader's opinion against elite universities such as Harvard and Stanford. Early in the article, Epstein mentions that he taught in a university for thirty years. This serves to establish him as an authority on the subject. By presenting this information first, Epstein predisposes the reader to become more accepting of his opinions on university students, and so he immediately presents his negative opinion of those students. Likewise, if he was a professor at a university, then the implication is that he understands universities better than someone who is not a professor; he mentions this very idea in the article's final paragraph.

The structural and organizational strategies Epstein uses in order to present his points are not the result of disjointed thought, though the article flits from point to point seemingly at the whim of the author. Epstein deliberately organizes his article in this way because it best suits his purpose. In writing for an audience already disposed to agree with him on the question of whether "good students" make good governors, the use of non-factual assertions does not hurt his cause. Epstein has probably chosen the best possible structure in writing an article in which hard facts are difficult to come by. ❦

Exercise Three:

Questions 11-15. Read the following passage carefully before you choose your answers.

This passage is an essay written by Emma Goldman (1869-1940), a notorious early twentieth-century political anarchist. During her life, she was often referred to as "the most dangerous woman in America," and she was jailed numerous times for "inciting to riots," "illegally distributing information," and "inducing persons not to register" for the draft. "The Tragedy of Women's Emancipation" was originally published in Anarchism and Other Essays *in 1910 by the Mother Earth Publishing Association. The following is as the essay appeared in the 1917 edition of the same book.*

The Tragedy of Woman's Emancipation
BY EMMA GOLDMAN

1   I BEGIN WITH AN ADMISSION: Regardless of all political and economic theories, treating of the fundamental differences between various groups within the human race, regardless of class and race distinctions, regardless of all artificial boundary lines between woman's rights and man's rights, I hold that there is a point where these differentiations may meet and grow into one perfect whole.

2   With this I do not mean to propose a peace treaty. The general social antagonism which has taken hold of our entire public life today, brought about through the force of opposing and contradictory interests, will crumble to pieces when the reorganization of our social life, based upon the principles of economic justice, shall have become a reality.

3   Peace or harmony between the sexes and individuals does not necessarily depend on a superficial equalization of human beings; nor does it call for the elimination of individual traits and peculiarities. The problem that confronts us today, and which the nearest future is to solve, is how to be one's self and yet in oneness with others, to feel deeply with all human beings and still retain one's own characteristic qualities. This seems to me to be the basis upon which the mass and the individual, the true democrat and the true individuality, man and woman, can meet without antagonism and opposition. The motto should not be: Forgive one another; rather, Understand one another. The oft-quoted sentence of Madame de Stael: "To understand everything means to forgive everything," has never particularly appealed to me; it has the odor of the confessional; to forgive one's fellow-being conveys the idea of pharisaical superiority. To understand one's fellow-being suffices. The admission partly represents the fundamental aspect of my views on the emancipation of woman and its effect upon the entire sex.

4   Emancipation should make it possible for woman to be human in the truest sense. Everything within her that craves assertion and activity should reach its fullest expression; all artificial barriers should be broken, and the road towards greater freedom cleared of every trace of centuries of submission and slavery.

5   This was the original aim of the movement for woman's emancipation. But the results

so far achieved have isolated woman and have robbed her of the fountain springs of that happiness which is so essential to her. Merely external emancipation has made of the modern woman an artificial being, who reminds one of the products of French arboriculture with its arabesque trees and shrubs, pyramids, wheels, and wreaths; anything, except the forms which would be reached by the expression of her own inner qualities. Such artificially grown plants of the female sex are to be found in large numbers, especially in the so-called intellectual sphere of our life.

6   Liberty and equality for woman! What hopes and aspirations these words awakened when they were first uttered by some of the noblest and bravest souls of those days. The sun in all his light and glory was to rise upon a new world; in this world woman was to be free to direct her own destiny—an aim certainly worthy of the great enthusiasm, courage, perseverance, and ceaseless effort of the tremendous host of pioneer men and women, who staked everything against a world of prejudice and ignorance.

7   My hopes also move towards that goal, but I hold that the emancipation of woman, as interpreted and practically applied today, has failed to reach that great end. Now, woman is confronted with the necessity of emancipating herself from emancipation, if she really desires to be free. This may sound paradoxical, but is, nevertheless, only too true.

8   What has she achieved through her emancipation? Equal suffrage in a few States. Has that purified our political life, as many well-meaning advocates predicted? Certainly not. Incidentally, it is really time that persons with plain, sound judgment should cease to talk about corruption in politics in a boarding-school tone. Corruption of politics has nothing to do with the morals, or the laxity of morals, of various political personalities. Its cause is altogether a material one. Politics is the reflex of the business and industrial world, the mottos of which are: "To take is more blessed than to give"; "buy cheap and sell dear"; "one soiled hand washes the other." There is no hope even that woman, with her right to vote, will ever purify politics.

9   Emancipation has brought woman economic equality with man; that is, she can choose her own profession and trade; but as her past and present physical training has not equipped her with the necessary strength to compete with man, she is often compelled to exhaust all her energy, use up her vitality, and strain every nerve in order to reach the market value. Very few ever succeed, for it is a fact that women teachers, doctors, lawyers, architects, and engineers are neither met with the same confidence as their male colleagues, nor receive equal remuneration. And those that do reach that enticing equality, generally do so at the expense of their physical and psychical well-being. As to the great mass of working girls and women, how much independence is gained if the narrowness and lack of freedom of the home is exchanged for the narrowness and lack of freedom of the factory, sweat-shop, department store, or office? In addition is the burden which is laid on many women of looking after a "home, sweet home"—cold, dreary, disorderly, uninviting—after a day's hard work. Glorious independence! No wonder that hundreds of girls are willing to accept the first offer of marriage, sick and tired of their "independence" behind the counter, at the sewing or typewriting machine. They are just as ready to marry as girls of the middle class, who long to throw off the yoke of parental supremacy. A so-called independence which leads only to earning the merest subsistence is not so enticing, not so ideal, that one could expect woman to sacrifice everything for

it. Our highly praised independence is, after all, but a slow process of dulling and stifling woman's nature, her love instinct, and her mother instinct.

10   Nevertheless, the position of the working girl is far more natural and human than that of her seemingly more fortunate sister in the more cultured professional walks of life—teachers, physicians, lawyers, engineers, etc., who have to make a dignified, proper appearance, while the inner life is growing empty and dead.

11   The narrowness of the existing conception of woman's independence and emancipation; the dread of love for a man who is not her social equal; the fear that love will rob her of her freedom and independence; the horror that love or the joy of motherhood will only hinder her in the full exercise of her profession—all these together make of the emancipated modern woman a compulsory vestal, before whom life, with its great clarifying sorrows and its deep, entrancing joys, rolls on without touching or gripping her soul.

12   Emancipation, as understood by the majority of its adherents and exponents, is of too narrow a scope to permit the boundless love and ecstasy contained in the deep emotion of the true woman, sweetheart, mother, in freedom.

13   The tragedy of the self-supporting or economically free woman does not lie in too many but in too few experiences. True, she surpasses her sister of past generations in knowledge of the world and human nature; it is just because of this that she feels deeply the lack of life's essence, which alone can enrich the human soul, and without which the majority of women have become mere professional automatons.

14   That such a state of affairs was bound to come was foreseen by those who realized that, in the domain of ethics, there still remained many decaying ruins of the time of the undisputed superiority of man; ruins that are still considered useful. And, what is more important, a goodly number of the emancipated are unable to get along without them. Every movement that aims at the destruction of existing institutions and the replacement thereof with something more advanced, more perfect, has followers who in theory stand for the most radical ideas, but who, nevertheless, in their every-day practice, are like the average Philistine, feigning respectability and clamoring for the good opinion of their opponents. There are, for example, Socialists, and even Anarchists, who stand for the idea that property is robbery, yet who will grow indignant if anyone owe them the value of a half-dozen pins.

15   The same Philistine can be found in the movement for woman's emancipation. Yellow journalists and milk-and-water litterateurs have painted pictures of the emancipated woman that make the hair of the good citizen and his dull companion stand up on end. Every member of the woman's rights movement was pictured as a George Sand in her absolute disregard of morality. Nothing was sacred to her. She had no respect for the ideal relation between man and woman. In short, emancipation stood only for a reckless life of lust and sin; regardless of society, religion, and morality. The exponents of woman's rights were highly indignant at such representation, and, lacking humor, they exerted all their energy to prove that they were not at all as bad as they were painted, but the very reverse. Of course, as long as woman was the slave of man, she could not be good and pure, but now that she was free and independent she would prove how good she could be and that her influence would have a purifying effect on all institutions in society. True,

the movement for woman's rights has broken many old fetters, but it has also forged new ones. The great movement of *true* emancipation has not met with a great race of women who could look liberty in the face. Their narrow, Puritanical vision banished man, as a disturber and doubtful character, out of their emotional life. Man was not to be tolerated at any price, except perhaps as the father of a child, since a child could not very well come to life without a father. Fortunately, the most rigid Puritans never will be strong enough to kill the innate craving for motherhood. But woman's freedom is closely allied with man's freedom, and many of my so-called emancipated sisters seem to overlook the fact that a child born in freedom needs the love and devotion of each human being about him, man as well as woman. Unfortunately, it is this narrow conception of human relations that has brought about a great tragedy in the lives of the modern man and woman.

16   About fifteen years ago appeared a work from the pen of the brilliant Norwegian, Laura Marholm, called *Woman, a Character Study.* She was one of the first to call attention to the emptiness and narrowness of the existing conception of woman's emancipation, and its tragic effect upon the inner life of woman. In her work Laura Marholm speaks of the fate of several gifted women of international fame: the genius, Eleonora Duse; the great mathematician and writer, Sonya Kovalevskaia; the artist and poet-nature, Marie Bashkirtzeff, who died so young. Through each description of the lives of these women of such extraordinary mentality runs a marked trail of unsatisfied craving for a full, rounded, complete, and beautiful life, and the unrest and loneliness resulting from the lack of it. Through these masterly psychological sketches, one cannot help but see that the higher the mental development of woman, the less possible it is for her to meet a congenial mate who will see in her, not only sex, but also the human being, the friend, the comrade and strong individuality, who cannot and ought not lose a single trait of her character.

17   The average man with his self-sufficiency, his ridiculously superior airs of patronage towards the female sex, is an impossibility for woman as depicted in the "character study" by Laura Marholm. Equally impossible for her is the man who can see in her nothing more than her mentality and her genius, and who fails to awaken her woman nature.

18   A rich intellect and a fine soul are usually considered necessary attributes of a deep and beautiful personality. In the case of the modern woman, these attributes serve as a hindrance to the complete assertion of her being. For over a hundred years the old form of marriage, based on the Bible, "till death doth part," has been denounced as an institution that stands for the sovereignty of the man over the woman, of her complete submission to his whims and commands, and absolute dependence on his name and support. Time and again it has been conclusively proved that the old matrimonial relation restricted woman to the function of a man's servant and the bearer of his children. And yet we find many emancipated women who prefer marriage, with all its deficiencies, to the narrowness of an unmarried life; narrow and unendurable because of the chains of moral and social prejudice that cramp and bind her nature.

19   The explanation of such inconsistency on the part of many advanced women is to be found in the fact that they never truly understood the meaning of emancipation. They thought that all that was needed was independence from external tyrannies; the internal

tyrants, far more harmful to life and growth—ethical and social conventions—were left to take care of themselves; and they have taken care of themselves. They seem to get along as beautifully in the heads and hearts of the most active exponents of woman's emancipation, as in the heads and hearts of our grandmothers.

20   These internal tyrants, whether they be in the form of public opinion or what will mother say, or brother, father, aunt, or relative of any sort; what will Mrs. Grundy, Mr. Comstock, the employer, the Board of Education say? All these busybodies, moral detectives, jailers of the human spirit, what will they say? Until woman has learned to defy them all, to stand firmly on her own ground and to insist upon her own unrestricted freedom, to listen to the voice of her nature, whether it call for life's greatest treasure, love for a man, or her most glorious privilege, the right to give birth to a child, she cannot call herself emancipated. How many emancipated women are brave enough to acknowledge that the voice of love is calling, wildly beating against their breasts, demanding to be heard, to be satisfied.

21   The French writer, Jean Reibrach, in one of his novels, *New Beauty*, attempts to picture the ideal, beautiful, emancipated woman. This ideal is embodied in a young girl, a physician. She talks very cleverly and wisely of how to feed infants; she is kind, and administers medicines free to poor mothers. She converses with a young man of her acquaintance about the sanitary conditions of the future, and how various bacilli and germs shall be exterminated by the use of stone walls and floors, and by the doing away with rugs and hangings. She is, of course, very plainly and practically dressed, mostly in black. The young man, who, at their first meeting, was overawed by the wisdom of his emancipated friend, gradually learns to understand her, and recognizes one fine day that he loves her. They are young, and she is kind and beautiful, and though always in rigid attire, her appearance is softened by a spotlessly clean white collar and cuffs. One would expect that he would tell her of his love, but he is not one to commit romantic absurdities. Poetry and the enthusiasm of love cover their blushing faces before the pure beauty of the lady. He silences the voice of his nature, and remains correct. She, too, is always exact, always rational, always well behaved. I fear if they had formed a union, the young man would have risked freezing to death. I must confess that I can see nothing beautiful in this new beauty, who is as cold as the stone walls and floors she dreams of. Rather would I have the love songs of romantic ages, rather Don Juan and Madame Venus, rather an elopement by ladder and rope on a moonlight night, followed by the father's curse, mother's moans, and the moral comments of neighbors, than correctness and propriety measured by yardsticks. If love does not know how to give and take without restrictions, it is not love, but a transaction that never fails to lay stress on a plus and a minus.

22   The greatest shortcoming of the emancipation of the present day lies in its artificial stiffness and its narrow respectabilities, which produce an emptiness in woman's soul that will not let her drink from the fountain of life. I once remarked that there seemed to be a deeper relationship between the old-fashioned mother and hostess, ever on the alert for the happiness of her little ones and the comfort of those she loved, and the truly new woman, than between the latter and her average emancipated sister. The disciples of emancipation pure and simple declared me a heathen, fit only for the stake. Their blind

183

zeal did not let them see that my comparison between the old and the new was merely to prove that a goodly number of our grandmothers had more blood in their veins, far more humor and wit, and certainly a greater amount of naturalness, kind-heartedness, and simplicity, than the majority of our emancipated professional women who fill the colleges, halls of learning, and various offices. This does not mean a wish to return to the past, nor does it condemn woman to her old sphere, the kitchen and the nursery.

23   Salvation lies in an energetic march onward towards a brighter and clearer future. We are in need of unhampered growth out of old traditions and habits. The movement for woman's emancipation has so far made but the first step in that direction. It is to be hoped that it will gather strength to make another. The right to vote, or equal civil rights, may be good demands, but true emancipation begins neither at the polls nor in courts. It begins in woman's soul. History tells us that every oppressed class gained true liberation from its masters through its own efforts. It is necessary that woman learn that lesson, that she realize that her freedom will reach as far as her power to achieve her freedom reaches. It is, therefore, far more important for her to begin with her inner regeneration, to cut loose from the weight of prejudices, traditions, and customs. The demand for equal rights in every vocation of life is just and fair; but, after all, the most vital right is the right to love and be loved. Indeed, if partial emancipation is to become a complete and true emancipation of woman, it will have to do away with the ridiculous notion that to be loved, to be sweetheart and mother, is synonymous with being slave or subordinate. It will have to do away with the absurd notion of the dualism of the sexes, or that man and woman represent two antagonistic worlds.

24   Pettiness separates; breadth unites. Let us be broad and big. Let us not overlook vital things because of the bulk of trifles confronting us. A true conception of the relation of the sexes will not admit of conqueror and conquered; it knows of but one great thing: to give of one's self boundlessly, in order to find one's self richer, deeper, better. That alone can fill the emptiness, and transform the tragedy of woman's emancipation into joy, limitless joy. ☙

Emma Goldman, "The Tragedy of Woman's Emancipation," from Anarchism and Other Essays, *1917.*

Multiple-choice questions:

11. The structure of this essay can best be described as
   A. linear.
   B. cyclic.
   C. circular.
   D. desultory.
   E. tangential.

12. The sentence that most clearly asserts Ms. Goldman's main point is

A. "To understand one's fellow-being suffices." (paragraph 3).

B. "Emancipation should make it possible for woman to be human in the truest sense." (paragraph 4).

C. "Merely external emancipation has made of the modern woman an artificial being..." (paragraph 5).

D. "...woman is confronted with the necessity of emancipating herself from emancipation..." (paragraph 7).

E. "To take is more blessed than to give." (paragraph 8).

13. An opponent of Goldman's view could legitimately criticize this essay because of which of the following?

A. The essay's thesis is unclear.

B. The language is inappropriate.

C. The essay lacks illustration and support.

D. The complex organizational pattern is confusing.

E. The essay lacks closure.

14. Which of the following lines from the last two paragraphs most accurately summarizes Goldman's thesis?

A. "The demand for equal rights in every vocation of life is just and fair..."

B. "...man and woman represent two antagonistic worlds..."

C. "...to be loved, to be sweetheart and mother, is synonymous with being slave or subordinate."

D. "to give of one's self boundlessly, in order to find one's self richer, deeper, better."

E. "That alone can fill the emptiness, and transform the tragedy of woman's emancipation into joy, limitless joy."

15. Which of the following pairs of phrases best identifies that evolution of ideas from the beginning to the end of Goldman's essay?

A. superficial equalization—salvation

B. social antagonism—artificial stiffness

C. peace or harmony—equal civil rights

D. equal suffrage—inner regeneration

E. narrowness and lack of freedom—emancipation

Free Response Item:

Carefully read Emma Goldman's essay "The Tragedy of Woman's Emancipation," in which she argues what the true goal of the early-twentieth-century's first wave of feminism should be. Then, write a thoughtful and well-supported essay in which you analyze the structure and organization of the piece and explain how they help Goldman achieve her purpose and reach her intended audience.

Synthesizing information from multiple sources—The Synthesis Essay

CHAPTER 5

✖ What is a Synthesis Essay?

The Synthesis Essay, though it sounds foreboding and may instill some fear in your heart, is not an altogether different type of essay from anything else you've written for school or while working in this book. Put simply, a Synthesis Essay is an essay for which the writer has consulted one or more sources in order to gather information and learn what others have said about a particular subject matter.

Consider this: Every sample essay you've read in this book and every essay you've written while using this book has been based on a passage you read and then responded to. Perhaps, you had to analyze the passage's structure or organization, analyze the author's use of language, including literary and figurative devices, or evaluate the effectiveness of an author's writing choices. The Synthesis Essay asks for nothing terribly different. It simply requires you to consult and cite more sources.

Do not be tricked into thinking, however, that your Synthesis Essay is *about* your sources. Whatever you are asked to do—evaluate an argument; analyze a technique; trace the development of an idea—you will first need to construct a thesis, a statement of *your* argument, the central idea of your essay. You will then use information gleaned from your multiple sources to illustrate and support your thesis. In addition, you may present a source's argument as a point to refute or qualify.

The key to a successful Synthesis Essay, then, is to draw ideas from your sources, formulate some of your own ideas, and create, or *synthesize*, a new argument, which you will state and support in your own essay.

❖ The Purpose of a Synthesis Essay

First, consider that no professional writer will actually ever write anything he or she would call a "Synthesis Essay," so from that standpoint, this is a purely contrived form. All professional writers, however, unless their subject matter comes completely from their memories or imaginations, will draw on a number and variety of different sources for information, new ways of thinking about a subject, other persons' views and opinions. In that sense then, virtually everything a professional writer writes is a synthesis piece: synthesis news article, synthesis novel, synthesis editorial, etc.

Since nearly everything a writer writes is, to some degree, a synthesis piece, it makes sense that Synthesis Essays can be written for exactly the same purposes that any other pieces are written: to inform, to persuade, to express a personal view or opinion, to entertain. The *only difference* between a Synthesis Essay and any other piece of writing is the number and variety of sources you will consult in planning your essay and the care with which you will refer to and cite the sources you use.

The purpose of the Synthesis Essay on the Advanced Placement Exam in English Language and Composition, however, is to test whether you, as a writer, are able to glean information and insight from others' work and the extent to which you are able to credit other sources in your work for the ideas you got from them.

You will usually be able to determine the governing purpose (to persuade, to inform, etc.) from the specific language in the writing prompt, the section headed "Assignment." In the actual essay you are going to write, you may be asked to evaluate an argument, to argue a position on a topic (often you are asked to support, refute, or qualify someone else's thesis), to explain the nature of the relationships that exist among the various sources provided to you, or to compare and contrast different writers' views or approaches.

This part of the exam will require a different thought process and mindset for you to write a successful essay, but if you have based all of your other essays on your understanding of and response to the passages about which you were asked to write, the differences will not be huge.

❖ How to Use Your Sources

It is important to remember that your essay is not *about your sources*. The sources exist only as support or illustration for *your thesis*.

That said, your use of the source material in your Synthesis Essay should be governed by the same principles that govern your use of source material (whether a single or multiple sources). In other words, any time you use another person's words or ideas, you must give that person credit.

Generally speaking, researchers and writers use sources in various ways:

Direct Quotation: You actually use the words verbatim from the source. You must place the quotation within quotation marks (" "), and you *should* orient your reader to the fact that you are going to be quoting a source.

EXAMPLES: According to Klondike, "All whales under a certain age…"

Smythe writes, "The problem with egrets is…"

For a piece the length of your Synthesis Essay, you should keep all direct quotations short (no more than a sentence), and you should reserve quotation only for instances in which the source's language is so specific or technical that you cannot paraphrase or summarize it accurately.

Sprinkling your "own" writing with individual words in quotation marks, even if those "words" are "borrowed" from your source, is usually "very distracting to your reader." Save direct quotations for important occasions.

Paraphrase: You restate the source's content keeping the source's order and tone, cutting out no details, etc., *but you state it in your own words.*

EXAMPLE: You report what you learned from the source, in the same order, and tone. You don't eliminate any of the source's details, but you use your own words.

Paraphrase comes in handy when you need to present a larger portion of information from a source than you can reasonably quote (remember that direct quotations are limited to a single sentence in a good Synthesis Essay), but you still want to establish that you have not altered—abbreviated, evaluated, interpreted, misstated—the source's content in any way.

You must still credit the source for the ideas you are presenting.

EXAMPLES: While explaining the importance of whales to the environment, Klondike explains that whales are an important part of the food chain. They eat krill that could potentially clog the ocean's ecology, and they provide important nutrients to many varieties of plankton…

Smythe continues to describe the problems inherent in training a domesticated egret by insisting that egrets are too large and too solitary to be brought into close contact with people…

Summary: Using your own words, you provide your reader with a brief overview of the source's key point or points. Summary is most effective if you simply want to offer an entire essay's main point as support, or if time and space limitations will not allow you to provide a more detailed discussion of the source.

EXAMPLES: Klondike posits three key reasons for the preservation of whales: They are an important part of the food chain; they provide necessary oxygenation to ocean waters; and they are fun to observe.

Smythe insists that, due to both physiology and psychology, egrets simply do not make good pets.

Direct and Indirect Reference: This is generally an issue in a longer paper that includes footnotes or endnotes or in-text citation and a works cited page. To refer to your source directly, you simply name the source, by title or author, in the body of your essay. All of the previous references to Klondike and Smythe are direct references. Indirect reference includes the vague, anonymous reference to "sources" or "experts" without actually naming any. In a longer research paper, you would still be obligated to provide a note and a works cited entry. In your AP Synthesis Essay, it is a better idea simply to refer to whatever sources you use directly.

Interpretation: All of the previous techniques for incorporating source material into your essay presume you're presenting facts from the source or restating the source's viewpoint or opinion. In your essay, however, you might feel you need to explain what the material from the source means. For example, if you were examining a political cartoon and noticed that the caricature's left eye was closed and the right eye was open, it would probably not be enough simply to tell your reader that. You would want to include an interpretation: The closed eye suggests the half-blind nature of the self-satisfied politician who sees it as his sole responsibility to get reelected.

EXAMPLES: Klondike's frequent references to humanity in nature indicate her firm belief that humans are not above or apart from nature but are subject to the same laws and forces that govern every other living creature.

Smythe specifies that the egret can reach a height of five feet and a weight of forty-five pounds, clearly too large for a New York City apartment dweller to consider taking home and raising.

Analysis: Interpretation provides an explanation of what the source material means. Analysis, however, explains how it is constructed or how it works.

EXAMPLE: One cannot help, however, questioning Smythe's apparently naïve conclusion. The color of the snowy egret (pure white) might indeed suggest the bird's goodness and purity [*this statement is interpretation*], but it is equally possible to see a ghostlike cowardice in the bird's color, or lack thereof [*more interpretation*]. The bird's aloofness, its predatory nature and voracious appetite, and its banshee-like scream that make it unsuitable for both human and animal companionship [*this is analysis*] more accurately portray this water fowl as just plain foul [*this statement is interpretation*]. On the other hand, Klondike assesses the whale justly and accurately. Black and white, gregarious, and trainable [*analysis*], the killer whale is clearly the "good neighbor" of the animal kingdom [*interpretation*].

Evaluation: Once you have examined the meaning of the source (*interpretation*), and the method of the source (*analysis*), you may be asked to discuss the success or failure of the source, its effectiveness as a persuasive piece, its value as a representative of a given culture. This process is evaluation. Be aware that, when you are asked to evaluate an argument or a technique, it is very tempting to leap straight to a conclusion. The readers who will score your Synthesis Essay, however, will be much more concerned with the rationale behind your evaluation than in the evaluation itself.

EXAMPLES: The fact that Klondike cites numerous sources by an international array of scientists and relies on her own firsthand experiences throughout a lifetime of study and exploration can leave little doubt that her observations are accurate and her conclusions valid.

Smythe is certainly well-versed in egret lore, having apparently studied even the most obscure apocryphal texts, but there is no evidence that he has any firsthand experience with the bird or that he has even seen a live egret. His conclusions, therefore, must be taken with some degree of skepticism.

ENGLISH LANGUAGE AND COMPOSITION

SYNTHESIS ESSAY

Sample 1:

Directions: The following prompt is based on the accompanying five sources.

This question requires you to integrate information or views from a variety of different sources into a coherent, well-written essay. *Refer directly to the sources to support your thesis, but do not merely paraphrase or summarize the sources. Your own thesis should be the focus; the sources simply should support this argument.*

Remember that you must attribute both direct and indirect citations.

Introduction
Queen Elizabeth I inherited the throne of England in 1558 when her half-sister Mary I died. The daughter of King Henry VIII and his second wife, Anne Boleyn, Elizabeth was considered by many—especially the Catholics in England and Europe—to be an illegitimate ruler. Still others questioned the legality of having an unmarried woman on the throne. As a result, there had been several attempts on Elizabeth's life. In 1588, King Phillip of Spain sent a powerful Armada against Britain, his intent to destroy Elizabeth and the Protestant English. The Spanish Armada was ultimately blown out to sea by a powerful storm, but the "defeat" of the Armada was a pivotal moment in Elizabeth's reign, allowing her to rule over a Golden Age in England for the next fifteen years.

Assignment
Carefully study the following sources (including all introductory information). Then, write an essay that cites at least three of the sources for illustration, evidence, and support, in which you analyze the role of mythmaking in the recording and reporting of history.

Source A (Leigh)
Source B (Sharp)
Source C (Aske)
Source D (Gower)
Source E (Anonymous)

SOURCE A (Leigh):

William Leigh (1550-1639) was an English clergyman. Shortly after
the accession of James I (1603), he preached before the king and was
appointed tutor to James's eldest son, Henry Frederick,
Prince of Wales.

---

*The following, from a sermon by Leigh published in 1612, is the first published
account of the speech.*

Come on now, my companions at arms, and fellow soldiers,[1] in the field, now
for the Lord, for your Queen, and for the Kingdom. For what are these proud
Philistines, that they should revile the host of the living God?[2] I have been your
Prince in peace,[3] so will I be in war; neither will I bid you go and fight, but come
and let us[4] fight the battle of the Lord. The enemy perhaps may challenge my sex
for that I am a woman,[5] so may I likewise charge their mould for that they are but
men, whose breath is in their nostrils, and if God do not charge England with the
sins of England, little do I fear their force. We commend your prayers, for they
will move the heavens, so do we your powerful preaching,[6] for that will shake the
earth of our earthly hearts, and call us to repentance,[7] whereby our good God may
relieve us and root up in mercy his deserved judgments intended against us, only
be faithful and fear not. Si deus nobiscum quis contra nos?[*]

---

[*] From the Christian New Testament, Romans 8: 31—If God is with us, who can be against us?

Sample Student Commentary

[1] The speech begins with Elizabeth identifying herself with her soldiers, as one of their "fellow[s]."

[2] Biblical and doctrinal allusions. The Spanish are "Philistines," the legendary enemies of the Old Testament Israelites. The queen, the embodiment of England, is the "host," the body of the "Living God."

[3] Possibly an allusion to Isaiah 9:6, in which the Messiah is called "the Prince of Peace."

[4] Antithesis: not bid you go, but...let us."

[5] Elizabeth's gender was an issue during her reign. The Sharp version of this speech is even more eloquent about Elizabeth's gender.

[6] This version of the speech, written by an Anglican minister, cites prayer and preaching as the forces that will defeat the Armada.

[7] It also uses the queen's speech to call the nation to repentance.

SOURCE B (Sharp):

Dr. Leonel Sharp (1559-1631) was an English cleric and courtier. In 1588, while serving as chaplain to Robert Devereux, 2nd Earl of Essex, he was present at the Tilbury camp and reportedly chosen to repeat Queen Elizabeth's speech to the assembled army. This account of the speech was written in a letter from Sharp to the Duke of Buckingham in 1623. While it was written more than a decade later than Leigh's account, it comes from a presumed witness to the event and someone who would, allegedly, be very familiar with the text.

My loving people, we have been persuaded by some that are careful of our safety, to take heed how we commit our selves to armed multitudes, for fear of treachery;[1] but I assure you I do not desire to live to distrust my faithful and loving people. Let tyrants fear. I have always so behaved myself that, under God, I have placed my chiefest strength and safeguard in the loyal hearts and good-will of my subjects; and therefore I am come amongst you, as you see, at this time, not for my recreation and disport, but being resolved, in the midst and heat of the battle, to live and die amongst you all;[2] to lay down for my God, and for my kingdom, and my people, my honour and my blood, even in the dust. I know I have the body but of a weak and feeble woman; but I have the heart and stomach of a king,[3] and of a king of England too, and think foul scorn that Parma or Spain, or any prince of Europe, should dare to invade the borders of my realm; to which rather than any dishonour shall grow by me, I myself will take up arms, I myself will be your general, judge[4], and rewarder of every one of your virtues in the field. I know already, for your forwardness you have deserved rewards and crowns; and We do assure you in the word of a prince, they shall be duly paid you. In the mean time, my lieutenant general shall be in my stead, than whom never prince commanded a more noble or worthy subject; not doubting but by your obedience to my general, by your concord in the camp, and your valour in the field, we shall shortly have a famous victory over those enemies of my God, of my kingdom, and of my people.

Sample Student Commentary

[1] The warnings to which Elizabeth is allegedly alluding are not based on fear of danger in battle, but apprehension that her own armed soldiers would threaten her.

[2] While this version does not have Elizabeth identify herself as a soldier, she still, allegedly, offers to die with her soldiers.

[3] This phrasing of the gender issue is well known and often quoted.

[4] This sentence is a subjunctive construction—"[before] Parma…I [would] take."

SOURCE C (Aske):

Elizabetha triumphans: Containing the dammed practices, that the devilish popes of Rome have used ever since her Highness's first coming to the Crown, by moving her wicked and traitorous subjects to rebellion and conspiracies, thereby to bereave her Majesty both of her lawful seat, and happy life. With a declaration of the manner how her Excellency was entertained by her soldiers into her camp royal at Tilbury in Essex: and of the overthrow had against the Spanish fleet: briefly, truly, and effectually set forth. Declared, and handled by I.A.

While information from various sources disagree, James Aske was apparently a soldier who may or may not have been present at Tilbury. His account appears in the book indicated above, published in London in November 1588.

Then shall I [Aske] write in these my lines too rude
Her royal speech (though nothing like her speech)
Which in effect was it that here ensues.

"We will them know that now by proof we see
Their loyal hearts to us, their lawful Queen.
For sure we are that none beneath the *Heavens*
Have readier Subjects to defend their right:
Which happiness we count to us as chief.
And though of love their duties crave no less,
Yet say to them that we in like regard,
And estimate of this their dearest zeal,
(If time of need shall ever call them forth
To dare in field their fierce and cruel foes)
Will be ourself their noted General.
Not dear at all to us shall be our life,
Nor Palaces, nor Castles huge of stone
Shall hold, as then, our presence from their view:
But in the midst and very heart of them,
Bellona-like we mean, as then, to march.
On common lot of gain or loss to both,
They well shall see we reck shall then betide.*

---

* At that time, they shall see that we mean what we say.

And, as for honor with most large rewards,
Let them not care, though common they should be:
The meanest man who shall deserve a mite,
A mountain shall for his reward receive.
And this our speech, and this our solemn vow:
In servant love to those our Subjects dear,
Say Sergeant Major, tell them from ourself,
On Kingly faith we will perform it there."

SOURCE D (Gower):

This famous allegorical depiction of the victorious Queen Elizabeth is attributed to George Gower and is thought to have been painted sometime around 1588. (Note that 1588 is also the year that James Aske's book—Source C—was published).

Sample Student Commentary

Right hand on globe—covering the Americas—so far, only Spain had American colonies, but Elizabeth had imperial aspirations…England as master of the seas.

British crown over her head and the globe.

Clouds on Spanish fleet—stormy seas; sun on British fleet—placid seas.

The storm is behind her, and she looks ahead to the calm and sunshine.

A mermaid or mythological siren stands at Elizabeth's right hand…Elizabeth is the siren who charmed the Spanish fleet to its destruction…?

> ## SOURCE E (image):
>
> Elizabeth I addressing the Troops at Tilbury before the arrival of the Spanish Armada 1588.

Sample Student Commentary

Elizabeth is in a spot of bright light while most of the others in the foreground are in darker shadows.

In terms of size and positioning, Elizabeth takes up nearly a quarter of the painting.

On her horse, and with her right hand raised, Elizabeth's physical presence is the highest of any potentially recognizable human in the painting.

Before you write your essay, make certain you can answer the following questions:

1. Given your assignment, what will the central argument or thesis of your essay be? In other words, can you provide a one- or two-sentence statement on what you are going to say in your essay?

> *I'm going to argue that, while no historical account can be truly objective, there are times when the recording of historical accounts is intentionally biased. This is historical mythmaking, and it was done when British historians began to record the Spanish Armada and Elizabeth I's "victory" against the Spanish in the Battle of Tilbury.*

2. Which three sources resonate most strongly with you? Why?

    Source A: the William Leigh version of Elizabeth's Tilbury Address. It was written closer in time to the actual event, but the writer may have had an "agenda" in reporting this version of the speech.

    Source B: the Leonel Sharp version of the "same" speech. This was written by an alleged eyewitness to the actual speech.

    Source D: the famous "Armada Portrait." For those who can "read into" a painting, this portrait is full of symbolism and propaganda to portray Elizabeth in a favorable light.

3. What specific facts or insights does each of your chosen sources provide for you?

    William Leigh, an Anglican priest, uses the famous quote, "If God is with us, who can be against us?" He portrays Elizabeth as divine and minimizes her role as a military leader.

    Sharp presents Elizabeth as a leader, a fighter. A key point is asserting the equal abilities of a queen, a woman, and a king, a man, to be a strong ruler.

    The portrait emphasizes the belief that God favored Elizabeth—and, thus, England. It also emphasizes Elizabeth's—and, thus, England's—destiny to rule the world.

4. What facts, insights, or viewpoints will you provide to support and advance the thesis you drafted in response to question 1?

    It's already commonly accepted that "history is written by the winners." The distance of the historian from the history being recorded—and the values or biases of that historian—must be taken into account when trying to understand the history behind the account. Without being overly paranoid, one should remember that propagandists often toy with history to manipulate their audience."

Once you have considered all of the above, you are ready to write your essay.

    Contrary to common misconceptions, there is no truly objective, factual, or true account of the past. Everything we know—or think we know—about historical events or persons has been colored by the perceptions, opinions, and biases of the persons recording and reporting it. While, often, the subjectivity of historical accounts is unintended and minimal, there are instances in which the annals of history are intentionally tampered with so as to leave a specific impression to those who will study it.

    This is certainly the case with Queen Elizabeth I's famous "Tilbury Speech," which she allegedly delivered to the assembled English forces before the defeat of the Spanish Armada in 1588. The known facts are few: Philip of Spain had sent his *Armada* to destroy *Elizabeth* and subjugate the *English* people. The *British* did not really have sufficient military strength to defend themselves. An unexpected storm blew the *Armada* to sea, greatly assisting the *British* in their defeat of the *Spanish*.

The event was pivotal in seating *Elizabeth* solidly on the throne she had tenuously occupied for thirty years already. To many historians, the event ushered in *England's* "Golden Age," which would include some of the nation's most celebrated poets, musicians, and artists. Clearly, history would demand a record of such an event and the monarch's role in it, and, clearly, such a record would be arranged to highlight—possibly even exaggerate—her positive elements.

In short, records of *Elizabeth I's* speech at *Tilbury*, and artistic representations of the *Spanish* defeat border on propaganda, and begin to create an *Elizabethan Myth* that survives even into the twenty-first century.

Not only was the Battle of *Tilbury* itself fodder for historical mythmakers, so was the fact of the queen's speech. Two well-known versions of this speech survive, and their differences are very telling about how the recorder of each intended *Elizabeth* to be remembered. The one, written in a sermon as part of a collection compiled to compare *Elizabeth* with *David, Joshua,* and *Hezekia,* portrays a virtuous queen who rightfully likens herself to a Messiah. The second, better-known version presents *Elizabeth* as the epitome of valor, the fellow soldier of beloved subjects. Whether as valiant or virtuous, a Messiah or a warrior, however, both versions of the speech present the picture of a larger-than-life figure of faith and courage.

Both sources were written over a decade after the event—indeed, both were written after *Elizabeth's* death. The authenticity of both is, therefore, dubious, and one must approach each with caution, suspecting that each writer had an intent and purpose in recording the speech as he did.

While Source A, a sermon by clergyman *William Leigh*, was recorded closer in time to the historical event, Source B was written by an alleged eyewitness, who may actually have been the first to hear the speech. Source A is part of a collection with a blatant agenda. Both, however, are clearly written to elevate the late queen.

Source A focuses on the godly-queen aspects of *Elizabeth's* reign. "Si deus nobiscum quis contra nos?" she says in closing, "If God is with us, who can be against us?" (Romans 8: 31). This godly queen is addressing her troops before they engage the "Philistines" in battle. Her reference to herself as their "Prince in peace," is clearly an allusion to Christ himself, the "Prince of Peace." The English troops are not about to fight *Elizabeth's* battle, or England's battle, they are setting forth to fight Christ's battle—"the battle of the Lord." The writer of Source A is an Anglican writing for Anglicans, and his intent is to secure the memory of his queen, not as valiant, but virtuous, not depending on the valor of her military, but relying on the faith of her people.

Source B, *Dr. Leonel Sharp*, presents the problem of authentication in a different light. The text was recorded even later than Source A, but it was recorded by someone closer to the actual event. His agenda, while ostensibly simply recording a historically significant moment, is apparently to portray Elizabeth as strong, stalwart, and manlike more than godlike. The issue of Elizabeth's gender, which had been a matter of concern during Elizabeth's early reign, takes a much more central place in Source B: "I know I have the body but of a weak and feeble woman; but I have the heart and stomach of a king." She is addressing soldiers about to fight, and she has the spirit—if not the body—to fight with them: "rather than any dishonour shall grow by me, I myself will take up arms, I myself will be your general..."

Those who recorded the events at Tilbury wanted Elizabeth to be remembered as God's ambassador on Earth, as soldier, and as empress—ruler of the world.

Source D, the famed "Armada Portrait," is a symbolic representation of the glorious and victorious Elizabeth. She sits on her throne. Behind her, through one of two windows, we see the Spanish Armada struggling vainly against stormy skies and rough seas. Through the other window, we see the British fleet sailing on calm seas in brilliant sunshine. Most telling, however, is that, under Elizabeth's right hand, rests a globe. Her hand is spanning the Atlantic Ocean, her fingers resting on the Americas. The defeated Spain already had vast holdings in the Americas, and Elizabeth has imperial aspirations. The defeat of the Armada might allow this goddess-queen, this warrior-queen to realize this aspiration.

What is history, and what is myth? The Battle of Tilbury took place, and the Spanish Armada was defeated. That is well-established fact. That Elizabeth addressed her troops immediately before the battle is generally accepted as true. What exactly she said is less certain. It is just that uncertainty that allows those who record and report the past to color their reports however they choose, to derogate or glorify, demonize or canonize. In the case of Elizabeth I and the Battle of Tilbury, the myth of the rise of England's Golden Age was engendered and nurtured.

That myth survives to this day.

ENGLISH LANGUAGE AND COMPOSITION

SYNTHESIS ESSAY

Exercise One:

Directions: The following prompt is based on the accompanying five sources.

This question requires you to integrate information or views from a variety of different sources into a coherent, well-written essay. *Refer directly to the sources to support your thesis, but do not merely paraphrase or summarize the sources. Your own thesis should be the focus; the sources should simply support this argument.*

Remember to attribute both direct and indirect citations.

Introduction
Many historians assert that, rather than restoring the Union, the aftermath of the Civil War actually created a new and vastly different United States from the nation that had divided in 1861. The unconditional surrender of the states that had been in rebellion strengthened the national identity, so that one's identification as "American" began to overshadow his or her identification with an individual state. Likewise the victory of one ideology over another began to shape a national character that, many insist, is still in the process of developing. Others argue, however, that the national character that began to emerge in 1865 was simply the long-delayed manifestation of the nation that was intended in 1776 and 1787.

Assignment
Carefully study the following sources (including all introductory information). Then, write an essay that cites at least three of the sources for illustration, evidence, and support, in which you describe the national character suggested by the sources and argue whether the sources illustrate an actual change in national direction or simply show progress along the same path.

Refer to the sources as Source A, Source B, etc.; titles are included for your convenience.

Source A (Nast)
Source B (Jones)
Source C (Lincoln)
Source D (*Harper's Weekly*)
Source E (*Harper's Weekly* - 2)

SOURCE A (Nast):

The following cartoon appeared in *Harper's Weekly* on November 20, 1869. It was drawn by the *Harper's* famous cartoonist, Thomas Nast. By November 1869, the Fourteenth Amendment, which guaranteed citizenship and equal protection under the law to all Americans, had been ratified. The Fifteenth Amendment, forbidding racial discrimination in voting rights, was in the process of ratification by the states. Political and social optimists like Nast believed they had reason to celebrate the realization of the United States' great potential and the fulfillment of its promise to the peoples of the world.

SOURCE B (Jones):

A Thanksgiving Sermon, preached January 1, 1808, in St. Thomas's, or the African Episcopal, Church, Philadelphia: On Account of the Abolition of the African slave trade, on that day, by the Congress of the United States. By Absalom Jones, rector of the said church.

A THANKSGIVING SERMON.

EXODUS, iii. 7, 8.

And the Lord said, I have surely seen the affliction of my people which are in Egypt, and have heard their cry by reason of their task-masters; for I know their sorrows; and I am come down to deliver them out of the hand of the Egyptians.

THESE words, my brethren, contain a short account of some of the circumstances which preceded the deliverance of the children of Israel from their captivity and bondage in Egypt.

They mention, in the first place, their *affliction*. This consisted in their privation of liberty: they were slaves to the kings of Egypt, in common with their other subjects; and they were slaves to their fellow slaves. They were compelled to work in the open air, in one of the hottest climates the world; and, probably, without a covering from the burning rays of the sun. Their work was of a laborious kind: it consisted of making bricks, and travelling, perhaps to a great distance, for the straw, or stubble, that was a component part of them. Their work was dealt out to them in tasks, and performed under the eye of vigilant and rigorous masters, who constantly upbraided them with idleness. The least deficiency, in the product of their labour, was punished by beating. Nor was this all. Their food was of the cheapest kind, and contained but little nourishment: it consisted only of leeks and onions, which grew almost spontaneously in the land of Egypt. Painful and distressing as these sufferings were, they constituted the smallest part of their misery. While the fields resounded with their cries in the day, their huts and hamlets were vocal at night with their lamentations over their sons; who were dragged from the arms of their mothers, and put to death by drowning, in order to prevent such an increase in their population, as to endanger the safety of the state by an insurrection. In this condition, thus degraded and oppressed, they passed nearly four hundred years. Ah! who can conceive of the measure of their sufferings, during that time? What tongue, or pen, can compute the number of their sorrows? To them no morning or evening sun ever disclosed a single charm: to them, the beauties of spring, and the plenty of autumn had no attractions: even domestick endearments were scarcely known to them: all was misery; all was grief; all was despair.

Our text mentions, in the second place that, in this situation, they were not forgotten by the God of their fathers, and the Father of the human race. Though, for wise reasons, he delayed to appear in their behalf for several hundred years; yet he was not indifferent to their sufferings. Our text tells us, that he saw their affliction, and heard their cry: his eye and his ear were constantly open to their complaint: every tear they shed, was preserved, and every groan they uttered, was recorded; in order to testify, at a future day, against the authors of their oppressions. But our text goes further: it describes the Judge of the world to be so much moved, with what he saw and what he heard, that he rises from his throne—not to issue a command to the armies of angels that surrounded him to fly to the relief of his suffering children—but to come down from heaven, in his own person, in order to deliver them out of the hands of the Egyptians. Glory to God for this precious record of his power and goodness: let all the nations of the earth praise him. *Clouds and darkness are round about him, but righteousness and judgment are the habitation of his throne. O sing unto the Lord a new song, for he hath done marvelous things: his right hand and his holy arm hath gotten him the victory. He hath remembered his mercy and truth toward the house of Israel, and all the ends of the earth shall see the salvation of God.*

The history of the world shows us, that the deliverance of the children of Israel from their bondage, is not the only instance, in which it has pleased God to appear in behalf of oppressed and distressed nations, as the deliverer of the innocent, and of those who call upon his name. He is as unchangeable in his nature and character, as he is in his wisdom and power. The great and blessed event, which we have this day met to celebrate, is a striking proof, that the God of heaven and earth *is the same, yesterday, and to-day, and for ever.* Yes, my brethren, the nations from which most of us have descended, and the country in which some of us were born, have been visited by the tender mercy of the Common Father of the human race. He has seen the affliction of our countrymen, with an eye of pity. He has seen the wicked arts, by which wars have been fomented among the different tribes of the Africans, in order to procure captives, for the purpose of selling them for slaves. He has seen ships fitted out from different ports in Europe and America, and freighted with trinkets to be exchanged for the bodies and souls of men. He has seen the anguish which has taken place, when parents have been torn from their children, and children from their parents, and conveyed, with their hands and feet bound in fetters, on board of ships prepared to receive them. He has seen them thrust in crowds into the holds of those ships, where many of them have perished from the want of air. He has seen such of them as have escaped from that noxious place of confinement, leap into the ocean; with a faint hope of swimming back to their native shore, or a determination to seek early retreat from their impending misery, in a watery grave. He has seen them exposed for sale, like horses and cattle, upon the wharves; or, like bales of goods, in warehouses of West India and American sea ports. He has seen the pangs of separation between members of the same family. He has seen them driven into the sugar; the rice, and the tobacco fields, and compelled to work—in spite of the habits of ease which they derived from the natural fertility of their own country in the open air, beneath a burning sun, with scarcely as much clothing upon them as modesty required. He has seen them faint beneath the pressure of their labours. He has seen them return to their smoky huts in the evening, with nothing to satisfy their hunger but a scanty allowance of roots; and these, cultivated for themselves, on that day only, which God ordained as a day of rest for man and beast. He has seen the neglect with which their masters have treated their immortal souls; not only in withholding religious instruction from them, but, in some instances, depriving them of access to the means of obtaining it. He has seen all the different modes of torture, by means of the whip, the screw, the pincers, and the red hot iron, which have been exercised upon their bodies, by inhuman overseers: overseers, did I say? Yes: but not by these only. Our God has seen masters and mistresses, educated in fashionable life, sometimes take the instruments of torture into their own hands, and, deaf to the cries and shrieks of their agonizing slaves, exceed even their overseers in cruelty. Inhuman wretches! though You have been deaf to their cries and shrieks, they have been heard in Heaven. The ears of Jehovah have been constantly open to them: He has heard the prayers that have ascended from the hearts of his people; and he has, as in the case of his ancient and chosen people the Jews, *come down to deliver* our suffering country-men from the hands of their oppressors. He came down into the United States, when they declared, in the constitution which they framed in 1788, that the trade in our African fellow-men, should cease in the year 1808: He *came down* into the British Parliament, when they passed a law to put an end to the same iniquitous trade in May, 1807:

He came down into the Congress of the United States, the last winter, when they passed a similar law, the operation of which commences on this happy day. Dear land of our ancestors! thou shalt no more be stained with the blood of thy children, shed by British and American hands: the ocean shall no more afford a refuge to their bodies, from impending slavery: nor shall the shores of the British West India islands, and of the United States, any more witness the anguish of families, parted for ever by a publick sale. For this signal interposition of the God of mercies, in behalf of our brethren, it becomes us this day to offer up our united thanks. Let the song of angels, which was first heard in the air at the birth of our Saviour, be heard this day in our assembly: *Glory to God in the highest,* for these first fruits of *peace upon earth, and good will to man:* O! let us *give thanks unto the Lord:* let us *call upon his name, and make known his deeds among the people.* Let us *sing psalms unto him and talk of all his wondrous works.*

Having enumerated the mercies of God to our nation, it becomes us to ask, what shall we render unto the Lord for them? Sacrifices and burnt offerings are no longer pleasing to him: the pomp of public worship, and the ceremonies of a festive day, will find no acceptance with him, unless they are accompanied with actions that correspond with them. The duties which are inculcated upon us, by the event we are now celebrating, divide themselves into five heads.

In the first place, Let not our expressions of gratitude to God for his late goodness and mercy to our countrymen, be confined to this day, nor to this house: let us carry grateful hearts with us to our places of abode, and to our daily occupations; and let praise and thanksgivings ascend daily to the throne of grace, in our families, and in our closets, for what God has done for our African brethren. Let us not forget to praise him for his mercies to such of our colour as are inhabitants of this country; particularly, for disposing the hearts of the rulers of many of the states to pass laws for the abolition of slavery; for the number and zeal of the friends he has raised up to plead our cause; and for the privileges, we enjoy, of worshiping God, agreeably to our consciences, in churches of our own. This comely building, erected chiefly by the generosity of our friends, is a monument of God's goodness to us, and calls for our gratitude with all the other blessings that have been mentioned.

Secondly, Let us unite, with our thanksgiving, prayer to Almighty God, for the completion of his begun goodness to our brethren in Africa. Let us beseech him to extend to all the nations in Europe, the same humane and just spirit towards them, which he has imparted to the British and American nations. Let us, further, implore the influence of his divine and holy Spirit, to dispose the hearts of our legislatures to pass laws, to ameliorate the condition of our brethren who are still in bondage; also, to dispose their masters to treat them with kindness and humanity; and, above all things, to favour them with the means of acquiring such parts of human knowledge, as will enable them to read the holy scriptures, and understand the doctrines of the Christian religion, whereby they may become, even while they are the slaves of men, the freemen of the Lord.

Thirdly, Let us conduct ourselves in such a manner as to furnish no cause of regret to the deliverers of our nation, for their kindness to us. Let us constantly *remember the rock whence we were hewn, and the pit whence we were digged. Pride was not made for man*, in any situation; and, still less, for persons who have recently emerged from bondage. The Jews, after they entered the promised land, were commanded, when they offered sacrifices to the Lord, never to forget their humble origin; and hence, part of the worship that accompanied their sacrifices consisted in acknowledging, *that a Syrian, ready to perish, was their father*: in like manner, it becomes us, publickly and privately, to acknowledge, that an African slave, ready to perish, was our father or our grandfather. Let our conduct be regulated by the precepts of the gospel; let us be sober minded, humble, peaceable, temperate in our meats and drinks, frugal in our apparel and in the furniture of our houses, industrious in our occupations, just in all our dealings, and ever ready to honour all men. Let us teach our children the rudiments of the English language, in order to enable them to acquire a knowledge of useful trades; and, above all things, let us instruct them in the principles of the gospel of Jesus Christ, whereby they may become *wise unto salvation*. It has always been a mystery, Why the impartial Father of the human race should have permitted the transportation of so many millions of our fellow creatures to this country, to endure all the miseries of slavery. Perhaps his design was, that a knowledge of the gospel might be acquired by some of their descendants, in order that they might become qualified to be the messengers of it, to the land of their fathers. Let this thought animate us, when we are teaching our children to love and adore the name of our Redeemer. Who knows but that a Joseph may rise up among them, who shall be the instrument of feeding the African nations with the bread of life, and of saving them, not from earthly bondage, but from the more galling yoke of sin and Satan.

Fourthly, Let us be grateful to our benefactors, who, by enlightening the minds of the rulers of the earth, by means of their publications and remonstrances against the trade in our countrymen, have produced the great event we are this day celebrating. Abolition societies and individuals have equal claims to our gratitude. It would be difficult to mention the names of any of our benefactors, without offending many whom we do not know. Some of them are gone to heaven, to receive the reward of their labours of love towards us; and the kindness and benevolence of the survivors, we hope, are recorded in the book of life, to be mentioned with honour when our Lord shall come to reward his faithful servants before an assembled world.

Fifthly, and lastly, Let the first of January, the day of the abolition of the slave trade in our country, be set apart in every year, as a day of publick thanksgiving for that mercy. Let the history of the sufferings of our brethren, and of their deliverance, descend by this means to our children, to the remotest generations; and when they shall ask, in time to come, saying, What mean the lessons, the psalms, the prayers and the praises in the worship of this day? let us answer them, by saying, the Lord, on the day of which this is the anniversary, abolished the trade which dragged your fathers from their native country, and sold them as bondmen in the United States of America.

Oh thou God of all the nations upon the earth! We thank thee, that thou art *no respecter of persons*, and that thou *hast made of one blood all nations of men*. We thank thee, that thou halt appeared, in the fulness of time, in behalf of the nation from which most of the worshipping people, now before thee, are descended. We thank thee, that the sun of righteousness has at last shed his morning beams upon them. *Rend thy heavens*, O Lord, and *come down* upon the earth; and grant that *the mountains*, which now obstruct the perfect day of thy goodness and mercy towards them, may *flow down at thy presence*. Send thy gospel, we beseech thee, among them. May the nations, which now *sit in darkness*, behold and rejoice in its light. May *Ethiopia soon stretch out her hands unto thee*, and lay hold of the gracious promise of thy everlasting covenant. Destroy, we beseech thee, all the false religions which now prevail among them; and grant, that they may soon *cast their idols, to the moles and the bats* of the wilderness. O, hasten that glorious time, when the knowledge of the gospel of Jesus Christ, shall cover the *earth, as the waters cover the sea; when the wolf shall dwell with the lamb, and the leopard shall lie down with the kid, and the calf and the young lion and the fatling together, and a little child shall lead them; and, when, instead of the thorn, shall come up the fir tree, and, instead of the brier, shall come up the myrtle tree: and it shall be to the Lord for a name and for an everlasting sign that shall not be cut off.* We pray, O God, for all our friends and benefactors, in Great Britain, as well as in the United States: reward them, we beseech thee, with blessings upon earth, and prepare them to enjoy the fruits of their kindness to us, in thy everlasting kingdom in heaven: and dispose us, who are assembled in thy presence, to be always thankful for thy mercies, and to act as becomes a people who owe so much to thy goodness. We implore thy blessing, O God, upon the President, and all who are in authority in the United States. Direct them by thy wisdom, in all their deliberations, and O save thy people from the calamities of war. Give peace in our day, we beseech thee, O thou *God of peace!* and grant, that this highly favoured country may continue to afford a safe and peaceful retreat from the calamities of war and slavery, for ages yet to come. We implore all these blessings and mercies, only in the name of thy beloved Son, Jesus Christ, our Lord. And now, O Lord, we desire, with angels and archangels, and all the company of heaven, ever more to praise thee, saying, *Holy, holy, holy, Lord God Almighty: the whole earth is full of thy glory.*

Amen.

> ## SOURCE C (Lincoln):
>
> Lincoln, Abraham, *Second Inaugural Address*. Saturday, March 4 1865.
>
> For weeks prior to Lincoln's second inauguration, heavy rain flooded
> Pennsylvania Avenue. Spectators stood in ankle-deep mud before the
> Capitol to watch the inauguration and hear their President's speech.
> In little more than a month, President Abraham Lincoln would be
> assassinated.

Fellow-Countrymen:

At this second appearing to take the oath of the Presidential office there is less
occasion for an extended address than there was at the first. Then, a statement
somewhat in detail of a course to be pursued seemed fitting and proper. Now,
at the expiration of four years, during which public declarations have been
constantly called forth on every point and phase of the great contest which
still absorbs the attention and engrosses the energies of the nation, little that is
new could be presented. The progress of our arms, upon which all else chiefly
depends, is as well known to the public as to myself, and it is, I trust, reasonably
satisfactory and encouraging to all. With high hope for the future, no prediction
in regard to it is ventured.

On the occasion corresponding to this four years ago all thoughts were anxiously
directed to an impending civil war. All dreaded it, all sought to avert it. While
the inaugural address was being delivered from this place, devoted altogether to
saving the Union without war, urgent agents were in the city seeking to *destroy*
it without war—seeking to dissolve the Union and divide effects by negotiation.
Both parties deprecated war, but one of them would *make* war rather than let the
nation survive, and the other would *accept* war rather than let it perish, and the
war came.

One-eighth of the whole population were colored slaves, not distributed generally
over the Union, but localized in the southern part of it. These slaves constituted a
peculiar and powerful interest. All knew that this interest was somehow the cause
of the war. To strengthen, perpetuate, and extend this interest was the object for
which the insurgents would rend the Union even by war, while the Government
claimed no right to do more than to restrict the territorial enlargement of it.
Neither party expected for the war the magnitude or the duration which it has

already attained. Neither anticipated that the cause of the conflict might cease with or even before the conflict itself should cease. Each looked for an easier triumph, and a result less fundamental and astounding. Both read the same Bible and pray to the same God, and each invokes His aid against the other. It may seem strange that any men should dare to ask a just God's assistance in wringing their bread from the sweat of other men's faces, but let us judge not, that we be not judged. The prayers of both could not be answered. That of neither has been answered fully. The Almighty has His own purposes. "Woe unto the world because of offenses; for it must needs be that offenses come, but woe to that man by whom the offense cometh." If we shall suppose that American slavery is one of those offenses which, in the providence of God, must needs come, but which, having continued through His appointed time, He now wills to remove, and that He gives to both North and South this terrible war as the woe due to those by whom the offense came, shall we discern therein any departure from those divine attributes which the believers in a living God always ascribe to Him? Fondly do we hope, fervently do we pray, that this mighty scourge of war may speedily pass away. Yet, if God wills that it continue until all the wealth piled by the bondsman's two hundred and fifty years of unrequited toil shall be sunk, and until every drop of blood drawn with the lash shall be paid by another drawn with the sword, as was said three thousand years ago, so still it must be said "the judgments of the Lord are true and righteous altogether."

With malice toward none, with charity for all, with firmness in the right as God gives us to see the right, let us strive on to finish the work we are in, to bind up the nation's wounds, to care for him who shall have borne the battle and for his widow and his orphan, to do all which may achieve and cherish a just and lasting peace among ourselves and with all nations.

SOURCE D (Harper's Weekly):

Harper's Weekly. Saturday, 8 March, 1865.

THE PRESIDENT'S INAUGURAL.

The first inauguration of President Lincoln was under circumstances of most intense interest. The people were wrought up to a high pitch of expectation. They were eager with apprehension, which was partially relieved by the eagerness of the hope that balanced with their fear. The apprehension related to the revolutionary excitement which was already culminating in the gulf States the hope wavered toward some deep resource of statesmanship, as yet unknown, which might master the storm and save the Republic. In the election of Mr. Lincoln, the people, though they issued no writ of ejectment against slavery in States, yet forbade its extension over the national territory. By his election the Government became national without doing the least violence to the reserved immunities of the States ; it became national instead of sectional. But the necessity had already long existed for a sectional government in order to the perpetuation of slavery. A national creed was, therefore, unacceptable to the South. She required that every issue in which all the people were interested should be decided in the interest of a part, and that part a minority. Because in a single instance the people had decided otherwise a revolution of terrible import was growing rapidly toward its crisis. And the watch word of the revolutionists was this paradox : That the Republic was invading certain States because it would no longer suffer their invasion on its own most sacred immunities.

For two reasons the popular expectation centred upon Mr. Lincoln. His election was in some sort the pretext of the revolutionists, and his attitude toward the revolution must now represent the decision of the people. Up to the time of his inauguration Mr. Lincoln was very reticent. But in his inaugural address his voice was clear and decided. The peculiar feature of the address was its nationality. Up to that moment the national consciousness of our people had found little expression of itself. Now we were one people, with a common boundary which we determined should be as inviolable by, traitors as by a foreign enemy.

Mr. Lincoln's second inaugural address was delivered under different circumstances from the first. In the one case the address was the principal thing. March 4, 1861, the people waited upon Mr. Lincoln's words; March 4, 1865, the solemn ceremonies of inauguration were inseparable from an expression of triumph it was the occasion itself and the spectacle which impressed the people. The most that was required of the second inaugural address was that it should befit the occasion. It was needless to reiterate statements already given as to the policy to be pursued in the conduct of the war, or as to the conditions necessary to peace. The President's views on these matters are well known to the people, and they are the views of the people. In fact, President Lincoln, in this second address, simply alludes briefly to the change of situation since his first inauguration, only dwelling for a moment upon the relation of slavery to the war, and then proceeds to take upon himself anew the vow of fidelity to the Constitution of the United States. The ceremony was an impressive one. The most hopeful thought connected with this event is that its next repetition will find us a united and happy people.

> ### SOURCE E (Harper's Weekly—2):
>
> *Harper's Weekly*. Saturday, 8 March, 1865.

THE INAUGURAL ADDRESS.

The inaugural address of the President is characteristically simple and solemn. He neither speculates, nor prophesies, nor sentimentalizes. Four years have revealed to every mind the ghastly truth that the Government of the United States is struggling in a death grapple with slavery; and as a new epoch of the Government opens in civil war, its Chief Magistrate states the vital point of the contest, and invokes God's blessing upon the effort of the country to finish its work in triumph. With a certain grand and quaint vigor, unprecedented in modern politics, the President says: "Fondly do we hope, fervently do we pray, that this mighty scourge of war may soon pass away. Yet, if God wills that it continue until all the wealth piled by the bondman's two hundred and fifty years of unrequited toil shall be sunk, and until every drop of blood drawn with the lash shall be paid with another drawn with the sword, as was said three thousand years ago, so, still it must be said: 'The judgments of the Lord are true and righteous altogether.'"

We are especially glad that the inaugural does not, as the *New York Tribune* wishes it did, "appeal to the rebels for a cessation of hostilities as pleadingly as its prototype [the first inaugural] urged forbearance from beginning them." Such a tone would have been neither politic nor humane. When the President speaks of "the progress of our arms upon which all else chiefly depends," every man is reminded of the peace history of the last year, and of the terms which have been constantly repeated, and which are perfectly well known to the rebels and to the world. Those terms are unconditional submission to the laws of the United States.

We are equally glad that the President indulges in no observations upon Mexico, England, France, and things in general. He was taking the oath to continue the work in which his conduct has so satisfied the country that he is continued in his office by general assent. With a fine sense of propriety he says, in the gravest and most impressive way, that he accepts the trust and prays for strength to do his duty. And all true American hearts say, Amen!

Before you write your essay, make certain you can answer the following questions:

1. Given your assignment, what will the central argument or thesis of your essay be? In other words, can you provide a one- or two-sentence statement on what you are going to say in your essay?

2. Which three sources resonate most strongly with you? Why?

3. What specific facts or insights does *each* of your chosen sources provide for you?

4. What facts, insights, or viewpoints will you provide to support and advance the thesis you drafted in response to question 1?

Once you have considered all of the above, you are ready to write your essay.

ENGLISH LANGUAGE AND COMPOSITION

SYNTHESIS ESSAY

Sample 2:

Directions: The following question is based on the accompanying seven sources.

This question requires you to synthesize a variety of sources into a coherent, well-written essay. When you synthesize sources, refer to them to develop your position and cite them accurately. *Your argument should be central; the sources should support this argument. Avoid merely summarizing, or responding to, the sources.*

Remember to attribute both direct and indirect citations.

Introduction

Even before the outbreak of the Revolutionary War in 1775 and the drafting of the Declaration of Independence in 1776, the question had been raised whether it was in the best interests of the British colonies in North America to maintain separate ties with England or to deal with certain domestic and international problems collectively. As early as 1754, seven of the thirteen colonies met to discuss the possibility of forming a union in order to handle affairs with the Native Americans more effectively and defend themselves against the French. At the Albany Congress in June and July of that year, Benjamin Franklin proposed the Albany Plan of Union. While this plan was rejected by the colonies, the issue of an American union never disappeared and resulted, eventually, in the formation of the United States of America. Even after the drafting of the Constitution in 1787, however, the question of whether it was best for a state to remain sovereign or allow itself to be absorbed into a stronger federation lingered. The issue is still argued today.

Assignment

Read the following sources (including any introductory information) carefully. Then, write an essay in which you evaluate the writers' or artists' arguments in favor of a strong union among the states. Synthesize at least three of the sources for support.

Refer to the sources by their titles (Source A, Source B, etc.) or by the descriptions in the parentheses.

Source A (Franklin)
Source B (*Massachusetts Centinel*)
Source C (Jay 1)
Source D (Jay 2)
Source E (Hamilton)
Source F (from: *The Constitution of the United States*)
Source G (from: *The Articles of Confederation and Perpetual Union*)

SOURCE A (image and Franklin):

Franklin, Benjamin. *Pennsylvania Gazette*, 9 May 1754.

Sample Student Commentary

Each of the eight sections is labeled with the initials of a colony, except the head, which is labeled for the region of New England.

Is Franklin suggesting anything by combining all of New England into a single segment? Were the colonies of New England already more unified than the other colonies? What might Franklin be suggesting by making New England the head of the snake?

This famous cartoon by Benjamin Franklin, which is often credited as the United States' first political cartoon, appeared in the May 9, 1754 Pennsylvania Gazette, accompanied by the following editorial, also by Franklin. Franklin probably chose the image of a snake to illustrate, first, that the snake's natural state was to be united; second, it was commonly believed at the time that a snake that had been cut to pieces could be restored to life if the pieces were reattached before sunset.

Join or Die

Friday last an Express arrived here from Major Washington, with Advice, that Mr. Ward, Ensign of Capt. Trent's Company, was compelled to surrender his small Fort in the Forks of Monongahela to the French, on the 17th past; who fell down from Venango with a Fleet of 360 Battoes and Canoes, upwards of 1000 Men, and 18 Pieces of Artillery, which they planted against the Fort; and Mr. Ward having but 44 Men, and no Cannon to make a proper Defence, was obliged to surrender on Summons, capitulating to march out with their Arms, &c. and they had accordingly joined Major Washington, who was advanced with three Companies of the Virginia Forces, as far as the New Store near the Allegheny Mountains, where the Men were employed in clearing a Road for the Cannon, which were every Day expected with Col. Fry, and the Remainder of the Regiment. —We hear farther, that some few of the English Traders on the Ohio escaped, but 'tis supposed the greatest Part are taken, with all their Goods, and Skins, to the Amount of near 20,000 pounds.[1] The Indian Chiefs, however, have dispatch'd Messages to Pennsylvania, and Virginia, desiring that the English would not be discouraged, but send out their Warriors to join them, and drive the French out of the Country before they fortify; otherwise the Trade will be lost,[2] and, to their great Grief, an eternal Separation made between the Indians and their Brethren the English. 'Tis farther said, that besides the French that came down from Venango, another Body of near 400, is coming up the Ohio; and that 600 French Indians, of the Chippaways and Ottaways, are coming down Siota River, from the Lake, to join them; and many more French are expected from Canada; the Design being to establish themselves, settle their Indians, and build Forts just on the Back of our Settlements in all our Colonies; from which Forts, as they did from Crown-Point, they may send out their Parties to kill and scalp the Inhabitants, and ruin the Frontier Counties.[3] Accordingly we hear, that the Back Settlers in Virginia, are so terrify'd by the Murdering and Scalping of the Family last Winter, and the Taking of this Fort, that they begin already to abandon their Plantations, and remove to Places of more Safety. —The Confidence of the French in this Undertaking seems well-grounded on the present disunited State of the British Colonies,[4] and the extreme Difficulty of bringing so many different Governments and Assemblies

---

Sample Student Commentary

[1] Franklin begins with exposition, a recitation of facts. He does not yet introduce his argument. Probably, he wants to lay out his case before risking alienating his reader with an unpopular thesis.

[2] Among the reasons for whatever action Franklin is going to suggest, there is the possibility of lost revenue.

[3] Among the facts are also statements of speculation and hearsay. Franklin clearly wants the cards stacked in his favor when he finally states his thesis.

[4] A clear suggestion of the thesis—the problems Franklin cites are caused by disunity, thus implying that the colonies need to unite.

to agree in any speedy and effectual Measures for our common Defence[5] and Security; while our Enemies have the very great Advantage of being under one Direction, with one Council, and one Purse.[6] Hence, and from the great Distance of Britain,[7] they presume that they may with Impunity violate the most solemn Treaties subsisting between the two Crowns, kill, seize and imprison our Traders, and confiscate their Effects at Pleasure (as they have done for several Years past) murder and scalp our Farmers, with their Wives and Children, and take an easy Possession of such Parts of the British Territory as they find most convenient for them; which if they are permitted to do, must end in the Destruction of the British Interest, Trade and Plantations in America.

Sample Student Commentary

[5] Common defense is clearly an important point—graphically illustrated by the snake that will die if the various segments do not join together.

[6] Emphasis is on the word one and the speed with which a single, united government can act, compared to the inefficiency of thirteen separate allies trying to come to consensus.

[7] Might Franklin be suggesting, not only the need for colonial unity, but also their autonomy from Britain as well?

SOURCE B (image)

The Massachusetts Centinel. 2 August 1790.

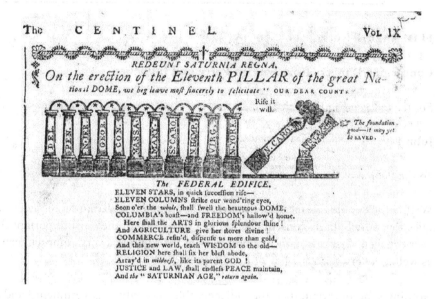

Sample Student Commentary

There is no real "argument" here beyond the suggestion that it was God's will that nine of the thirteen states ratify the Constitution, thus establishing it as the law of the land.

Rhode Island had been the most stubborn state, not even participating in the Constitutional Convention. Represented by the broken column, it will be the last state to ratify. This cartoon expresses hope that the thirteen might still be united into one.

SOURCE C (Jay)

B

Yale Law School. Lilian Goldman Law Library. *The Avalon Project: Documents in Law, History and Diplomacy.*

FEDERALIST No. 2

Concerning Dangers from Foreign Force and Influence

For the Independent Journal.

John Jay

To the People of the State of New York:

WHEN the people of America reflect that they are now called upon to decide a question, which, in its consequences, must prove one of the most important that ever engaged their attention, the propriety of their taking a very comprehensive, as well as a very serious, view of it, will be evident.

Nothing is more certain than the indispensable necessity of government,[1] and it is equally undeniable, that whenever and however it is instituted, the people must cede to it some of their natural rights in order to vest it with requisite powers. It is well worthy of consideration therefore, whether it would conduce more to the interest of the people of America that they should, to all general purposes, be one nation, under one federal government, or that they should divide themselves into separate confederacies, and give to the head of each the same kind of powers which they are advised to place in one national government.[2]

It has until lately been a received and uncontradicted opinion that the prosperity of the people of America depended on their continuing firmly united, and the wishes, prayers, and efforts of our best and wisest citizens have been constantly directed to that object. But politicians now appear, who insist that this opinion is erroneous, and that instead of looking for safety and happiness in union, we ought to seek it in a division of the States into distinct confederacies

---

Sample Student Commentary

[1] Unlike Franklin's earlier piece, Jay is absolutely transparent and immediate in stating his thesis.

[2] Jay asserts that the governments will be essentially the same, and the people will cede essentially the same rights, whether they agree to one central federal government or insist on their sovereign states' governments.

or sovereignties.[3] However extraordinary this new doctrine may appear, it nevertheless has its advocates; and certain characters who were much opposed to it formerly, are at present of the number. Whatever may be the arguments or inducements which have wrought this change in the sentiments and declarations of these gentlemen, it certainly would not be wise in the people at large to adopt these new political tenets without being fully convinced that they are founded in truth and sound policy.

It has often given me pleasure to observe that independent America was not composed of detached and distant territories, but that one connected, fertile, widespreading country was the portion of our western sons of liberty. Providence has in a particular manner blessed it with a variety of soils and productions, and watered it with innumerable streams, for the delight and accommodation of its inhabitants. A succession of navigable waters forms a kind of chain round its borders, as if to bind it together;[4] while the most noble rivers in the world, running at convenient distances, present them with highways for the easy communication of friendly aids, and the mutual transportation and exchange of their various commodities.

Sample Student Commentary

[3] Note the distinction: Those who support union are the "best and wisest citizens," while those who oppose union are "politicians."

[4] The point of this paper seems to be that God intended the nation to be unified, since He unified it geographically.

SOURCE D (Jay—2)

Yale Law School. Lilian Goldman Law Library. *The Avalon
Project: Documents in Law, History and Diplomacy.*

FEDERALIST No. 3

**The Same Subject Continued: Concerning Dangers From Foreign Force and
Influence**

For the Independent Journal.

John Jay

. . .

At present I mean only to consider it as it respects security for the preservation
of peace and tranquillity, as well as against dangers from FOREIGN ARMS AND
INFLUENCE, as from dangers of the LIKE KIND arising from domestic causes.[1]
As the former of these comes first in order, it is proper it should be the first
discussed. Let us therefore proceed to examine whether the people are not right in
their opinion that a cordial Union, under an efficient national government, affords
them the best security that can be devised against HOSTILITIES from abroad.

. . .

Because, under the national government, treaties and articles of treaties, as well
as the laws of nations, will always be expounded in one sense and executed in
the same manner,—whereas, adjudications on the same points and questions,
in thirteen States, or in three or four confederacies, will not always accord or be
consistent; and that, as well from the variety of independent courts and judges
appointed by different and independent governments, as from the different local
laws and interests which may affect and influence them.[2] The wisdom of the
convention, in committing such questions to the jurisdiction and judgment of

---

Sample Student Commentary

[1] Jay argues that a central government is necessary so that individual states will not be able to act as agitators against
outside groups.

[2] This argument harkens back to Franklin's cartoon and editorial, which asserted that separate entities cannot act with
the effectiveness and efficiency of a single, centralized entity.

courts appointed by and responsible only to one national government, cannot be too much commended.

. . .

Because the prospect of present loss or advantage may often tempt the governing party in one or two States to swerve from good faith and justice;[3] but those temptations, not reaching the other States, and consequently having little or no influence on the national government, the temptation will be fruitless, and good faith and justice be preserved. The case of the treaty of peace with Britain adds great weight to this reasoning.

Because, even if the governing party in a State should be disposed to resist such temptations, yet as such temptations may, and commonly do, result from circumstances peculiar to the State, and may affect a great number of the inhabitants, the governing party may not always be able, if willing, to prevent the injustice meditated, or to punish the aggressors. But the national government, not being affected by those local circumstances, will neither be induced to commit the wrong themselves, nor want power or inclination to prevent or punish its commission by others.

. . .

Because such violences are more frequently caused by the passions and interests of a part than of the whole; of one or two States than of the Union. Not a single Indian war has yet been occasioned by aggressions of the present federal government, feeble as it is; but there are several instances of Indian hostilities having been provoked by the improper conduct of individual States, who, either unable or unwilling to restrain or punish offenses, have given occasion to the slaughter of many innocent inhabitants.[4]

The neighborhood of Spanish and British territories, bordering on some States and not on others, naturally confines the causes of quarrel more immediately to the borderers. The bordering States, if any, will be those who, under the impulse of sudden irritation, and a quick sense of apparent interest or injury, will be most likely, by direct violence, to excite war with these nations; and nothing

---

Sample Student Commentary

[3] Jay is suggesting that, if left to themselves, individual states might act in their own best interests and actually betray their sister states in negotiations with other nations.

[4] While not necessarily an earth-shattering contention, Jay does have a legitimate, factual example to support his point about the safety of a central government versus the potential dangers of a collection of sovereignties.

can so effectually obviate that danger as a national government, whose wisdom and prudence will not be diminished by the passions which actuate the parties immediately interested.[5]

Sample Student Commentary

[5] Thus, a federal government will be less likely to engage in armed conflict with Spain than a sovereign Georgia would.

SOURCE E (Hamilton)

Yale Law School. Lilian Goldman Law Library. *The Avalon Project: Documents in Law, History and Diplomacy.*

FEDERALIST No. 6

Concerning Dangers from Dissensions Between the States

For the Independent Journal.

Alexander Hamilton

To the People of the State of New York:

THE three last numbers of this paper have been dedicated to an enumeration of the dangers to which we should be exposed, in a state of disunion, from the arms and arts of foreign nations. I shall now proceed to delineate dangers of a different and, perhaps, still more alarming kind—those which will in all probability flow from dissensions between the States themselves, and from domestic factions and convulsions.[1] These have been already in some instances slightly anticipated; but they deserve a more particular and more full investigation.

A man must be far gone in Utopian speculations who can seriously doubt that, if these States should either be wholly disunited, or only united in partial confederacies, the subdivisions into which they might be thrown would have frequent and violent contests with each other.[2] To presume a want of motives for

---

Sample Student Commentary

[1] Hamilton is talking, of course, about wars between the states—civil war, as it were.

[2] The argument is clear, but one wonders what the basis of Hamilton's claim is.

such contests as an argument against their existence, would be to forget that men are ambitious, vindictive, and rapacious. To look for a continuation of harmony between a number of independent, unconnected sovereignties in the same neighborhood, would be to disregard the uniform course of human events, and to set at defiance the accumulated experience of ages.[3]

Sample Student Commentary

[3] Perhaps, if the paper continued, Hamilton would provide specific examples, but the passage as presented here simply provides an unsupported generalization.

SOURCE F

Yale Law School. Lilian Goldman Law Library. *The Avalon Project: Documents in Law, History and Diplomacy.*

---

from: *THE CONSTITUTION OF THE UNITED STATES*

Preamble:

We the People of the United States, in Order to form a more perfect Union, establish Justice, insure domestic Tranquility, provide for the common defence...[1]

. . .

Article I, Section 10 - Powers prohibited of States

No State shall enter into any Treaty, Alliance, or Confederation; grant Letters of Marque and Reprisal; coin Money; emit Bills of Credit; make any Thing but gold and silver Coin a Tender to Payment of Debts; pass any Bill of Attainder, ex post facto Law, or Law impairing the Obligation of Contracts; or grant any Title of Nobility.[2]

No State shall, without the Consent of Congress, lay any Imposts or Duties on Imports or Exports, except what may be absolutely necessary for executing its inspection laws: and the net Produce of all Duties and Imposts, laid by any State

Sample Student Commentary

[1] The document proposed to unify the states begins by asserting "domestic tranquility" and "common defence" as key values.

[2] All of these prohibitions are items that could threaten or destroy the Preamble's concept of "domestic tranquility."

on Imports or Exports, shall be for the Use of the Treasury of the United States; and all such Laws shall be subject to the Revision and control of the Congress.

No State shall, without the Consent of Congress, lay any duty of Tonnage, keep Troops, or Ships of War in time of Peace, enter into any Agreement or Compact with another State, or with a foreign Power, or engage in War, unless actually invaded, or in such imminent Danger as will not admit of delay...[3]

Amendment 10: Powers of the States and People.

The powers not delegated to the United States by the Constitution, nor prohibited by it to the States, are reserved to the States respectively, or to the people.[4]

. . .

Sample Student Commentary

[3] The powers prohibited here threaten "common defence."

[4] By not enumerating the powers retained by the states and the people, the Constitution actually implies that these powers are almost unlimited.

SOURCE G

Yale Law School. Lilian Goldman Law Library. *The Avalon Project: Documents in Law, History and Diplomacy.*

from: *THE ARTICLES OF CONFEDERATION AND PERPETUAL UNION*

To all to whom these Presents shall come, we the undersigned Delegates of the States affixed to our Names, send greeting...

Whereas the Delegates of the United States of America, in Congress assembled, did, on the 15th day of November, in the Year of Our Lord One thousand Seven Hundred and Seventy seven, and in the Second Year of the Independence of America, agree to certain articles of Confederation and perpetual Union between the States of New-hampshire, Massachusetts-bay, Rhode-island and Providence Plantations, Connecticut, New York, New Jersey, Pennsylvania, Delaware, Maryland, Virginia, North-Carolina, South-Carolina, and Georgia in the words following, viz.

"Articles of Confederation and perpetual Union between the states of New-hampshire, Massachusetts-bay, Rhode-island and Providence Plantations,

Connecticut, New-York, New-Jersey, Pennsylvania, Delaware, Maryland, Virginia, North-Carolina, South-Carolina and Georgia".[1]

Article I. The Stile of this confederacy shall be "The United States of America".

Article II. Each state retains its sovereignty, freedom, and independence, and every Power, Jurisdiction and right, which is not by this confederation expressly delegated to the United States, in Congress assembled.[2]

Article III. The said states hereby severally enter into a firm league of friendship with each other, for their common defence,[3] the security of their Liberties, and their mutual and general welfare,[4] binding themselves to assist each other, against all force offered to, or attacks made upon them, or any of them, on account of religion, sovereignty, trade, or any other pretence whatever.

Article IV. The better to secure and perpetuate mutual friendship and intercourse among the people of the different states in this union, the free inhabitants of each of these states, paupers, vagabonds and fugitives from justice excepted, shall be entitled to all privileges and immunities of free citizens in the several states; and the people of each state shall have free ingress and regress to and from any other state, and shall enjoy therein all the privileges of trade and commerce, subject to the same duties impositions and restrictions as the inhabitants thereof respectively...[5]

. . .

Article VI. No state, without the Consent of the united states in congress assembled, shall send any embassy to, or receive any embassy from, or enter into any conference agreement, alliance or treaty with any King prince or state; nor shall any person holding any office of profit or trust under the united states, or any of them, accept of any present, emolument, office or title of any kind whatever from any king, prince or foreign state;[6] nor shall the united states in congress assembled, or any of them, grant any title of nobility.

Sample Student Commentary

[1] Note the phrase "perpetual union" as part of the official title of the document.

[2] The Tenth Amendment to the Constitution echoes the terms in this provision.

[3] Again, "common defence" is a key issue.

[4] "Security of Liberties" and "general welfare" are issues in the Declaration of Independence and are referenced in the preamble to the Constitution.

[5] Domestic tranquility.

[6] This prohibition has implications for common defense.

No two or more states shall enter into any treaty, confederation or alliance whatever between them, without the consent of the united states in congress assembled, specifying accurately the purposes for which the same is to be entered into, and how long it shall continue.[7]

No state shall lay any imposts or duties, which may interfere with any stipulations in treaties, entered into by the united states in congress assembled, with any king, prince or state, in pursuance of any treaties already proposed by congress, to the courts of France and Spain.[8]

No vessels of war shall be kept up in time of peace by any state, except such number only, as shall be deemed necessary by the united states in congress assembled, for the defence of such state, or its trade; nor shall any body of forces be kept up by any state, in time of peace, except such number only, as in the judgment of the united states, in congress assembled, shall be deemed requisite to garrison the forts necessary for the defence of such state; but every state shall always keep up a well regulated and disciplined militia, sufficiently armed and accoutered, and shall provide and constantly have ready for use, in public stores, a due number of field pieces and tents, and a proper quantity of arms, ammunition and camp equipage.[9]

No state shall engage in any war without the consent of the united states in congress assembled, unless such state be actually invaded by enemies,[10] or shall have received certain advice of a resolution being formed by some nation of Indians to invade such state, and the danger is so imminent as not to admit of a delay till the united states in congress assembled can be consulted: nor shall any state grant commissions to any ships or vessels of war, nor letters of marque or reprisal, except it be after a declaration of war by the united states in congress assembled, and then only against the kingdom or state and the subjects thereof, against which war has been so declared, and under such regulations as shall be established by the united states in congress assembled, unless such state be infested by pirates, in which case vessels of war may be fitted out for that occasion, and kept so long as the danger shall continue, or until the united states in congress assembled, shall determine otherwise.

Sample Student Commentary

[7] This provision touches on the issue of domestic tranquility.

[8] Common defense.

[9] Notice that, under the Articles of Confederation, there would be no national army. Each state would maintain a militia for its defense.

[10] Congress did not have the power to declare war. The states could declare war, but only with the consent of Congress.

Article XI. Canada acceding to this confederation, and joining in the measures of the united states, shall be admitted into, and entitled to all the advantages of this union: but no other colony shall be admitted into the same, unless such admission be agreed to by nine states.

Article XII. All bills of credit emitted, monies borrowed and debts contracted by, or under the authority of congress, before the assembling of the united states, in pursuance of the present confederation, shall be deemed and considered as a charge against the united states, for payment and satisfaction whereof the said united states, and the public faith are hereby solemnly pledged.

Article XIII. Every state shall abide by the determinations of the united states in congress assembled, on all questions which by this confederation are submitted to them. And the Articles of this confederation shall be inviolably observed by every state, and the union shall be perpetual;[11] nor shall any alteration at any time hereafter be made in any of them; unless such alteration be agreed to in a congress of the united states, and be afterwards confirmed by the legislatures of every state.

And Whereas it hath pleased the Great Governor of the World to incline the hearts of the legislatures we respectively represent in congress, to approve of, and to authorize us to ratify the said articles of confederation and perpetual union. Know Ye that we the undersigned delegates, by virtue of the power and authority to us given for that purpose, do by these presents, in the name and in behalf of our respective constituents, fully and entirely ratify and confirm each and every of the said articles of confederation and perpetual union, and all and singular the matters and things therein contained: And we do further solemnly plight and engage the faith of our respective constituents, that they shall abide by the determinations of the united states in congress assembled, on all questions, which by the said confederation are submitted to them. And that the articles thereof shall be inviolably observed by the states we respectively represent, and that the union shall be perpetual. In Witness whereof we have hereunto set our hands in Congress. Done at Philadelphia in the state of Pennsylvania the ninth day of July in the Year of our Lord one Thousand seven Hundred and Seventy-eight, and in the third year of the independence of America.[12]

Sample Student Commentary

[11] The Articles of Confederation do not allow for secession.

[12] Given the portion of the document presented here, one wonders what the benefits of union would be. These articles do not even guarantee common defense, as there is no national army, only alliances between individual states' militias.

Before you write your essay, make certain you can answer the following questions:

1. Given your assignment, what will the central argument or thesis of your essay be? In other words, can you provide a one- or two-sentence statement on what you are going to say in your essay?

My essay will explain that the most powerful argument the writers and artists present in favor of a strong union is that of the necessity for a common defense. All other considerations follow from this initial idea.

2. Which three sources resonate most strongly with you? Why

The Franklin cartoon and corresponding editorial are effective because they encapsulate the idea that a loosely connected group of colonies is less able to stand against attack.

Similarly, Jay (2) is effective because it explains why a united government will better moderate the actions of individual states, thereby protecting them from harm by outsiders.

Hamilton provides another reason to unite: to protect the states from violent disagreements with one another.

3. What specific facts or insights does each of your chosen sources provide for you?

Franklin explains that the French and French Indians are attacking outposts of the colonies. The implication from the image and the corresponding editorial is that Franklin believes that a united government would be better able to respond quickly to such threats.

Jay (2) makes the claim that the individual states would be best served by a central, moderating influence, one that would restrict states from making foolish decisions that lead to violence. Further, the federal government would have no conflict of interest in preventing these decisions or punishing those who made them.

Hamilton makes the point that if the states are to be disunited, they will likely have violent disagreements with one another. This, of course, proved true in the Civil War, but the disagreements led to the dissolution, not the other way around.

4. What facts, insights, or viewpoints will you provide to support and advance the thesis you drafted in response to question 1?

To establish a common defense was the most important aspect of the decision to unite, whether that defense was against threats from abroad or within. Without centralized decision-making, this defense would be impossible, as responses would be painfully slow, and it is possible that some states would not agree to assist others.

Once you have considered all of the above, you are ready to write your essay.

It is well established that during the 18th century, the fledgling United States was threatened repeatedly and on many fronts. Given the manifold threats to the survival of the individual colonies and, later, the United States as a whole, the argument in favor of a common defense was particularly cogent. Several writers and authors of the period enumerated many reasons for uniting—and maintaining the unity of—the states, ease of trade and travel being among these reasons; however, freedom of trade and travel would be impossible were there no common defense in place to secure these freedoms. Recognizing this, those who would come to be known as Federalists often made the need for a common defense a cornerstone of their arguments. There are three major components to the argument in favor of a federal government that would provide a common defense: protection from external threats, protection from internal threats, and the prevention of unilateral action against outside forces which would result in retaliation against the whole.

As to protection from external threats, Franklin (Source A) explains why a centralized government is needed. Though Franklin does not explicitly state that the formulation of such a government is necessary in his editorial, his meaning is obvious in the woodcut that accompanies it. Franklin identifies a major weakness of the current organization: The various colonies are dreadfully slow to agree on any action—there is too much deliberation involved; they are also disconnected from one another, as illustrated in the woodcut. To help make his point, he contrasts this sluggishness with the speed with which the French opposition carries out its attacks. Franklin believes that because the French forces do not have multiple leaders giving them multiple directions, they have an advantage over the colonies, who are not united in purpose. A centralized government would be able to act swiftly and decisively. Jay makes a similar argument in Source D: A centralized government will take one approach toward a problem; if thirteen different states try to solve the same problem, there may be thirteen different solutions, none of which agree. The argument seems to be one made strictly from a logistical perspective: Reduce the number of people involved in decision-making so that the colonies can respond to threats more efficiently.

Source E (Hamilton) is concerned with the second component of the argument, protection from internal threats. Hamilton believes that, were the United States dissolved into several smaller "independent, unconnected sovereignties," there would be continual strife among them. Hamilton's major argument is this: Mankind inherently tends toward deplorable behavior, especially toward those that are outsiders; therefore, a strong moderating influence is necessary to keep these base instincts in check. This argument is not as effective as Franklin's. Hamilton believes that relations between independent countries in close proximity to one another must dissolve into violent conflict. This is not necessarily true; great differences in cultures or great disparities in natural resources may, indeed, cause violent conflict, but simple proximity combined with a tendency toward ambition and greed cannot be cited as viable causes of war. Plenty of countries who share borders are peaceful and cooperative trade partners, and Hamilton is assuming that each of these countries would be led by a group of "ambitious, vindictive, and rapacious" people. The occurrence of the Civil War does not vindicate Hamilton, either. He claims that the dissolution of the union will lead to disagreement and violent conflict, but in the case of the Civil War, the opposite occurred: Disagreement between confederations of states led to dissolution. In the end, the idea of a centralized government working as a moderating influence makes sense, but the way in which Hamilton chooses to portray this is perhaps less effective than it could have been.

Source D also touches upon the theme of the moderating influence, but does so somewhat more successfully. In this case, Jay argues for a centralized government so that individual states will not act as agitators against outside groups. A centralized government would ensure that individual states would not have the authority to act as aggressors; Jay mentions that no conflict with Indian peoples has been instigated by the federal government, but several conflicts have been initiated through the "improper conduct of individual States." Giving the authority to make war to the national government alone ensures that individual states cannot make poor decisions that affect the whole union. Jay's argument is that because states that feel injured by outside agitators may retaliate, an objective observer should have oversight to ensure that rash actions are not taken. He places this argument in the context of protecting the lives of innocent inhabitants, with no other considerations. By taking the position of protecting innocent life above everything else, Jay places himself in a position that is difficult to assail. It is also important to note that Jay echoes a sentiment expressed decades earlier by Benjamin Franklin—that thirteen separate sovereignties, or a smaller number of individual confederacies, will not always agree, will not always arrive at the same terms of peace with outside powers, and, generally, will not be able to act with the efficiency and effectiveness of a single, central government.

The common thread throughout all these arguments, explicit or implicit, is that the states are stronger when united than they are as individuals. Though the arguments have varying levels of efficacy, the ideas behind them are well founded and reflect a realistic outlook on the issues of the time. In identifying the need for a common defense, the writers and artists who produced the sources described here drew the correct conclusion that, without that common defense, all other considerations would have been impossible. ❧

ENGLISH LANGUAGE AND COMPOSITION

SYNTHESIS ESSAY

Exercise Two:

Directions: The following question is based on the accompanying five sources.

This question requires you to integrate information or views from a variety of different sources into a coherent, well-written essay. *Refer directly to the sources to support your thesis, but do not merely paraphrase or summarize the sources. Your own thesis should be the focus; the sources should simply support this argument.*

Remember to attribute both direct and indirect citations.

Introduction
The issue of whether part time employment is beneficial or harmful to high school students, their academic achievement, and their future careers has been an ongoing debate for decades. The recent focus on educational reform and increasing educational standards and requirements has intensified the debate. Among the proponents are those who argue that part time employment increases a student's confidence and character, while the opponents insist that the student's focus should be on his or her academics.

Assignment
Read the following sources (including any introductory information) carefully. Then, write an essay in which you argue for or against the advisability of holding a part time job during the high school academic year. Synthesize at least three of the sources for support.

Refer to the sources by their titles (Source A, Source B, etc.) or by the descriptions in the parentheses.

Source A (Prestwickhouse)
Source B (Parent Blog)
Source C (Chart)
Source D (Yoder)
Source E (Adolescent Journal)

SOURCE A (Prestwickhouse):

from: *The Journal of Research on Educational Issues* © 2009
Prestwickhouse, Inc.

Abstract

The effect of part-time employment on academic performance in U.S. high school students is being examined in an ongoing study performed by the Prestwickhouse Educational Research Foundation (PERF). The first cohort of selected students (N = 2,500) were examined Grade 8 (2004), Grade 10 (2006), and Grade 12 (2008). A second cohort was examined in Grade 8 (2006) and Grade 10 (2008). This is a pivotal year because it represents the school year during which the majority of students who are going to be employed while in school will seek and procure their first part time position. It was found that student employment during the school year had an overall negative and curvilinear effect on academic performance. Students who worked fewer than 12 hours per week achieved higher GPAs than their cohorts who were not employed. However, students who worked more than 11—13 hours per week achieved significantly lower GPAs.

SOURCE B (Parent Blog):

from: *How to be the Perfect Parent of Perfect Kids.* Parent Blog

---

Today, teenagers and young adults constitute one of the largest consumer groups in the United States. Teens, especially those who maintain part time employment while they are in high school, have ready funds to spend on clothing and entertainment. Once they attain legal employment age, some are required to buy their own cars or pay for their own car insurance. In fact, in survey after survey, students report that it is the need for a car that precipitates the need for part time employment.

The converse of the issue is that employed high school students make up a significant portion of the American work force, filling especially low-earning, menial, and entry-level jobs in the food and service industries.

Parents and teachers, however, debate the advisability of students working while in school. There are those who argue that part time employment helps teens build character and self-esteem, while others argue that the time and energy students expend on working would be better spent in school.

Proponents of both sides generally propose the following arguments.

The benefits of working part time while in high school include:

1. Student dependence on parents is lessened. This can help build a sense of independence and improve self esteem.

2. Being accountable to an employer and a paycheck can help students develop important character traits like reliability, loyalty, and perseverance.

3. Once they are spending money they themselves have earned, students may learn to be more responsible spenders and savers.

4. Experiencing the hard work and minimal payback of menial jobs may encourage students to stay in school and apply themselves harder to their school work.

5. Teens and their parents may actually grow closer, as the teens learn to appreciate their parents' hard work and parents see their children acting like responsible adults.

There are, however, a few possible drawbacks the need to be considered as well.

1. Students may be seduced by the immediate reward of the paycheck, versus the delayed gratification of good grades and an education. As a result, they may neglect their school responsibilities in order to meet their employers' demands.

2. Working nights, weekends, and holidays might interfere with the student's non-academic, extracurricular school life, as well as family commitments.

3. Students who grow to enjoy their newfound independence and increased purchasing power, may be seduced into leaving school altogether for the sake of full time employment. Statistics clearly show a positive relationship between level of education and income potential, with high-school dropouts consistently falling below the poverty level.

4. Many studies suggest that the time and energy spent at work contribute to adolescent fatigue and depression. These conditions can have lifelong consequences for the affected teenagers.

5. The types of jobs available to high school students are not likely to teach skills or provide experience necessary for advancement or for higher-paying, professional-level jobs.

My own personal opinion is that a student's "job" is to be a student. Teenagers have their entire lives to work and earn money, but they have only the first 18 or 19 years of their lives to be high school students. Unless there is a genuine need for the additional income generated by a student's part time work, parents should step up and meet their parental responsibilities to their kids.

And let the kids be kids.

I'm just saying…

—Dexter Truth

<table>
<tr><td colspan="9" align="center">SOURCE C (Chart):

Table: Employment Status and Hours Worked Per Week in Grades 10 and
12 Compared with Curriculum Track and Drop-out Rate</td></tr>
</table>

Employment in grade 10				Employment in grade 12			
Full Sample	**Not Employed**	**1 to 15hr/week**	**>15hr/week**	**Full Sample**	**Not Employed**	**1 to 15hr/week**	**>15 hr/wk**
13,965	10,432	1,273	2,269	13,965	7,126	2,846	3,993
Full Sample							
100%	74.2%	8.6%	17.2%	100%	49.1%	21.3%	29.6%
Curriculum Track, Grade 12							
College Preparatory							
2,133	75.1%	9.0%	15.9%		50.0%	20.6%	29.4%
General							
1,572	70.4%	9.5%	20.1%		45.3%	19.5%	35.2%
Vocational							
517	65.6%	6.7%	27.7%		40.0%	16.0%	44.0%
Undetermined							
174	77.5%	5.4%	17.1%		59.9%	14.5%	25.6%
Percentage Who Dropped Out Before Grade 12							
5,256	5.5%	1.5%	7.5%				
GPA at End of Target Year							
Full Sample	**Not Employed**	**1 to 15hr/week**	**>15hr/week**	**Full Sample**	**Not Employed**	**1 to 15hr/week**	**>15 hr/wk**
4.0 – 3.1				**4.0 – 3.1**			
2,792	2,574	218	0	3,491	2,046	921	524
3.0 – 2.1				**3.0 – 2.1**			
6,236	5,772	400	64	6,005	2,690	854	2,461
2.0 – 1.1				**2.0 – 1.1**			
3,285	2,697	350	238	2,977	1,500	525	952
1.0				**1.0**			
1,652	0	305	1,347	1,492	893	246	353

Analysis and Conclusions

- In tenth grade, only 25.8% of students hold part time jobs after school. By twelfth grade, that percentage nearly doubles to 50.9%.

- At the same time, approximately 65% of tenth-graders finish their sophomore year with Grade Point Averages of 2.1 or better.

- Only 25% of twelfth-graders earn GPAs of 2.1 or better.

- Of tenth-graders who completed the year with a GPA of 3.1 or better, 92% were not employed after school.

- Of twelfth-graders who completed the year with a GPA of 3.1 or better, 58% were not employed after school.

- No tenth-graders who reported working more than 15 hours per week earned GPAs of 3.1 or better.

- Only 15% of twelfth-graders who reported working more than 15 hours per week earned GPAs of 3.1 or better.

- Of tenth-graders who reported working more than 15 hours per week, 82% earned GPAs of 1.0, effectively failing for the year.

- Of twelfth-graders who reported working more than 15 hours per week, 8% earned GPAs of 1.0, effectively failing for the year.

SOURCE D (Yoder)

Yoder, Gabriel. "In What Way and to What Extent Does Student Part Time Employment During High School Affect Students' Academic Performance?" *Educational Issues Quarterly*. Washington, DC: Department of Education and Progress, 2007.

The following is the abstract for a longer article that appeared in a scholarly, professional journal several years ago.

ABSTRACT

A four-year study examined how part time employment during the school year (Labor Day through Memorial Day weekend) affected high school academic performance among a representative, national sample of students in grades 10 through 12. Regular employment at moderate weekly hours (15 hours per week on average) was associated with higher grades within each grade level. Regular employment at more than 15 hours per week, however, seemed to result in a significant drop in grades.

The average effect of school year employment was, on the whole, unremarkable, and summer employment (Memorial Day weekend through Labor Day) had no impact on grades whatsoever.

Among some demographic populations, regular employment was accompanied by drops in both school attendance and grades, suggesting that employment during the school year exhausted student time and energy that might otherwise have been available to study.

It is generally acknowledged that, in the Western world, teenagers mature and develop the character and the skill sets necessary for adult success and fulfillment through formal education. In the United States, however, the number of hours worked per week during the school year are suspected of negatively impacting these important aspects of adolescent development.

Numerous studies indicate that almost two-thirds of high school students are employed at some time during their junior year. Of this two-thirds, students work 71% of the weeks in the school year at an average of 18 hours per week. The numbers for high school seniors are even higher: Three-fourths work at some point during the year, working an average of 76% of the school year's weeks, for an average of 23 hours per week.

It may seem likely that paid employment during the school year would increase the student-worker's competencies and abilities and, by helping the student develop skills, also cultivate work habits, and increase "real world" knowledge and experience; it is not clear whether this increase comes as the expense of what the student gains while participating in his or her school experiences.

Obviously, working during the school year will reduce study time. This is a two-fold loss, as the student sacrifices not only the physical time spent at work, but also non-work and non-school time that is usually devoted to leisure and not to academics. In addition, the student who is fatigued by long hours and distracted by work-related issues will also benefit less from his or her time in class and out-of-school study time.

On the other hand, however, school-year employment might actually enhance the amount and value of study time for students whose after school jobs complements their studies. Employed students might also develop an awareness of the future and feel more motivated to build that future, whether it were to include advancement in the field of part time employment or an escape from a menial, no-advancement job.

It is impossible, then, to predict whether part time employment during the school is likely to have a positive or negative effect on the student and his or her future.

SOURCE E (Adolescent Journal)

---

from: *The New Adolescent Journal.* 2000 April-June; 20(97): 327-34.

"Social aspects of high school student employment: How adolescents' view of the role of part time employment impacts their achievement."

Abstract

The vast majority of lower- and middle-class high school students work part time during the school year. In the course of an eight-year study, juniors and seniors at a predominantly middle-class high school were studied and interviewed regarding their attitudes toward after school employment and their decisions whether to work or not to work. Student responses were examined, and their attitudes toward the workplace, as well as their interpretations of the work ethic were analyzed in order to determine the role of part time employment in their lives. Our findings suggest that there exists a negative stereotype of the employed high school student, that such students are viewed as indifferent to their education, and are focused exclusively on the present, and insist on immediate gratification. Our findings further suggest that this negative stereotype is not justified. Instead, after school employment reinforces values commonly associated with the middle class, especially that which is called the American (or the Protestant) work ethic.

Before you write your essay, make certain you can answer the following questions:

1. Given your assignment, what will the central argument or thesis of your essay be? In other words, can you provide a one- or two-sentence statement on what you are going to say in your essay?

2. Which three sources resonate most strongly with you? Why?

3. What specific facts or insights does *each* of your chosen sources provide for you?

4. What facts, insights, or viewpoints will you provide to support and advance the thesis you drafted in response to question 1?

Once you have considered all of the above, you are ready to write your essay.

APPENDICES

APPENDIX 1: List of rhetorical devices and logical fallacies: names, definitions, and examples

ALLITERATION: is the repetition of a consonant sound at the beginning of successive words. It differs from consonance in that the repeated sound may come anywhere in the word for consonance, but it must come at the beginning of the word for alliteration.

Examples:

Friday found the freeloaders facing frustration.

We went to the well where we wished for a wheelbarrow.

ALLUSION: a reference to a person, event, or other work outside of the text; allusions—whether current, historical, fictional, etc.—are usually intended to clarify or emphasize points in the passage in which they are included. Of course, the writer is relying on the reader's recognition of the allusion and its significance.

Examples:

It rained so much that spring, we began to talk of building an ark.

Like Juliet, Meghan found herself wondering wherefore Simon was a member of the rival team.

Hannibal had his elephants, Ford his Edsel, and Mayor Ogdenberry will have her Muckswamp Park.

AMPLIFICATION: the repetition of a word or phrase, followed by additional information; it is used both to clarify and intensify the meaning of the original word.

Examples:

The Constitution established that the United States would be a nation of laws, laws that protected the rights of the weak as well as the mighty.

Few things are as undervalued as aloneness, that utter and uncorrupted aloneness that pits self against self and allows self to emerge the victor.

All Ethan asked for was a chance, a chance to prove his hard-won ability, a chance to overcome the hardship of his youth.

ANAPHORA: the repetition of the same word or phrase at the beginning of series of clauses, or sentences; the device links the ideas in the series and often contributes to structural devices like PARALLELISM and CLIMAX.

Examples:

No amount of money, no amount of labor, no amount of sacrifice will be sufficient to repay the debt we owe to these great men and women.

The time has come to put aside petty differences, to put aside personal grudges, to put aside biases and prejudices of every kind and come together for the greater benefit of all humankind.

Let me remind those who now claim a share of the finished product that no one else helped to till the soil or plant the grain. No one else helped to harvest the ripened wheat. No one else carted the wheat to the mill. No one else ground the grain into flour, and no one else mixed the dough and baked the bread. The law of justice, therefore, demands that no one else should eat the bread but me!

ANTITHESIS: the emphasis of two contrasting ideas by placing them adjacent to one another in a sentence or clause, often in parallel structure

Examples:

To try admits the potential for success; not to try ensures failure.

Success makes men proud; failure makes them wise.

"To err is human; to forgive, divine." —Alexander Pope

APOSTROPHE: the direct address of a person or personified concept; apostrophe is most commonly used to communicate intense emotion.

Examples:

O wild West Wind, thou breath of Autumn's being...—Percy Bysshe Shelley

America! America! God shed His grace on thee...—Katharine Lee Bates

And know that it is for you, Future Generations of America, that we stand here today and make this pledge.

ASSONANCE: the repetition of vowel sounds in successive words. As a sound device, assonance is related to alliteration and consonance.

Examples:

You know "the show must go on."

The stray took the bait and ate the sprayed grapes.

ASYNDETON: the omission of conjunctions that would normally separate the items in a list or series; the effect is usually a slowing of the pace with which the list is read. Asyndeton also contributes an informal, unplanned tone to the list.

Examples:

In Oz, Dorothy was amazed and amused by the Scarecrow, the Tin Woodsman, the Cowardly Lion, the Wicked Witch of the West, the Wizard, Glinda.

Children's literature is filled with unlikely anthropomorphisms: talking lions, kindly badgers, beleaguered frogs, insolent caterpillars.

North, south, east, west, the food at home is always best.

BEGGING THE QUESTION: a logical fallacy in which the asserted conclusion is based on a prior question that is only presumed settled

Examples:

Since all men are liars, it is obvious that you cannot take Jared's word for anything.

Given women's overemotional natures, Laura's outburst is probably nothing to worry about.

Once the accused is found guilty, it will be important to impose the harshest sentence allowable under the law.

CHIASMUS: is a kind of inverted PARALLELISM; the structure or word order of two closely placed phrases or clauses is the reverse of each other.

Examples:

To voice an opinion is always easy, but it is often a challenge to support it with facts.

Humans pamper their pets; animals in the wild must fend for themselves.

"...ask not what your country can do for you—ask what you can do for your country." —President John F. Kennedy

CONSONANCE: the repetition of consonant sounds in close succession, thus linking and emphasizing similarities

Examples:

"And the silken sad uncertain rustling of each purple curtain." —Edgar Allen Poe

At what price do we value a human life—whether prince or pauper, poet or priest?

Worry not, neither wonder nor rage; life's fullest measure is more than an age.

ENUMERATIO: Specific examples clarify and illustrate the point being established.

Examples:

The university bookstores sells many items besides textbooks. It has current nonfiction, popular fiction, CDs, DVDs, a large selection of periodicals, and office and classroom supplies.

The benefits of an education are almost limitless: exposure to a variety of ideas and views, broadened experience, enhanced knowledge and skill, and increased employment opportunities.

Math is easy except for the numbers, the formulas, and the terminology.

EPISTROPHE: The repetition of a word or phrase at the end of successive phrases, clauses, or sentences. Epistrophe might be considered the counterpart to ANAPHORA. The repetition of the closing words emphasizes their meaning. As with ANAPHORA, the epistrophe may be used in combination with PARALLELISM and CLIMAX.

Examples:

The Ford Edsel was an abysmal failure because the name was unpopular, the design was unpopular, and the price unpopular.

Your dissertation is exemplary, except that your thesis is weak, your support is weak, and your writing style is weak.

"...that government of the people, by the people, for the people..." — President Abraham Lincoln, 1863.

FALSE DICHOTOMY: presents two alternatives that are not necessarily mutually exclusive as if they were. Often, the false dichotomy ignores other alternatives beyond the two that are presented as the "either/or."

Examples:

We either pass Global Warming legislation now, or we will face the extinction of all life on earth later.

It seems you must either deplete your life savings and go into debt or go without medical care.

You're either a supporter of our cause or a traitor.

HYPERBATON: variations or inversions in conventional word order, usually for the sake of emphasis and aesthetic impact

Examples:

He was a loyal friend and true.

At the sound of the alarm, arose the village, to the news of the attack.

"To the victor belong the spoils of the enemy."— Senator William Marcy, 1832.

HYPERBOLE: an intentional, usually obvious, exaggeration

Examples:

The drive to Florida was endless.

Never has so heinous an act been perpetrated.

The University of Blogosfier is famous for accepting anyone who can walk and chew bubblegum at the same time.

HYPOPHORA: resembles a rhetorical question in that it raises a question in the text, but hypophora follows the question with an answer. It is a common introductory or transition device.

Examples:

Why would someone innocent of a crime agree to a plea agreement? Consider the emotional, physical, and economic drain of a long trial.

Where would the lonely and brokenhearted go for solace and a reprieve from their sorrow? Poets, sages, and philosophers have for centuries praised the healing properties of the ocean.

How does one get to Carnegie Hall? Practice! Practice! Practice!

LITOTES: is the use of a double negative to generate a positive understatement.

Examples:

The homework assignment was not unreasonable.

This speeding ticket certainly won't do your driving record any good.

The king did not fail to appreciate the young prince's treachery.

METAPHOR: is a direct comparison between two unlike objects, stated in such a way as to emphasize the one or two key traits they have in common.

Examples:

Money is power.

After navigating a sea of paperwork, they finally filed their mortgage application.

"Life [i]s but a walking shadow, a poor player, / That struts and frets his hour upon the stage, / And then is heard no more." —William Shakespeare, Macbeth, Act V, scene v

PARALLELISM: is the use of similar word choice, syntax, and/or structure in successive parts of a sentence, or successive sentences; the primary purpose is to communicate that the parts or sentences are related in meaning and equal in importance. Parallelism also adds balance, rhythm, cohesion, and clarity to a passage.

Examples:

It has long been my goal, but never my achievement, to climb Mount Everest.

The first person to arrive in the morning should unlock the door, set up the coffee pot, check the phone messages, and turn on the lights.

"For the end of a theoretical science is truth, but the end of a practical science is performance." —Aristotle

PARATAXIS: is essentially the creating of a compound sentence, with or without coordinating conjunctions.

Examples:

Time is money, and I have enough of neither.

The lightning flashed, the thunder rolled, and the rain came down in buckets.

The die is cast, the Rubicon is crossed, there is no retreat.

POLYSYNDETON: is the opposite of ASYNDETON, the inclusion of a conjunction before every item in a list or series (except the first); the effect is usually to speed up the pace with which the list or series is read.

Examples:

"And neither snow, nor rain, nor heat, nor gloom of night, nor the winds of change, nor a nation challenged will stay us from the swift completion of our appointed rounds." Herodotus, *Histories* (unofficial creed of the United States Postal Service)

"If solitude, or fear, or pain, or grief, / Should be thy portion…" —William Wordsworth *Lines Composed a Few Miles Above Tintern Abbey*

"We must change that deleterious environment of the 80's, that environment which was characterized by greed and hatred and selfishness and mega-mergers and debt overhang…." —Barbara Jordan, 1992 Democratic National Convention Keynote Address

PROCATALEPSIS: anticipates a reader's objection, addresses it, and then moves on with the writer's thesis.

Examples:

There are, of course, those who will complain that such a move would be too costly but the question remains, can we afford not to act?

Naysayers and prophets of doom will no doubt want proof that this new energy source is both safe and effective, but the proof will be in the product's success. How can the future be proven?

The argument that wiretapping and satellite photography violate citizens' privacy holds no validity since the Bill of Rights offers no specific protection of a "right" to privacy.

SCESIS ONOMATON: creates emphasis by repeating the same idea in a series of essentially synonymous statements.

Examples:

"Friends, Romans, countrymen, lend me your ears…" William Shakespeare, *Julius Caesar*, Act III, scene 2

"I have fought the good fight, I have finished the race, I have kept the faith." —2 Timothy 4:7

"I'm continuing to spread our agenda globally, and around the world, as well as internationally." —President George W. Bush, 2006

SENTENTIAL ADVERB: is an adverbial use that modifies the meaning of an entire sentence, often accomplished by interrupting the normal syntax of the sentence by single word or short phrase. When used effectively, the tone of the sentential adverbs helps to establish the writer's attitude toward the subject and the reader.

Examples:

The loss suffered by the victim is, undoubtedly, the only factor that matters.

James Madison was, perhaps, the United States' greatest statesman.

"All truth is not, indeed, of equal importance; but if little violations are allowed, every violation will in time be thought little." —Samuel Johnson

SLIPPERY SLOPE: a logical fallacy that claims a series of intensifying consequences will inevitably follow a seemingly safe incident

Examples:

If we agree to this 10% rent increase, eventually they'll demand a 20% increase, and then a 40%, 50%, and eventually we'll be driven from our homes.

Today, the Organization of Dispute wants to distribute pamphlets. Tomorrow, they'll want to hold a rally. Before you know it, they'll be swarming the streets and abducting our women and children.

We can't ease up on the children's bed times or we'll eventually lose all parental control.

APPENDIX 2: Answer keys

Chapter 1, Exercise One

1. The essay begins with a variation of the *sententia* (A), the pithy (and now famous) "These are the times that try men's souls." Among the similes (B) is, "Tyranny, like hell, is not easily conquered" (paragraph 1). Among the metaphors (C) is "the summer soldier and the sunshine patriot" (paragraph 1). There are several examples of antithesis (E), among them, "the harder the conflict, the more glorious the triumph. What we obtain too cheap, we esteem too lightly" (paragraph 1). For all of Paine's criticisms of the king, however, he does not, in this paragraph, provide a single specific example. **Thus, (D) is the best answer.**

2. Paine uses the word *superstitious* to contrast or qualify his "secret opinion," and this secret opinion has to do with the will of "God Almighty." While (A), (B), and (C) are all points expressed in the paragraph, they do not touch on the essential contrast between superstition and his opinion, or faith. (D) might be tempting, in that it does touch on the will of the Divine, but Paine's assertion that "God Almighty" is unwilling to deal unjustly with the United States more strongly supports (E). **Thus, (E) is the best answer.**

3. The antecedent, of course, must be a noun that immediately precedes the pronoun. *Nations* (A) occurs much too early, and makes no syntactic sense in the sentence. Likewise, *countrymen* (B) is too early and syntactically unworkable. *Traitors* (D) and *curses* (E) come after the pronoun and, therefore, cannot be the antecedents. The basic gist of the paragraph, however, is *panics*, the surprising fact that they occur and the equally surprising fact that they can be beneficial ("They are the touchstones of sincerity..."). **Thus (C) is the correct answer.**

4. The first four paragraphs, while expressing Paine's opinions about the cause of liberty and the timing of the Americans' actions, are not worded strongly enough to be interpreted as persuasive (C) or inspirational (D). The statements of opinion, however, are too blatant to consider the paragraphs as merely informative (B) or academic (E). The opening paragraphs are simply expressive of Paine's personal opinion—and he is frank about that; he then shifts to informing his readers of certain proceedings in the war which the reader may not know. **Thus, (A) is the best answer.**

5. The sentence, "The heart that feels not now is dead," might be read as ardent (A), but "the blood of his children will curse his cowardice" is hardly the language of "friend to friend." It is, possibly, stronger than "fervent" (B) as well. (C) is almost a giveaway answer as "torpid" is the opposite of Paine's tone. (E) is tempting, as it denotes a stronger tone than *ardent* and *fervent*, but before the end of this paragraph, Paine eventually equates loyalty to Britain as "were I to make a whore of my soul," and the

king of Britain as a "sottish, stupid, stubborn, worthless, brutish man." Such language, stronger than *ardor, fervor, or hostility*, can best be described as **vitriolic (D)**.

Chapter 1, Exercise Two

6. Anaphora (A) is the beginning of successive clauses or sentences with the same word or phrase. One of the most famous and effective uses of anaphora in twentieth-century literature is this speech, which Churchill ended with the powerful repetition of "We shall fight..." One use of amplification that, thus, eliminates (B) is in paragraph 11: "All of our types—the Hurricane, the Spitfire and the new Defiant—and all our pilots have been vindicated as superior to what they have at present to face." There are numerous metaphors (D), including, "an almost ceaseless *hail of bombs*." (paragraph 9). Likewise there are several similes (E), including: "the German eruption swept *like a sharp scythe*...") paragraph 2. Throughout the speech, however, Churchill frequently addresses Parliament directly, and by extension the British people, but even in his final, rousing paragraph, he does not address any non-human or abstract being. **Thus, (C) apostrophe is the correct answer.**

7. The two uses of the word *communications* in close proximity suggest that Churchill means something different in each use. The first, being more general ("cut off all communications") would suggest (B), (C), and (D). (E) is eliminated by the fact that Churchill qualifies his second use of the word with the phrase, "our own." These are not overall communications, but are "communications for food and ammunition," and run a specific geographic route—"first to Amiens and afterwards through Abbeville." **Therefore, (A) is the best answer. The routes by which food and ammunition were transported had been "severed."**

8. Churchill was a skilled orator, and he certainly does indulge in (A) and (B) in this speech, but neither alone can be said to dominate. While he suggests future victories, in this speech, there are no recent victories (D) to recount. In fact, more than once, he refers to the initiative as a disaster. (C) might be tempting, but Churchill does not "forecast" defeat (C) as much as he acknowledges the possibility of at least a partial defeat. He is, however, very careful to number the losses, for example, from paragraph three: "1,000 Frenchmen, in all about four thousand strong...30 unwounded survivors...") **Thus, (E) is the best answer.**

9. Churchill never assumes a conciliatory (A) tone in this address. If anything, he lays down a challenge. (C) might be tempting, as the specific factual and numerical data he provides in the bulk of the speech are informative and instructive, but the data cannot really be interpreted as "reflective." Even if a student views the early admissions that the event was a disaster, and the vast numbers of casualties make the opening of the speech

"pessimistic," the second portion—especially the closing paragraph—cannot be said to be "resigned." Likewise, even if the beginning is seen as "mournful" (E), the closing looks to an optimistic future; it does not celebrate an already-achieved victory. **(B), however, is the best answer.** The first several paragraphs are informative—explaining to Parliament and the British people what the situation was, what had occurred, and what the results were. The speech then ends on the famous inspirational note that, regardless of what happens in the near future, Britain will never cease to fight.

10. (A) is certainly an underlying purpose of the entire address but is not specifically the focus of the closing sentence. Earlier in the address, Churchill acknowledges that he had asked for additional resources (B) from Parliament. Churchill promises that help will come "in God's good time," but he does not invoke divine aid (C). Earlier, he referred to—and apologized for—a certain suspension of civil liberties (E), especially for those who sympathized with the Nazis, but, again, this is not a topic of the final sentence, nor does he ever seek permission in this speech. His closing line, however, "until, in God's good time, the New World…steps forth to the rescue and the liberation of the old," is clearly addressed to the United States, suggesting—requesting—her assistance in defeating the Nazis. **Thus, (D) is the best answer.**

Chapter 1, Exercise Three

11. Given the full context of the essay, it is clear that *corking* has a connotation of pleasant, happy, or fun. (A) is suggested in the second paragraph when Marquis suggests that an adult with the freedom of an infant or adolescent would be happy. (B) might tempt some, but Marquis admits that "an old age of dissipation and indolence and unreverend disrepute" (paragraph 5) is precisely what he desires. (C), while general, includes all of the connotations suggested by the passage. (D) is established with the description of his desired life in the seventh paragraph. Only (E) is not suggested by the passage. In fact, Marquis goes to great length describing the years of hard work and sacrifice that typically precede the years of one's "perfectly corking time." **Thus, (E) is the best answer.**

12. Marquis's use of first person plural refers only to himself, not to himself and the reader ("we have determined to die at the age of one hundred two," "We used sometimes to walk over the Brooklyn Bridge…," etc.), thus eliminating (A). While this first person is clearly self-referential, Marquis's personal illustrations and examples cannot be interpreted to intrude on the narrative, thus eliminating (B). Likewise, the first person is self-referential, not patronizing to the reader (E). (C) applies to the use of the third person, not first. As a journalist of the first half of the twentieth century, however, Marquis would be familiar with the convention of referring to himself in the plural. **Thus, (D) is the correct answer.**

13. Marquis hypothesizes the existence of Martians in Part II as a means of illustrating humankind's propensity to undervalue itself while idealizing that which is foreign or unknown. (B) might tempt some students, but, while Marquis does suggest that humankind's achievements like cities and bridges liken us to deities, he makes no such claim of the Martians. (C) and (D) are both parts of the point of the comparison, but neither explains the full point. (E) might also be tempting but is a gross and inaccurate oversimplification of the issue, especially when compared to the best answer. Marquis does suggest, however, that while we look to the stars and envision a higher culture, the Martians may do this as well. He specifically notes, "If we tumbled into Mars or Arcturus of Sirius this evening we should find the people there discussing the shimmy, the jazz, the inconstancy of cooks and the iniquity of retail butchers, no doubt…and they would be equally disappointed by the way we flitter, frivol, flutter and flivver." **Thus, (A) is the best answer.**

14. Marquis's use of words like "corking" and off-the-cuff comments like "suffer for lack of beer," eliminate (A) and (B). The times he does directly address his reader ("if you should ask us suddenly…") eliminate (D). Certainly, Marquis employs a number of colloquialisms (E) in his essay ("…not what it is cracked up to be…," "Hanged if we know…"), but these contribute to the tone rather than define it. Clearly, informal and colloquial words and phrases, occasional direct reference to the reader, and Marquis's own admission of "dissipation"—evidenced by the old age he envisions for himself and his assertion that humankind suffers "for lack of beer"—all contribute to a lighthearted, conversational tone that can accurately be described as cordial. **Thus, (C) is the best answer.**

15. (A) might tempt some because Marquis does refer to humans as "subtle deities" and "demi-gods," but he also compares New York City to a "pigsty." Likewise, (C) accounts for only one half of the issue. The few metaphors that involve Martians (D) do not constitute the "overall contribution" of metaphors to the piece. (E) is easily eliminated by the fact that the entire essay stresses this potential, not only the metaphors. In the metaphors, however, bridges are songs "in stone and steel," the New York skyline is a "mighty hieroglyphic." The comparisons that exaggerate the foulness of human failings are, for the most part, similes. **Thus, (B) is the best answer.**

Chapter 2, Exercise One

1. Henry's use of the word *patriotism* in this sentence is certainly ambiguous, even ironic. He begins by acknowledging the "patriotism" of the gentlemen who have apparently spoken before him, and one might infer from Henry's call to arms that these gentlemen were advocating loyalty to Great Britain (A, E). Henry's rhetorical questions and his use of first person plural—especially in references to "our country," "our petition"—clearly suggest that even the previous speakers were arguing for what they considered the best path

for some entity *other than* Britain. (C) is tempting, but Henry calls the men in other states who have been fired upon "brothers."—" Our brethren are already in the field!" Thus, he is concerned with more than merely Virginians. (B) and (D) might appear to be equally tempting, but every reference in the speech to liberty or to the need to fight is on the personal level, the desire for freedom, and the abhorrence to slavery to Britain. There is no mention of a collective "United States." **Thus, (D) is the best answer.**

2. (A) is eliminated by Henry's asking whether the pacifists in the assembly will listen to the "song of that siren till she transforms us into beasts," which is a slightly inaccurate allusion to Homer's *Odyssey*, in which Henry conflates the episodes of the Sirens (who sang the irresistible song) and Circe (who transformed Odysseus's men into swine). (B) is eliminated by the clear references to Psalm 115: "having eyes, [they] see not, and, having ears, [they] hear not"; Psalm 119: "one lamp by which my feet are guided"; and the book of the prophet Amos: "cover our waters and darken our land." (C) is eliminated by the reference to the Gospel accounts of Judas Iscariot's betrayal of Jesus with a kiss: "Suffer not yourselves to be betrayed with a kiss." (D) might alarm some students as it is such a specific choice, but the speech is identified as having been delivered in 1775, nearly a year after the 1774 petition, and Henry makes numerous references to "our petition." Thus, whether Henry is referring to this specific petition or any others that were drafted and sent prior to March 1775, his references to petitions, entreaties, and efforts at reconciliation eliminate (D). There is, however, no direct reference to any specific document like the Magna Carta (E) that grants British subjects the rights that Henry warns against losing. **Thus, (E) is the best answer.**

3. Like his use of *patriotism* in his opening sentence, this use raises the question of whether the treason being committed is against the lawful government (Parliament and the king) or against the insurrectionists (the American revolutionaries). While there is sarcasm in many of Henry's rhetorical questions and uses of hypophora, his specific and limited use of this word is sincere. Likewise, his speech is indeed fervent (B), and his use of the word *treason* is sincere, so this is not the best answer. Certainly, Henry is using the word to express exactly the betrayal it means, so (C) is eliminated, and nothing in this speech, redolent with rhetorical devices and near-propaganda, can be described as understated (E). **Thus, (D) is the best answer.**

4. One might expect use of the first person to be personally revealing (A), but the Patrick Henry delivering this speech is a thoroughly public persona with no real evidence of his private self. Wherever Henry acknowledges that his views might be antagonistic, he rhetorically apologizes, and his use of first person seems intended actually to *lessen* antagonism, to allege that he is speaking only for himself. Thus (C) is eliminated. (D) might be tempting, but Henry is unyielding in his views; he simply does not claim to be speaking for anyone else. (E) is likewise tempting if one recognizes the rhetorical strength of the speech. Henry is speaking "for only himself," but there is a tone of judgment to those who believe or would act differently. Whatever tacit accusations

he makes, however, cannot really be considered "broad" (E). In the mild accusation of his personal references—"as for me, give me liberty, or give me death!"—Henry sets himself up almost as an archetype, an example to be followed: "I have but one lamp by which my feet are guided; and that is the lamp of experience. I know of no way of judging of the future but by the past. And judging by the past, I wish to know what there has been in the conduct of the British ministry for the last ten years..." **Thus, (B) is the best answer.**

5. (A) is an example of inductive reasoning, in which Henry is basing his mistrust of the future by referring to the series of British atrocities in the past. Whether completely accurate or not, it is logical, and therefore not propaganda. (B) is an allusion to Judas Iscariot's betrayal of Jesus as portrayed in the Christian gospels. Henry is using the allusion metaphorically to describe his fear of the consequences of American pacifism. (C) is a series of rhetorical questions that point to the current British actions that cause Henry alarm. (D) is an anaphora, summing up the recent American response to British actions. (E), however is a strong statement, a false dichotomy, or fallacy of false choice. As Henry knows he is presenting this "choice" in an attempt to persuade his colleagues to arm and fight, he is not committing a legitimate fallacy, but employing a technique of propaganda. **Thus, (E) is the best answer.**

Chapter 2, Exercise Two

6. The paragraph contains all of the listed devices, but most are simply present and cannot be said to "control" the paragraph. The paragraph begins, however, with the impassioned address to "America!" and continues throughout with the direct address, speaker including himself with his audience in asking, "Let us..." **Therefore, (A) is the best answer.**

7. The references to Concord, Gettysburg, Normandy, Khe Sahn are clearly historical allusions (A), but they appear in only the one paragraph and cannot be said to connect this to any other paragraphs. References to sweatshops and "the lash of the whip" may be metaphoric (B) but are probably literal. While the progression of events enumerated in the three paragraphs may be chronological, it is not necessarily climactic (C), and the use of conjunctions throughout the paragraphs adheres to normal conventions, thus eliminating (E). **Each of the paragraphs begins with the phrase "For us," linking the paragraphs by establishing a common motivation for all the events listed. Thus, (D) is the correct answer.**

8. (A) is clearly a simple expression of humility, not necessarily exaggerated. (B) might be tempting, but "precious" and "noble" are evaluations that may be accurate. (C), likewise, might tempt some but may also be a literal and accurate evaluation. (D) is too abstract to

be tempting. **(E), however, is a metaphor and is clearly exaggerated, possibly to the point of bathos or melodrama.**

9. While the ideas of *price* and *promise* in this sentence are clearly almost contradictory, the consonant repetition of the *pr* sound links the ideas in the hearer's (or reader's) mind (A), creating a tension for the reader/hearer between what is being heard and what is being communicated (D), (E). By the same token, the creation of a pleasing sound effect (C) is one of the primary reasons a writer or speaker would employ consonance. **Ultimately, the use of the sound device lessens the difference between the two disparate ideas—in this case making them sound almost synonymous—so (B) is the best choice.**

10. Certainly, the quotation, from George Washington during the winter of 1777 at Valley Forge contributes to the overall optimistic, future-looking tone of the speech, but this is true of most of the speech. Thus, (A) is not the best answer. Likewise, the quotation does allude to Washington (B), but the allusion is a means to an end, not an end in itself. (C) is also minimally tempting because it is too general to satisfy. Clearly, we are approaching the end of the speech, as indicated by a number of structural and linguistic signs, but the transition to the conclusion actually began (E) in the paragraph previous to this quotation. The next paragraph, however, relies on the extended metaphor of the nation's current "winter of our hardship" with its "icy currents" and the storms that are yet to be endured. **Without the Valley Forge quotation, the audience is likely to understand the references as a general metaphor rather than a specific allusion to the nation's past. Thus, (D) is the best answer.**

Chapter 2, Exercise Three

11. **(A) is, of course, the primary purpose or effect of direct address.** (B) might tempt some, as the essay is indeed didactic, but exclusive use of third person would probably lend a more academic or didactic tone. (C) is eliminated by the fact that the hypothesis could be effectively introduced in the second or third person as well. (D) is eliminated by the fact that, in the original, Eagleton uses first person without direct address. (E) is the least tempting choice, as it addresses neither the hypothesis of the essay, nor the point of the opening paragraphs.

12. This fairly easy comprehension question is answerable by examining the summary's section headings. (A) is eliminated by the section titled "Literature Is Pragmatic Speech." (C) is eliminated by the section "Literature Is 'Good' Writing." (B) is eliminated by the section, "Literature is Extraordinary Language." (E) is eliminated by the section titled "Literature Is Imaginative Writing." **Only (D) is not an included characteristic of literature.**

13. There is the occasional use of enumeratio (A), but there are far more rhetorical questions (E). **In fact, some of the points are developed exclusively by Laga's asking a series of rhetorical questions.** Further, some of the questions explicitly invite the students to consider and address the issues themselves. Direct address (B) and apostrophe (D) are techniques of appealing to the reader, but do not have implications for the topics being developed. Laga does not rely on connotative understandings (C) unless he employs the same distinctio as Eagleton. **Thus, (E) is the best answer.**

14. (A) is eliminated by the fact that a summary, by definition, cannot be better detailed than the original on which it is based. (B) is tempting, as Laga does use a good deal of direct address and several rhetorical questions, but the overall impact of the summary is not an intimate address. Eagleton's original, while detailed, cannot really be considered pedantic (C) as his case is well reasoned and supported. Thus, it is difficult to consider the summary less "pedantic." (E) is eliminated since the summary of a subjective hypothesis cannot be said to be less subjective than its original. (D) is the best answer as, despite his frequent direct address and rhetorical questions, there are times in the summary in which Laga simply states the information presented by Eagleton without overt style or voice. While Eagleton's original is often flip and sarcastic, Laga's is, at times, simply informative. **Thus (D) is the best answer.**

15. The sentences referred to in this question read, "Lists of 'masterpieces,' 'essential reading,' or tables of contents in anthologies are *not* benign and innocent. *Instead*, they display cultural values." **The juxtaposition of *not* and *instead* clearly suggests opposition** rather than fulfillment or completion (A, C). That Laga contrasts the two concepts is not merely coincidental (D). (E) might tempt students who find the closing paragraph of the essay surprising or refreshing, but the revelation about the amorphous definition of *literature* in not expressed in the juxtaposition of these two concepts. The opposition established by the use of *not* and *instead*, suggests the antithetical nature of the two concepts. **Thus, (B) is the correct answer.**

Chapter 3, Exercise One

1. (A), (C), (D), and (E) are all eliminated by the sentence that follows the one in question: *To be sure, other armies had yet to surrender, and for a few days the fugitive Confederate government would struggle desperately and vainly...Catton continues, "But in effect it was all over when Grant and Lee signed the papers."* **Thus (B) is the best answer.**

2. (A) is hopefully too obvious and simplistic to be truly tempting. (B) might tempt some, but the symbolic qualities attributed to Grant and Lee are not shown to be primal or cross-cultural in the way that archetypes are. (D) is more tempting, but the political references are details in the development of the symbols, not the symbols'

meaning itself. Clearly, Catton is sympathetic or respectful to both men, so (E) is easily eliminated. As Catton suggests that Lee came to symbolize the Aristocratic ideals of the Confederacy, a relic of the Age of Chivalry; and Grant came to symbolize the new, expanding, industrial America, it is clear that each typifies his culture. **Thus, (C) is the best answer.**

3. Although the passage itself develops a contrast between the two men, the antithetical ideals that each represents are not juxtaposed closely enough to be considered the rhetorical device of antithesis (A). While Catton does occasionally indulge in mild exaggeration, *"a great new chapter began,"* these exaggerations are too few and too mild to be considered hyperbole (B) and to be said to be "prevalent" in the passage. (C) is eliminated by the fact that, even when Catton begins to assert the generals' similarities, the differences and similarities discussed in the passage are not mutually exclusive and, thus, not paradoxical. Sentences like, *"a great chapter on American life came to a close, and a great new chapter began"* add new information, not merely emphasize what has already been said, thus eliminating (D). While the passage is, by no means, chock full of metaphors, this is the most frequently employed device. In fact, the passage opens with the metaphor; comparing the antebellum and post-bellum eras as chapters is a metaphor—if, perhaps, a cliché. **Thus, (E) is most compelling answer.**

4. While Catton's discussion of the energetic and forward-looking Grant might be interpreted as optimistic (B), his tone when discussing Lee is tinged with regret or reminiscence. (C) might tempt some students because Catton does not criticize either man outright; there is a clear slant toward Grant, whom Catton associates with energy, democracy, expansion, and everything that is modern American. Even in his portrayal of Lee as a fading aristocrat and something archaic, Catton does not condemn the Southern General (D), and while he does describe Grant in positive terms, his treatment can hardly be described a laudatory (E). Given the imagery with which Catton associates Lee, the nobility he attributes to the Southern General, and even the idealistic notions of "belonging" and "community" which he associates with Grant; given the sense of reminiscence mingled with the optimism of the closing of the "great chapter" and the opening of a "great new chapter," the overall tone of the passage can best be described as poignant. **Thus, (A) is the best answer.**

5. The equation of the symbol with its referent (Lee and the Confederacy) is not the same relationship as exists between the source and target of an analogy (A). The assertion that Confederate soldiers fought for Lee *"as if he himself was the Confederacy"* is subjunctive (if contrary to fact), not hypothetical (C). The unsupported, unillustrated statement might be considered a broad generalization (D), but this is not the best answer available. There is no allusion (E) in the sentence. Catton is, however, literally informing the reader that the young Confederate soldiers did indeed fight as if they considered their general to be the cause for which they fought. **Thus, (B) is the correct answer.**

Chapter 3, Exercise Two

6. The opening of the lecture is clearly a narrative. Fables (A) tend to involve anthropomorphized animals or personified inanimate objects. They typically state a direct moral. Although Wiesel calls the opening narrative "a Hasidic legend," legends (C) are generally rooted in actual or perceived historical fact. They contain strong elements of verisimilitude. (D) is not incorrect, but is far too broad and vague. (E) is eliminated by the fact that Wiesel offers the story as an introduction, not as an illustration for a point he is trying to establish. The story is, however, a parable, an instructive tale that illustrates a religious or moral lesson. **Thus, (B) is the best answer.**

7. Statements like, "*if memory helps us to survive, forgetting allows us to go on living,*" and "*How are we to reconcile our supreme duty towards memory with the need to forget that is essential to life?*" eliminate (A). (B) is eliminated by: "*David, a great warrior…is not permitted to build the Temple; it is his son Solomon, a man of peace, who constructs God's dwelling place.… some wars may have been necessary or inevitable, but none was ever regarded as holy…a holy war is a contradiction in terms…The Talmud says,…It is the wise men who will bring about peace.*" (C) is eliminated by the paragraph that reads in part, "*If dreams reflect the past, hope summons the future. Does this mean that our future can be built on a rejection of the past? Surely such a choice is not necessary.*" (D) is eliminated by "*How could we go on with our daily lives, if we remained constantly aware of the dangers and ghosts surrounding us? The Talmud tells us that without the ability to forget, man would soon cease to learn. Without the ability to forget, man would live in a permanent, paralyzing fear of death.*" There is nothing antithetical between wisdom and memory. Further, Wiesel himself writers, "*It is the wise men who will bring about peace. Perhaps, because wise men remember best.*" **Thus, (E) is the correct answer.**

8. This passage is clearly about the Nazis. Before the outbreak of World War I, Germany had been a center of scientific exploration and artistic and cultural development. The "metamorphosis" Weisel cites is from "*doctors of law or medicine or theology, all those lovers of art and poetry, of Bach and Goethe*" to "*who coldly, deliberately ordered the massacres and participated in them.*" (B), (C), (D), and (E) might suggest the pre-metamorphic state, but **only (A) approaches the intent of the post-metamorphic state.**

9. The sentence, "*Our abhorrence of war is reflected in the paucity of our literature of warfare,*" is followed by the facts that famous Jewish warriors receive either no mention or negative mention in Jewish literature. Even Scripturally, David is denied the building of the Temple, the honor given to a man of peace. (A) and (D) do not seem at all likely in this context. (B) and (E) might tempt, but (E) would result in a vague, redundant, and meaningless sentence. (B) would assume a literature that had existed and been censored, and Wiesel's references to the Talmud do not support this interpretation. **Given the few mentions of Jewish war heroes, therefore, (C) is the best answer.**

10. A linear (A) pattern would lead us to a new and different point. Wiesel uses illustrations, but his speech cannot be said to be episodic (B). He does employ the rhetorical device of antithesis, but his lecture is not antithetical (C), nor does his argument, once it returns to its beginning, cycle into new and undeveloped subject matter (D). Weisel says in his final paragraph, "*I began with the story of the Besht. And, like the Besht, mankind needs to remember more than ever.*" He uses the story of the Besht at the beginning in order to emphasize "*the mystical power of memory.*" As he begins and ends on essentially the same point, **(E) is the most compelling answer.**

Chapter 3, Exercise Three

11. While the first account is comprehensible, it cannot be considered "intellectual." In fact, Truth admits in the speech that she cannot read, and that she had only heard the Bible. Thus, (B) is eliminated. (C) is also eliminated, since none of the accounts can be considered formal, and the second account is clearly more colloquial than the third. (D) is unclear and meaningless. All three accounts are purposeful, and the presumed delivery of none of them could be considered ambivalent. While the second and third accounts are indeed passionate, neither of them can be considered provocative (E). (A) is the best answer. The first account is a measured and well-supported appeal to logic (if women have only a pint of intellect, then let them have their pint's full) and consistency (the biblical reasons cited by the opponents of women's rights do not really hold). The final two accounts are impassioned, the emotion highlighted by the refrain, "Ain't I a woman?" **Thus, (A) is the correct answer.**

12. Both anaphora (A) and epistrophe (B) involve repeated words or phrases, but these are very specific repetitions at the beginning or end of succeeding sentences or paragraphs. The repetition "Ain't I woman?" is not that measured or regular. A prologue (C) is the equivalent of an introduction, and an epigram (D) is indeed a pithy statement, but one more used as an allusion or reference beyond the work. The repetition of "Ain't I a woman?" is more like a refrain, a repeated line that lends structure and emphasis to the text. **Thus, (E) is the correct answer.**

13. While Sojourner Truth cannot be accused of speaking rudely or insultingly, there is no evidence of affection (A) for her audience. She clearly is not confused (B) as every account of her speech shows it to be poised, organized, and well structured. She speaks with passion but no rancor (D). She is also unwavering in her intent and message. Thus, (E) is eliminated. She does, however, suggest that she believes the men in the audience—the opponents of women's rights—are "mean," and she clearly points out the inconsistency and illogic of the opponents' arguments. **Thus, (C) is the best answer.**

14. (A) might tempt those who notice that most of the brackets are missing from the third account, but the text within the brackets in the second account reads more like stage directions than explanatory side notes. (C) might also be tempting but is not the best answer. (D) is simply inaccurate as all three accounts are designed to show Truth as strong, purposeful, and persuasive. (E) might also tempt some students, but while the second and third accounts may have been altered to present Truth in a more heroic light, they cannot be said to "glamorize" her. The bracketed comments, however, in that they describe audience comment and reaction, are clearly intended to recreate for the reader the experience of hearing Truth speak. **Thus, (B) is the best answer.**

15. (A) might explain the changes in language and the addition of the "Ain't I a woman?" refrain, but the transposition of the second account into modern, more standard English would not enhance reader sympathy. The changes from the second account to the third might have been motivated by (B), but this reason does not explain the changes from the first to the second. Public approval (D) is too vague and general a response. (E) might be more tempting but is also, ultimately, too unclear or vague. The imitation of Truth's alleged dialect and the content expanded to include the woman's children and physical labor, and the creation of the powerful refrain, "Ain't I a woman?" is clearly intended to take a powerful speech and make it even more powerful. Whoever might be moved to support black and women's rights after hearing the first version of the speech is so much more likely to do so after the third. **Thus, (C) is the best answer.**

Chapter 4, Exercise One

1. The first paragraph, including the greeting, is clearly an introduction (A), and the second and third paragraphs as well contain introductory elements. Beginning with the fourth paragraph, Kennedy transitions into a section identifiable by the opening phrase of each paragraph: "Let every nation," "To those old allies," "To those new states," "To those peoples," "To our sister republics," "To that world assembly," and "...to those nations who would make themselves our adversary." This is clearly an address to the world (B). The section that reads, "So let us begin anew," continues through paragraphs that all begin, "Let both sides," which contain a desire to work in unity toward solutions and enlightenment is clearly a conciliation (D). The closing section, which begins, "Now the trumpet summons us again" and is characterized by Kennedy's famous declaration: "ask not what your country can do for you—ask what you can do for your country" is clearly a challenge to the American people (E). There is, however, no challenge to America's enemies. The section that addresses our enemies is conciliatory yet strong: "to those nations who would make themselves our adversary, we offer not a pledge but a request: that both sides begin anew the quest for peace." **Thus, (C) is the best answer.**

2. The oxymoron, "man holds in his mortal hands the power to abolish all forms of human poverty and all forms of human life" is also a zeugma, linking two vastly different direct objects to the same verb. This power to abolish for good or for ill is new. It emphasizes (A). (B) looks at the past that still influences the present. (C) is a call for unity, but does not involve either of the terms of the zeugma. (D) looks to the past but offers no apparent contradiction to be reflected in the oxymoron. Similarly, (E) looks to the future, but does not clarify or elaborate upon a contrast. **Thus, (A) is the best answer.**

3. (A) might tempt some students who focus on the fact that this sentence is beginning a new section of the speech, but "and more" does not establish what the new topic is going to be, so it fails as an introduction. Likewise, (B) might tempt those who see the sentence as providing closure for the section that has gone before, but it is not the best answer of the five available. (C) and (D) are easily eliminated because the sentence is too vague to be considered the main point or statement to be argued. **(E) is clearly the best answer.** The sentence closes the discussion that has come before and looks toward something different that is going to come.

4. This is almost purely an identification question. Epistrophe (A) might tempt those students who know the device involves repetition but confuse where the repetition occurs. (B) is something of a homonym for (A) but the direct address it names does not have implications for structure. (D) and (E) do both affect the structure of a piece, but neither is the best choice available. The anaphora (C), however, the repetition of "To those…" in the one section and "Let both…" and "My fellow…ask" in the closing sections clearly establish the structure of Kennedy's address. **Thus, (C) is the best answer.**

5. Kennedy never really states any specific examples or instances, so (A) does not work. (B) simply does not satisfy as it is impossible to infer the relative importance of the "old allies" versus the "new states," or the increasing magnitude from "explore what problems unite us" to "seek to invoke the wonders of science." (C) is quite tempting if one considers the final challenge, beginning first with "fellow Americans" and widening to "fellow citizens of the world," but it does not explain the earlier progression of ideas. (D) is apparent only in the oxymoron examined in question 2, but does not follow for the rest of the speech. (E), however is evident from the first paragraph when Kennedy connects himself to the other thirty-four men through history who have sworn the same oath. It is emphasized when he compares the complexity and danger of "the world…now" with the past, and his famous assertion that "the torch has been passed to a new generation of Americans." The progression of ideas through the rest of the speech is similar: "to those old allies," "to those new states," "we offer…a request: that both sides begin anew." Indeed, throughout the entire speech, Kennedy looks to the past, to what has been, to what has shaped the present; and then he looks to that present and to the future: "All this will not be finished in the first 100 days. Nor will it be finished in the first 1,000 days, nor in the life of this Administration, nor even perhaps in our lifetime on this planet. But let us begin." **Thus, (E) is the best answer.**

Chapter 4, Exercise Two

6. Because King has written his letter in response to something he has read in the newspaper, he really has no thesis to prove. His point is simply to refute the previous writers' assertions. Thus, (A) is eliminated. (C) is tempting, but King's contrasts between violence and non-violence, justice and injustice, etc., go deeper than merely stating how they are similar and how they are different. (D) and (E) are eliminated by the realization that King is essentially responding to the original writers in the same order in which they presented their sentiments. **The preponderance of contrasts, however: outsider versus colleague and invited guest, justice versus injustice, lawful versus moral, and so on, establish (B) as the best answer.**

7. (A) should be easily eliminated by the understanding that this published letter is clearly not a rough draft and is not unstructured or random. (B) and (E) might tempt some but are ultimately too vague to satisfy. (C), likewise, is clearly not wrong but is so vague a statement as to be virtually meaningless. Transitional clues like "You deplore the demonstrations...," "One of the basic points in your statement is...," and "In your statement you assert" clearly suggest that King is responding point by point to the original letter. **Thus, (D) is the best answer.**

8. (B) certainly explains a significant source of King's development but does not, ultimately, contribute to the letter's overall unity. (C) is eliminated by the fact that the first response King offers the clergymen is to establish that he was not an "outsider" but an invited guest. (D) certainly is a unifying theme, but is not the best choice available. (E) is likewise mentioned toward the beginning and again toward the end of the letter, but it is also not the best choice available. King begins his letter, "My Dear Fellow Clergymen." In his final paragraph, he expresses the desire to meet them "as a fellow clergyman and a Christian brother." Throughout the letter, King describes his family history, establishing himself as "the son, the grandson and the great grandson of preachers." His identifying himself closely as a colleague of the first letter's writers, in addition to his frequent biblical allusions, strongly suggests that **(A) is the best answer.**

9. (A) is tempting, as the letter does close on a point different from the one on which it begins, but there are frequent and long sections in which King pauses in his linear progression to develop and elaborate on his point. This explanation tempts (B), but the divergent passages do return to the main point, and the letter does not lose itself in a random series of tangents. (C) better explains the organization plan of the information within the individual paragraphs than it does the overall structure of the letter. (E) is tempting, but, again, each divergent discussion does cycle back to the main idea and then progress to the next point. **Thus, (D) is the best answer.**

10. (A) is relatively easily eliminated by the fact that, throughout the entire letter, King is disagreeing with the concerns of the writers of the original letter. (B) is eliminated by the fact that he does not have a true thesis, and his conclusion leads to a different point from which he began. King does not offer a summative statement (D). (E) might tempt some students, as King does predict a time when his efforts will succeed, but this is not the main thrust of the paragraph. Until this point, however, King has responded to the clergymen's assertions. He has provided historical and biblical facts and interpretations of those facts. His statement, "I wish you had commended the Negro," is the first time in the letter that he expresses a personal sentiment. Thus, he is clearly beginning to conclude his response, and **(C) is the best answer.**

Chapter 4, Exercise Three

11. While (A) is tempting as the essay clearly does not cycle back to earlier points or return to its starting point, it is not the best answer. (B) and (C) are both excluded for the reason stated above. (D) and (E) seem equally tempting, but while the structure is an unpredictable series from point to point to point, it does follow a logical progression, so (E) is eliminated, and **(D) is the best answer.**

12. (A) might tempt some because it does point to what is at the root of Goldman's view of emancipation, but it is too vague and general to be the best answer. (C) is another statement of her point, but it is fully clear only because the point has been established earlier. (D) is as vague and general as (A), and (E) is a quotation Goldman attributes to industry and commerce, and she is criticizing those endeavors and their motto. **Thus, (B) is the best answer. Emancipation, to Goldman, is not the imposition of superficial equalities of circumstances; it is the freedom of a woman to know who she is and to be herself.**

13. While the thesis is not fully established until toward the end of the essay, the final two paragraphs are very clear about the main point of Goldman's essay. Thus (A) is eliminated. (B) is too ambiguous and vague, as one is left with the question, "Inappropriate for what?" The topic? The age, gender, or education level of the reader? Without knowing these aspects, (B) is not a viable choice. (D) is eliminated by the fact that there is no discernable organizational pattern. It may be purely linear, or it may be conversational or desultory. The pattern may, in fact, be confusing, but it cannot be said to be confusing because if its complexity. (E) is eliminated by the strong closure in the sentence, "That alone can fill the emptiness, and transform the tragedy of woman's emancipation into joy, limitless joy." (C), however is a valid criticism. The essay contains observations, assertions, and opinions, but there are no facts or examples to persuade a skeptical reader to accept Goldman's point. **Thus, (C) is the best answer.**

14. (A) is tempting, but it is too general to be the best answer from among the five choices. (B) is easily eliminated by the realization that this statement is the antithesis of what Goldman is saying. This is a notion that, according to Goldman, must be abandoned. Likewise, (C) is antithetical and a notion that Goldman wishes to see discarded. (E) might tempt some students who don't recognize that it is a summative statement whose meaning is dependent upon whatever is stated in the previous sentence. The reader does not know what the relative pronoun "that" refers to. **(D), then, is the best answer.** All of Goldman's points, all of her criticism of the shortcomings of the current emancipation, lead to the notion that true emancipation is the fulfillment of one's humanity, which is clearly summed up in this penultimate sentence.

15. Social antagonism (B) is one of the difficulties that results from a movement to change, but it is not the overall point on which Goldman begins. Salvation may summarize her concluding point, but there is a better, more specific choice available. Peace or harmony (C) is not the beginning point; it is an early suggestion at the goal; nor are "equal civil rights" the goal, but only a part of that goal. Similarly, "Inner regeneration" (D) does express the end goal, but equal suffrage is a part of that goal, not the point at which Goldman begins and from which she departs. (E) might tempt some as "narrowness and lack of freedom" might indeed be Goldman's beginning point, but "emancipation" is the main point of the essay, not only the idea to which the essay leads. **(A) is the best answer.** The problem with the "current" emancipation, according to Goldman, is that it is shallow, superficial, and is possibly even more restricting on women than their previous status had been. The essay ends with a description of emancipation that is, indeed, tantamount to salvation for both men and women.